TEACHING ACROSS CULTURAL STRENGTHS

A Guide to Balancing Integrated and Individuated
Cultural Frameworks in College Teaching

Alicia Fedelina Chávez and

Susan Diana Longerbeam

Foreword by Joseph L. White

Copublished in association with
NISOD

1996-2016 20TH ANNIVERSARY

Stylus
PUBLISHING, LLC.

STERLING, VIRGINIA

Published by Stylus Publishing, LLC.
22883 Quicksilver Drive
Sterling, Virginia 20166-2102

Library of Congress Cataloging-in-Publication Data

Chavez, Alicia Fedelina.

Teaching across cultural strengths : a guide to balancing integrated
and individuated cultural frameworks in college teaching / Alicia
Fedelina Chvez and Susan Diana Longerbeam ; foreword by Joseph
L. White. -- First edition.
    pages cm
    Includes bibliographical references and index.

ISBN 978-1-62036-323-2 (cloth : alk. paper)
ISBN 978-1-62036-324-9 (pbk. : alk. paper)
ISBN 978-1-62036-325-6 (library networkable e-edition)
ISBN 978-1-62036-326-3 (consumer e-edition)
    1. College teaching--Social aspects.   2. Culturally relevant
pedagogy.   I. Longerbeam, Susan Diana.   II. Title.
    LB2331 .C5125
    378.1'25--dc23
                                                            2015022283

13-digit ISBN: 978-1-62036-323-2 (cloth)
13-digit ISBN: 978-1-62036-324-9 (paperback)
13-digit ISBN: 978-1-62036-325-6 (library networkable e-edition)
13-digit ISBN: 978-1-62036-326-3 (consumer e-edition)

Bulk Purchases

Quantity discounts are available for use in workshops and for
staff development.
Call 1-800-232-0223

First Edition, 2016

I would like to dedicate this book to my first and most incredible teachers—my parents, Josefita Gonzales Chávez and Gabriel Venceslado Chávez.

Alicia Fedelina Chávez

I dedicate this book to all the teachers who have reflected my culture back to me—my parents, Esther and Gordon Longerbeam, who give me my culture. And to those who give me windows, Rosa Maria Zayas, Osa Hidalgo-de la Riva, Larry Roper, Dawn Johnson, Ryan Holmes, Deb Burke, Marylu McEwen, and, of course, Alicia Fedelina Chávez.

Susan Diana Longerbeam

CONTENTS

FOREWORD

*T*eaching Across Cultural Strengths: A Guide to Balancing Integrated and
Individuated Cultural Frameworks in College Teaching is a brilliant
and engaging book written by Alicia Fedelina Chávez and Susan
Diana Longerbeam, two associate professors at the University of New Mexico
and Northern Arizona University, respectively. The primary focus of this
excellent book is the influence of culture on college teaching and learning.

As we move through the Browning of America in the twenty-first century
toward a time when people of color will become the majority American
population, increasing numbers of Native Americans, African Americans,
Hispanics, Asian Americans, and immigrant undergraduate students will be
entering our colleges and universities. In many cases, the teachers and students will be from different cultural frameworks. Culture as the way of life
of a people is characterized by ways of behaving, ways of learning, norms of
conduct, skills and behavior, and patterns of interpersonal relationships and
conduct passed from generation to generation.

An imbalance in the teaching and learning situation exists when the
teacher teaches from one cultural perspective and the student's primary
learning experiences come from another. To enhance the possibility that the
student will master the learning situation and achieve its deep objectives, it
is important that college teachers expand their cultural reach and include
multicultural perspectives in the teaching and learning situation that recog-
nize the cultural assets that students bring to the classroom.

This book offers a comprehensive set of guidelines based on a sound
theoretical foundation, as well as empirical research that will enable college
teachers to narrow the gap in cross-cultural teaching and student learning
and assist teachers in transforming learning for all students across the many
cultures that exist in the classroom. By following the steps outlined in this
book, teachers can progressively learn about the role of culture in learning
while transforming their teaching through introspection, reflection, practice,
and the application of new teaching pedagogies that deepen student learning.

Through eight well-written chapters, the authors present their ideas on
course design, offer pragmatic insights, provide a guide for faculty to pursue
cultural self-analysis, examine their assumptions about teaching, and review

narratives from students and faculty on cultural influences in teaching and learning rhythms.

This book has the potential to literally change the face of college teaching and learning from a multicultural perspective. No one who reads this text and reflects on its message can continue to teach in the old monocultural ways of teaching and learning.

Joseph L. White, PhD
Professor Emeritus
Psychology and Psychiatry
University of California, Irvine

PREFACE

This book guides faculty to integrate a diversity of cultural strengths in teaching and learning processes. We strove to bring together an understanding of both strengths-based and culturally resonant teaching in the direction of facilitating student learning. Teaching in U.S. colleges and universities remains patterned primarily on Oxford and Germanic models brought to the United States early in its higher education history. Cultural influences of these models are evident in the linear, oratorical, modular ways most teaching takes place on U.S. college campuses. Ensuring learning and success among students overall—and especially among students of color who originate in cultures centered in interrelational, cyclical, integrated, and contextual ways of learning—is a challenge and an opportunity. Enhancing and integrating learning inclusively for all students is becoming a larger priority—especially as student enrollments diversify ethnically and as external pressures are increasing to graduate students and prepare them for a global society. We understand from our own efforts that transforming teaching practices takes a kind of academic courage to reimagine things we hold dear and to face our own cultural assumptions and patterns of practice. We understand that it takes openness and a kind of humility to try to understand teaching and learning from student perspectives and to join those of us who strive to develop a culture of belief in students. And we understand that it takes strength and perseverance to change in the face of dominant norms and pressures to teach in profoundly new forms. We welcome you to this journey that has meant so much to us and the students and faculty we have listened to and worked with over the years. We wish you well in the journey.

What matters most to student learning, success, and increased retention and graduation rates is for faculty to teach from a strengths-based approach. Strengths-based approaches begin with recognizing cultural and other strengths that students bring to higher education and to their own learning. These approaches cultivate and draw on student strengths to engage and facilitate inclusive learning and are derived from positive psychology and social work (Schreiner & Anderson, 2005). It also matters that we continue to bring strengths from our own cultural origins to balance the strengths of others.

We thought it might be helpful for you to gain a sense of our own individual culture and teaching and learning journeys as well as our shared learning across our cultural strengths. The following are individual musings about the influence of culture in our own college teaching and learning and then a discussion about some of what we learned from ongoing writing, faculty development facilitation, scholarship, and a deep friendship across our integrated and individuated assumptions and ways of being.

Musings From Alicia . . .

During our beginning conversations about this book, Susan asked me how I would describe equity among students in college. I responded, *We will be equitable when all populations of students are learning and graduating at similar rates.* For me it is not about getting a little bit better or a little more equitable. It is purely and simply about a responsibility I feel for the learning and success of *all* of our students. Culture is an important factor that has been largely overlooked in relation to learning in college. I believe we must draw on the cultural strengths in student backgrounds and identities; blend them with our own cultural strengths; and systematically transform our teaching, classrooms, and campuses to balance across integrated and individuated cultural norms. Until we do this across higher education institutions, profound inequities in student learning and success will continue.

My name is Alicia Fedelina Chávez, and I am *Mestiza*, a mixing of Spanish and Native American cultures from the time my ancestors began to intermarry in the late 1500s in what is now New Mexico. I share this with you because it matters. Culture matters. The norms, values, beliefs, assumptions, priorities, and behaviors that came down through the lives of my ancestors influence my teaching and learning in profound ways. I teach with the strengths of my mother and grandmothers—searching for interconnections and relationships among ideas, places, events, and people. I teach with the strengths of my father and grandfathers—facilitating learning through experiences of doing, reflecting, simulating, and imagining.

I am fortunate that my family emphasized and consciously taught us about our cultures and the meaning of them in our lives. I realize now what a gift this is in a country where not everyone is consciously aware of the rich cultures of their origins. Yet culture comes down through the lives of our ancestors into our everyday lives regardless of whether we are conscious of its presence or influence. Many of my own cultural norms became more and more obvious to me as I left home for college, as I bumped unknowingly into others' cultures and sometimes met with delighted response, yet, more often, disapproving reactions to my own.

As I journeyed through my own college education at four universities in disparate parts of the country, I became adept at identifying and negotiating cultural differences and similarities. I learned when I took on the role of teacher for the first time that collegiate classrooms are usually highly monocultural in nature. Student and faculty expectations jarred and shocked me, even with many years of experience in predominantly White universities and colleges. I entered a new country in many ways as I began to teach and over time developed a synergy among who I am, who my students are, and the subject matter. Even after my first class session, students of color inquired how it was that I taught as their elders had, sharing their relief at learning within cultural norms similar to their own. A few students of Northern European cultural origins also found relief and joy in experiencing new ways of learning and some in finding their own unique learning rhythms in my teaching. Yet more than a few challenged my ways of teaching in very direct, sometimes belligerent, cruel, or even highly inappropriate ways. I will always remember learning that one student made an appointment with the provost to complain. Fortunately, the provost, an anthropologist, pointed out to this young man he was privileged to be learning in new ways that would assist him to negotiate a global society. What developed in me from this journey was an ever increasing passion for understanding culture and drawing on its diverse strengths and a fascination with how culture manifests in both student learning and teaching practice.

My sense of urgency about teaching more systematically across cultural frameworks actually happened in a roundabout way. One semester I was faced with teaching a group of graduate students in which more than half identified as learning disabled. I strive to facilitate learning in ways effective for all students, so I made an appointment to see the director of the Office of Accessibility at that university. She introduced me to Gardner's theories of multiple intelligences (see Gardner, 2006) and explained that teaching across intelligences would help all of my students learn better. This changed my life as a teacher in many ways, including my systematic ability to design courses and facilitate learning more effectively across cultures.

I began to balance pedagogies across multiple intelligences when facilitating my class sessions. I also began to inquire more purposefully of students how they learn naturally and then modify assignments, introduce students to Gardner's intelligences at the beginning of courses, and work differently when assisting struggling students. I remember one student who came to me and shared that he had never been a good writer and yet our program required mostly extensive papers. He said that other faculty kept giving him writing exercises and sending him to the campus writing center; it wasn't helping him. I had a flash of insight to work with him from his learning strengths and asked him to share with me his two top intelligences. He said they were discussion (interpersonal) and visual/spatial. So I asked him to bring a tape recorder to our next appointment where I had crayons and newsprint ready. It occurred to me that perhaps *the way to learning* for this student wasn't through any kind of writing but rather *through his more natural intelligences first as a way into writing.* So I interviewed him about the assignment (interpersonal), asked him to share some of his thoughts and ideas, and had him tape-record the interview to take home. Then I gave him crayons and newsprint and asked him to draw or chart out his ideas (visual/spatial). I encouraged him to transfer ideas from both the recording and his newsprint to write his paper.

This student did well in my class, but I didn't see him much as he finished his master's. What startled me was that he ended up winning the writing award for our program, and when he got up to share at our program's graduation celebration, he shared this story and said that finding nonwriting ways into his ideas was a turning point in his learning and gave him a way, using his own strengths, to do things he hadn't been able to do before—even things at which he had never been good, like writing.

I learned almost immediately that diversifying my pedagogies across intelligences and working with students from their strengths also made a difference in my ability to teach across cultures as students of color, both domestic and international, began approaching me after classes to share that I was often their first professor who included learning processes from the ways they were taught in their families, tribes, countries, and communities. Student reactions served as a catalyst for my research on cultural strengths in college teaching and my work with faculty on teaching across cultural frameworks.

I am profoundly changed through transforming my teaching for diverse learners, and my journey continues as I develop more overt ways to transform pedagogy, interactions, communications, and facilitations across cultural frameworks to enhance student learning and success.

Like mine, your culture(s) of origin influence your teaching—regardless of whether culture is consciously held in your life or not. In addition, students' learning is influenced by their cultures of origin. Like culture, teaching and learning are in many ways learned phenomena, which means that we can transform our teaching to integrate a balance of cultural norms and enhance student learning.

As teachers we have a responsibility to design and facilitate responsively to the needs of a diversity of students. It is helpful to understand that how we learn is greatly influenced by the cultural norms, epistemologies, and worldviews in which we were raised, regardless of whether they are consciously understood as culture. It is crucial subsequently to assess ways our teaching reflects one or more worldviews from our own ways of learning and begin to incorporate a wider diversity of cultural norms into our practice. This is critical especially to those students whose cultures originate outside those prevalent in college and university teaching. It is also critical that all of our students become adept at learning within a wider cultural context because learning has become an essential skill in the workplace and the wider global society. Individuals will need to negotiate many cultural influences as they learn repeatedly in emerging work, social, and familial contexts. When we integrate pedagogies, interactions, and ways of being from across cultural frameworks, we assist our students in gaining skill and comfort that will help them negotiate a diverse global society. In the process, we develop our own understandings and transform our teaching to balance across cultural strengths.

Musings From Susan . . .

Alicia and I share a sense of urgency about higher education success, particularly in Latino and Native populations in the U.S. Southwest. Alicia's response to my question about equity reminded me that my passion for college students is in the promise they present: Equity has a chance when the same families do not stay in poverty through generation after generation (L. Roper, personal communication, n.d.). The question of how to seek equity for future generations is humbling in its vastness. I am learning through this work on culture and college teaching that part of the answer lies in the question of cultural influences on our early learning.

My name is Susan Diana Longerbeam, and I am of Northern European Caucasian descent. I was raised in a geographic region of rapidly increasing newcomers, and my family was among them: California, specifically the San Francisco area of the 1960s and 1970s, a land of the human potential movement whose messages to people of my cultural origin included the unlimited potential of the individual, unbounded by cultural ties. Everything was new. We were about pushing rules and boundaries; it was a deeply optimistic and hopeful time. I had liberal White parents who taught me I could be anything I wanted to be. I learned from my mother and father, who learned from their parents, that individual striving would lift us to the middle class, to a better life. I was encouraged to exercise discipline through music lessons, homework lessons, and athletics. Born into poverty in the Dust Bowl and Depression-era Oklahoma, my father earned the privilege of a college degree through the U.S. Navy. My mother was raised in Los Angeles and, after she had earned her community college degree, created a stable and loving home as a homemaker. We lived in a new suburb, with other new nuclear families uprooted from their extended family roots. I don't remember any of my childhood friends living with grandparents. Most of our learning was abstract, at school, and doing well in school was expected of us. At home, we did not learn predominantly by doing because we lived in tract homes with shiny new appliances. Our chores were few; we were not living from the land. In our spare time, we visited city parks and watched TV. On weekends, we visited theme parks and went car camping.

I don't remember conscious lessons about my cultures of origin, though I do remember references to the past. I visited grandparents twice a year, in Southern California. My maternal and paternal grandparents were living in Los Angeles from the time of my parents' childhood. Our earlier roots were in Scandinavia by way of Wisconsin and in Germany and England by way of the U.S. South. Though my parents were raised differently, my father in Oklahoma poverty and my mother in California middle class, from adolescence onward they shared the cultural influences of the 1950s White and (striving toward) middle-class Los Angeles.

My formal education was in California public schools. It was a time before large tax cuts, when K–12 and public higher education were thriving. I was encouraged to create my own learning in high school and in undergraduate learning at the University of California, Santa Cruz. I thrived in educational environments that encouraged me to explore my own learning through many cultures. My best learning occurred through friendships with peers, sharing cultures different from my own. In Santa Cruz, for instance, my greatest teachers were Latina. My passion for culture developed there. I continued the search for community, mostly through culture and spiritual and intellectual mentors. The struggle for connection continues to drive me. I am individualistically earnest to do a small part for human freedom and opportunity, yet I yearn for community. Mine is a common dominant White liberal American narrative.

I believe culture describes real differences in the ways people learn. For me, discovering my cultural ways is part of a long process I think of as the proverbial onion peel of Whiteness. The discovery is a process of becoming more aware of culture's influence and requires of me ongoing compassion and humility toward my culture and toward others who share my culture. Developing compassion and humility, I find, has allowed me to stay with the discovery, with more openness and less defensiveness.

I now know and acknowledge, for example, that I do better with segmented learning. In discrete steps, I write to a timed clock. It works for me. Also, I am comfortable with learning through abstract theory, though I prefer when application to personal story is included in theoretical learning. Discrete stage theory is especially easy for me to remember. The ways that we make sense of our world are deeply culturally influenced. In the case of predominantly European American higher education culture, for example, I continually ask these questions: What are the teaching and learning implications of competitive, earnest individualism? What are more possibilities, more ways to teach and learn? Further, what are the learning and life experiences that encourage openness to diversity? These are the kinds of questions that remain core in my life and my work. When Alicia invited me to share in the culture and teaching project, I said yes immediately; I knew I wanted to do this work, especially with her. I keep saying yes to culture in my work, and saying yes comes from and keeps me rooted in my purpose to understand culture as a way to understand myself and others—ultimately so that I may better support all of our successes.

I have been blessed with mentors who are committed to human transcendence over oppression and to expanded opportunities for all people, especially people of color and women in the U.S. education system. I live in Arizona, a land of restriction of immigrants and gays in the early twenty-first century. Yet I work with many colleagues who are committed to equity and opportunity for all students. Through compassionate work with faculty, my hope is to contribute a small part to student success. One way I do this now is to encourage faculty (especially European Americans) to explore our own cultures of origin, to open up a pedagogy that reaches all students and gives hope for educational equity—and for ourselves, more rewarding relationships with students and more enriching professional lives.

Our Shared Story of Learning Across Cultural Strengths

For us, much of this journey has been one of compassionate questions of each other about our cultured selves: Why do you do it that way? Explain how doing things that way is helpful to you. Where did that come from in how you were raised? What is the meaning of that to your learning? What assumptions are you making when you teach that way?

Writing retreats, numerous phone discussions, and daily e-mail queries make it possible for us to engage in a continuous dialogue to strive toward understanding across our cultural strengths. We work fundamentally from contrasting ends of the cultural continuum, Susan from a primarily individuated cultural framework and Alicia from a deeply integrated one. What has made our cross-cultural collaboration possible and powerful is our willingness to ask, reflect, and share—sometimes we need to go inward and reflect for a moment to figure things out before making sense of our daily ways of being so that we can explain. Whitt (1993) refers to this as "making the familiar strange" (p. 81), a process of studying something in our everyday lives as though we were visitors in a foreign land.

Our goal is to provide a guide for faculty to draw from the cultural strengths of *all* peoples in service toward equitable and effective teaching and learning in colleges and universities. Our partnership across our own cultural strengths made it possible for us to strive toward weaving together cultural norms of students and faculty from cultures that are underserved in U.S. higher education by currently dominant cultural norms in teaching. Our willingness to learn from each other, sometimes facing discomfort to explore differing assumptions about learning, about students, about teaching, about education, and about life has proved essential.

We continue to find joy and challenge in our journey. It is our *shared* cultural strengths that fashioned this book. We hope you find it helpful in your journey to develop your teaching across cultural strengths.

Chapter Overview

We designed this book as an incremental and pragmatic guide for faculty to transform teaching practices for the purpose of inclusively drawing from a balance of cultural strengths to enhance student learning over time. This section provides a brief overview of each chapter and the appendices.

Chapter 1, "Balancing Cultural Strengths in Teaching," presents an empirically derived and practically applied model of integrated and individuated cultural frameworks in eight continua of college teaching and learning. Understanding cultural frameworks in our own and student lives helps us strive toward a balance of learning processes and techniques in teaching. This model is useful for transforming pedagogical design and practice and reflecting on one's own cultural manifestations in teaching. Teaching scenarios, vignettes, and narratives offer readers a guide to balancing cultural norms in pedagogy, interactions with and among students, and purposeful, ongoing, reflective development of practice. Examples highlight key principles for transforming teaching over time across cultural norms and worldviews.

Chapter 2, "Culture in College Teaching," provides a context for culture in college teaching and the need for the transformation of college teaching to balance multiple cultural epistemologies to enhance student learning. Sections include cultural demographics of faculty and students in higher education and the demands and expectations for teaching that they engender; a definition of *culture* and its importance in teaching and learning; a short history on specific cultural norms in U.S. society and implications for higher education and student learning, retention, and success; short discussions of learning and the neuroscience of learning; and the underlying and often unconscious influence of culture in faculty teaching and student learning.

Scenarios include integrated and individuated teaching approaches and their strengths. These teaching examples are presented to illustrate cultural realities in student learning, faculty teaching, and classroom environments.

Chapter 3, "Rewards, Dilemmas, and Challenges of Teaching Across Cultural Frameworks," presents key principles and rewards for balancing cultural strengths in college teaching. Some dilemmas and hazards faculty are likely to face are offered as well. Teaching examples and narratives are provided throughout the chapter to assist in negotiating through hazards and dilemmas.

Chapter 4, "Applying Cultural Introspection to Teaching and Learning," assists faculty with cultural introspection to identify ways that cultural norms, beliefs, values, and assumptions manifest in their teaching and in student learning. This introspection enables faculty to develop a more balanced teaching practice across cultural norms. Faculty are guided in systematically analyzing teaching practices, design, and interactions. Emphasis is placed on authentic teaching through honoring and integrating a diversity of cultural norms in teaching and learning. Faculty are encouraged to find ways within and outside their own cultural norms to teach across cultures.

Chapter 5, "Strengths-Based Teaching in Cultural Context," focuses on the critical practice of assuming and working from students' cultural strengths. Cultural strengths from a variety of student origins provide a basis for facilitating student learning in teaching practice so that all students benefit from some of their natural ways of learning—as well as adapt to the challenges of learning in multiple ways. This chapter focuses in two primary areas. The first is on reimagining teaching philosophy on learning, student success, and retention with subsections on starting where students are developmentally and on balancing cultural capital. The second is targeted toward when everyone's learning *is* the objective—pedagogy, facilitation, and interaction across cultural frameworks with subsections on course syllabi; individual needs; evaluations and assignments; time, timing, and scheduling; the facilitation of a multiculturally empowering climate from the first class; student engagement across cultures; ways to balance activities across cultural norms, learning processes, and personalities; and finally a section on additional considerations.

Chapter 6, "Top 10 Things Faculty Can Do to Teach Across Cultures," addresses the common pressure faculty experience to gradually transform their teaching within busy professional lives. Over time, faculty can take on one or two strategies at a time, trying on different practices, observing student responses and learning, and transforming in a sustained manner over the life of their teaching. In our Culture and Teaching Faculty Development Project, faculty often engaged during a specific academic term in one fundamental or profound transformation in their teaching. By taking on one small yet profound change, faculty experienced renewal and were empowered to continue with small changes over time.

Chapter 7, "Spreading the Cultural Word: Faculty Development on a Larger Scale," offers suggestions for working with faculty colleagues over time in developing teaching practices that address differences across cultures. In addition, it offers suggestions for how faculty can influence colleagues in their own departments and academic communities to transform teaching across cultures for the benefit of student learning, success, and retention.

Chapter 8, "The Story of Our Work With Faculty," provides, for those who are interested, the story of our yearlong faculty development project on culture and college teaching, including how we conceptualized, funded, organized, and facilitated the project throughout the year. This section includes some of the varied ways we worked with faculty in the two universities.

"Final Reflections: Toward Learning Equity: Cultivating a Culture of Belief in Students" provides some closing reflections on the journey forward.

A Call to Faculty

We call upon faculty to take on the growing challenge to teach effectively across cultures, to learn culturally about ourselves and the students we teach, and to continually transform teaching and learning at our institutions. Culture matters in teaching, and we encourage everyone to facilitate learning and the success of *all* students by harnessing the strengths of our own culture(s) as well as those of our students.

Our hope is not that you remember our names; our hope is that something in this volume resonates with you and helps you facilitate learning more deeply and inclusively among students. Our hope is also that you ripple out through higher education by sharing your insights about culture and college teaching with faculty colleagues and students.

We Are Deeply Grateful

Our deepest thanks go to the many students who shared their narratives of learning with us over the years and especially to those who find the courage each day to negotiate college learning environments through cultural frameworks not so common to academic halls.

Our humble esteem, commendations, and thanks go to those individual faculty who care deeply about students as human beings, as learners, and as important contributors to our society and the world. Faculty with these qualities at the University of New Mexico and Northern Arizona University assisted us in this project through conversations and interviews, in their willingness to engage in and share insights from their own cultural introspection, by allowing us to observe and discuss their teaching, by engaging in our yearlong Culture and Teaching Faculty Development Project, with a willingness to take risks and develop new pedagogies, and through their passion for students, teaching, and learning. We are forever in your debt.

Thank you as well to the provost at NAU and the five academic deans at UNM who provided stipends for participating faculty.

Thank you to Linda Shadiow and Gary Smith for your support of and partnership in our faculty development projects at NAU and UNM.

Thank you to Joseph White for taking the time and offering your wisdom in writing a foreword for this book. We are honored by your insights.

Thank you to John von Knorring at Stylus Publishing for your enthusiasm for and support of this book, your quick and positive responses to our many queries during the process, and your insightful suggestions, which made this book as strong as possible. We could not have asked for a better partner for this project.

Thank you to Florence M. Guido, Jane Fried, Gary Smith, Don Trahan, Laura Rendón, and Robert Ibarra. Your insights, critique, and suggestions on the first draft of our manuscript helped us make this book stronger, and we are forever grateful for your wisdom and the gift of time and expertise you gave to us in the service of improving teaching across cultures in college.

Finally, we wish to thank our families for their unending love and support over the five years of this project.

A Note About the Cover

The symbols on the cover of this book represent the concept of strength in five cultures. We believe that our world is in need of the wisdom of every culture and wish to honor and draw from the many strengths of all peoples in our teaching.

I

Balancing Cultural
Strengths in Teaching

*I feel like I have to leave my culture at the door to be taken seriously, to not startle people, to have
a chance at being seen as intelligent. Trying to learn through someone else's cultural traditions
makes getting my education even tougher. I grew up discussing things and comparing my ideas to
others', but classrooms are mostly just hours of listening. I want to apply what I'm learning at least
hypothetically to serve my own communities, but mostly we just regurgitate facts, ideas, and theory
in the abstract. I've learned over time how to negotiate this reality, yet I wonder sometimes what it
would have been like to learn within my own cultural epistemologies. My hope is that when I am
a professor, I can teach in ways that embody many cultures, not just my own or the ones that are
so prevalent in college and university classrooms.*

—African American doctoral student in education[1]

Culture is interwoven through teaching and learning (Banks & Banks,
1997; Gay, 2000; Tisdell, 2003). Like the student quoted previously,
all college students bring with them into collegiate learning environments culturally influenced ways of learning, communicating, and behaving
as well as expectations about teaching (Chávez, Ke, & Herrera, 2012; Ibarra,
2001; Rendón, 2009). Likewise, faculty bring cultural influences into teaching practices and into the interpretation and evaluation of students (Chávez,
2007; Ibarra, 2001). Teaching-learning relationships between faculty and
students are embedded in culture. We propose that faculty apply a cultural
lens to teach more inclusively across cultural frameworks. By doing so, we
make possible teaching across a diversity of cultural strengths to enhance
learning for everyone.

This book is designed as a guide for teaching faculty to apply a cultural lens to college teaching and learning for the purpose of understanding how culture manifests in our own teaching and to enhance student learning. We crafted it to help faculty design and facilitate learning by drawing from a wide variety of cultural strengths across student populations. Our belief and our assumption guiding this book are that we as faculty can learn how to balance our own cultural norms alongside a full spectrum of cultural norms in teaching and learning practices. Because culture is embedded so foundationally and often unconsciously in how individuals interpret and behave in the world, this text is designed to assist faculty in systematically reflecting on, observing, analyzing, uncovering, and considering ways to develop teaching using a range of cultural approaches, while balancing those approaches. Applying a cultural or anthropological lens to college teaching and learning unleashes a powerful tool to develop our teaching over time and to understand the great diversity in students as learners. We encourage everyone to try. Some would say that you need to understand every culture before you can move to application. But we encourage you to try, not to feel like you need to know every culture thoroughly in order to be completely sensitive. It is important to start and to just try. We understand that this takes a kind of academic courage, to face who we are and to reimagine our teaching in fundamental ways. Insights, sensitivity, awareness, and cultural responsiveness develop through our efforts over time. And through this process we learn about different cultures and different ways that students learn.

> We encourage everyone to try, not to feel like you need to know every culture thoroughly in order to be completely sensitive. . . .
> Just try. . . . Insights, sensitivity, awareness, and cultural responsiveness develop through our efforts over time.

Within the field of anthropology, *culture* is characterized as a learned foundation of individual and collective assumptions, values, beliefs, priorities, and behaviors developed by a population over time (Deal & Peterson, 2009; Kuh, 1993; Mead, 1971). Peoples around the world and in the United States live within distinctive frameworks of culture. This book is designed to assist us in developing greater cultural responsiveness to students as learners by balancing across cultural frameworks in our teaching. Applying an anthropological or cultural lens to teaching practice is helpful in developing our acuity in cultural responsiveness to learners. (For a deeper discussion of culture, see Chapter 2.) Purposefully applying a balance of cultural frameworks in teaching will help faculty foster more complex learning processes among students.

Learning can be conceptualized as a layering or weaving of many ways of understanding and knowing. The more rich and diverse our exploration of knowledge and ideas, the more complex our learning. Balancing teaching across cultural frameworks centers student learning in natural and dissonant ways; teaching techniques sometimes feel familiar to students of a particular upbringing and sometimes feel unfamiliar, challenging them with new experiences and the resulting disequilibrium. Balancing teaching across familiar and unfamiliar cultural frameworks offers a healthy dynamic tension of challenge and support. This dynamic tension of challenge and support is essential to facilitating greater complexity in thinking and processing (Baxter Magolda, 1999). Further, teaching across cultural frameworks engages the mind as well as the heart, spirit, intuition, and body to develop greater understandings and encourages consideration of multiple perspectives or lenses. A balance across cultural frameworks in course design and teaching practices makes it possible for individual students to apply at least some of their own cultural strengths to learning. It makes it possible for all students regardless of their origins and experiences to find themselves in the mirror of collegiate learning.

Our intent in this chapter is to expediently introduce the Cultural Frameworks in Teaching and Learning model (a detailed discussion of the model begins on p. 11), including a discussion of the empirical studies undergirding its development. The model describes integrated and individuated cultural frameworks, discussed through eight continua of teaching and learning. For readers who want background information on the concept of culture and worldviews in pedagogy or who desire a thorough description of and definitions for our use of *culture* and related concepts, such as *race* and *ethnicity*, please read Chapter 2.

Reimagining Teaching Toward a Culturally Strengths-Based Approach

Promoting learning among college students is an elusive challenge for faculty, especially when faculty and students originate in differing cultures, an increasingly relevant actuality as campuses diversify. Though many factors come into play when facilitating learning in collegiate contexts, faculty and student cultural norms engender a significant influence. As teachers we have the opportunity to draw from and balance cultural strengths originating in highly differentiated cultural frameworks. This may take a kind of reimagining of our teaching toward a culturally strengths-based approach, balanced with pedagogies outside our own cultural framework or worldview. We understand that reimagining teaching and learning across cultural frameworks can be uncomfortable, and faculty often believe that expertise is necessary in something before we apply it to our practice. Yet we believe that teaching across cultural frameworks is an area where the opposite is necessary. We learn as we try. In the process we become more adept at reimagining our teaching, developing new practices, and honing our abilities as teachers who work with learners from a culturally strengths-based approach.

This book offers an opportunity to consider the role of culture, especially cultural strengths, to enhance student learning through the development of faculty teaching and cultural introspection. Integrating a variety of cultural norms into teaching practices complexifies learning activities and contexts, deepening learning among students by offering each student a balance of naturally comfortable techniques as well as naturally dissonant ways of learning. Following this practice, faculty develop in cross-cultural proficiency, awareness, and understanding (Chávez, 2007). This volume offers an opportunity to consider the role of culture, especially cultural strengths, in enhancing student learning through development of faculty teaching and cultural introspection.

Through accessing strengths in cultures of origin, whether consciously or unconsciously, learners may favor or even assume individual or collective ways of learning; may forefront the mind, body, spirit, or heart as avenues for taking in and processing knowledge; may think and communicate in linear or circular patterns; and may process from applied to conceptual or conceptual to applied pedagogies. Similarly, faculty bring culturally influenced design, pedagogy, evaluations, assumptions, interactions, and facilitation of learning into teaching practice. Because collegiate learning benefits from a variety of modes of taking in, processing, and applying knowledge, it is beneficial for all students to experience a diversity of teaching modes. Applying a balance of techniques, interactions, and relationships to teaching practice is helpful in developing pedagogical diversity. Using a cultural lens as one means to diversify pedagogy assists in including natural ways of learning from across cultures and addressing the cultural frameworks within which students live.

A fundamental shift to a more strengths-based approach is important for faculty who wish to facilitate learning effectively for all students across cultures, learning processes, and personalities. Research on college student retention suggests that at colleges where faculty believe students have what it takes to learn and consider it their job to make sure students learn, students are more likely to learn and to stay in college (Woodard, Mallory, & DeLuca, 2001). Alternatively, at colleges where faculty consider it their job to "weed students out," students learn and retain in much lower numbers, even when controlling for student intake factors such as GPAs, test scores, and demographics (Woodard, Mallory, & DeLuca, 2001).

As faculty we make assumptions based in our own cultures about students as learners. For example, our cultural upbringing may lead us to interpret student silence in a learning environment as a sign of deep thought, apathy, reflection, disinterest in the subject, respect, disengagement, idea gathering prior to speaking, active listening, wisdom, or even rudeness. Silence in learning contexts carries different meanings according to the cultural individualities and backgrounds of teachers and learners.

Many behaviors among students and faculty are interpreted individually through lenses developed during our upbringing. The following vignettes from a faculty member and student illustrate interpretation of similar behaviors from very different perspectives. The faculty member is concerned by the student's personal sharing, worrying that the student may ask for special considerations, while the student wants to find a sense of connection and worries that this may be interpreted negatively and that the professor will not understand that the student is trying to learn while negotiating many responsibilities.

> *I am always on my guard when a student comes to see me and tells me about what is going on in their personal lives. It usually leads to them asking for some special consideration.*
> —British American communications professor

> *I like making appointments with my professors to get to know them a bit, and I often start by sharing some things about my own life. It still throws me off, though, when the professor looks taken aback when I share anything about my kids or my job. I always feel like they immediately start suspecting me of trying to get away with something or that they really don't want to know me. Even when I do need to ask for a bit more time or something, I am not trying to be irresponsible, just juggling many different responsibilities as best I can.*
> —French-Italian American law student

As faculty we bring behavioral interpretations and judgments with us into collegiate learning environments, which affects how we design learning activities, how we interpret students, and sometimes even how we feel about students while teaching. It is a natural and common tendency to interpret cultural and other norms similar to ours in a positive manner while interpreting those different from ours negatively.

By developing cultural self-awareness and learning about differing cultural frameworks, we can cultivate the ability to reinterpret others' cultural norms as strengths and redesign our teaching and courses to engage these strengths among students. Balancing our teaching practices across cultural norms natural to a diversity of student learners then creates learning environments that are more inclusive of many ways of being. Both challenge and support are offered as a context within which a diversity of students can apply their own cultural strengths as well as experience other ways of learning and interacting. See Box 1.1 for an application exercise.

Box 1.1: Your Turn . . .

Think of one of the behaviors you often notice among students. It may be helpful to think of one that concerns or even irritates you.

- How might this behavior be interpreted differently? Perhaps as a strength?

Consider approaching students and asking them about the meaning of this behavior in their lives and in relation to their learning.

- Can you find out the "why" behind the behavior for students?

Notice your own behaviors and how students respond to them.

- How might students interpret your specific behaviors?
- What different messages might you be sending with your behavior to students from integrated and individuated cultural backgrounds?

Acknowledging a World With Many Oppressions

We would like to take a moment to acknowledge, honor, thank, and commend the many critical, feminist, race, Indigenous thought, womanist, and other scholars and activists in education and beyond for their deep, reflective work on racism, sexism, homophobia, and all other forms of oppression and discrimination in classrooms specifically—and in education and society more widely. This important work continues, and much of the discourse is eloquent and powerful. In this book we strive to build on the critical work of these powerful minds and hearts to offer further pragmatic guidance in the area of teaching and learning across cultures.

Our experience is that the hearts and minds of faculty, staff, and students in higher education often begin to open as we become more reflective about our own identities and more questioning of our assumptions about others (Chávez, Guido-DiBrito, & Mallory, 2003). This often seems to happen as individuals strive to work more effectively across cultures and other identities, perhaps because then we come face-to-face in very pragmatic ways with our own humanity as well as with the humanity of others. This book is written with pragmatism in mind. With it we attempt to add to existing works on what to *do* about these oppressions specifically within our professional practices as teachers: building a sense of agency and instilling hope for and development toward a better world.

We acknowledge that our book, while including examples from many cultures, is primarily rooted in U.S. ethnic cultures. There are many cultures we did not include, because we made a choice to focus our examples on the cultures with which we primarily work and from which our empirical data primarily derive. The scope of this book is not inclusive of all culture—especially global cultures and cultures of religion, gender, sexual orientation, age, and socioeconomic class, among many others. We encourage others to pursue work on using cultural strengths in college teaching and learning within these identities, as work across all cultures is greatly needed.

We firmly believe and have seen it borne out repeatedly that when faculty strive to balance teaching practices across cultural frameworks, they usually grow in understanding, empathy, and awareness. We urge you to continually seek out and learn from the deep body of literature and other works about social equity and diversity.

Cultural Frameworks, Epistemologies, and Worldviews

Cultural frameworks (see Tables 1.1 and 1.2), epistemologies, and worldviews are the underlying tenets of assumptions, beliefs, and values that influence our behavior in everyday life. Much of this is unconscious until we bump up against someone or something that is based in a very different underlying cultural framework. Many individuals experience this immediate sense of different cultural frameworks when traveling in other countries and, to a lesser extent, to other regions or cities in their own countries. Each of us grows up being taught both subtly and overtly about appropriate and inappropriate ways to do things, values to live by, and beliefs to espouse. Though we make many choices about how to live our lives as we grow older, we continue to carry with us our earliest teachings and interpret the world through these foundational underlying cultural lenses or frameworks.

Anthropological and psychological work on the relationship between culture and learning (Hall, 1959, 1966, 1981, 1984, 1993) and on cultural contextuality in higher education (Ibarra, 2001) enhance understanding of the role of culture in everyday life and in higher education. Multicultural education K–12 literature (Banks & Banks, 1997; Gay, 2000; Gilliland, 1999; Nieto, 1999) and some adult learning across cultures literature (Rendón, 2009; Tisdell, 2003) provides a theoretical base for teaching and learning. Our focus is on college teaching and adult learning. See Chapter 2 for a synopsis of some of this theory and wider literature on cultural epistemologies, worldviews, and strengths in relation to collegiate teaching and learning.

TABLE 1.1
Cultural Frameworks in Teaching and Learning Model

Individuated		Integrated
In a culturally <u>individuated</u> framework, a private compartmentalized, linear, contextually independent conception of the world is common, assumed, and valued.	⟷	*In a culturally <u>integrated</u> framework, an interconnected, mutual, reflective cyclical, contextually dependent conception of the world is common, assumed, and valued*
Knowledge, individual competence, to move forward toward goals and the betterment of humanity	**Purpose of Learning**	Wisdom, betterment of the lives of those with whom we are connected—family, tribe, and community
Mind as primary, best, or only funnel of knowledge	**Ways of Taking in and Processing Knowledge**	Mind, body, spirit/intuition, reflection, emotions, relationships as important aspects and conduits of knowledge
Compartmentalized and separate; belief that understanding how the parts work separately, abstractly, and in isolation will lead to the greatest understanding	**Interconnectedness of What is Being Learned**	Contextualized and connected, belief that understanding how things affect each other within the whole and within family and community will facilitate understanding
Learning is a private, individual activity; responsible for one's own learning so that family and others are not burdened	**Responsibility for Learning**	Learning is a collective, shared activity, responsible for one's own as well as others' learning
Linear, task oriented, can be measured and used, to be on time shows respect	**Time**	Circular, seasonal, process oriented, dependent on relationships; to allow for enough time shows respect
Provider and evaluator of knowledge—best perspectives and ways of learning, predetermined or bounded learning; communication primarily between teacher and students	**Role of the Teacher**	Facilitator of learning experiences— multiple perspectives and ways of learning, emergent constructivist; wide variety of interactions among students and between teacher and students
Others' perspectives are optional for learning. Primarily rely on verbal messages; individuals are paramount, predominantly verbal in both written and oral communications	**Student Interactions**	Others' perspectives and interpretations are important, even essential to learning. High use of nonverbals, collective as paramount, and multiple streams of communication
Learning by mastering abstract theory first, followed by testing; unlikely to include application, experience, or doing in real life	**Sequencing**	Learning by doing, listening to others' experiences, imagining or experiencing first, then drawing out abstract theory

*Note. **Chávez & Longerbeam**. The earliest version of this model was presented in a paper at the 2009 ASHE Conference and developed from a later version of the model in Ke & Chávez (2013).*

Cultural worldviews or frameworks can be conceptualized as flowing along a continuum of behaviors, beliefs, assumptions, and priorities from individuated to integrated worldviews. The development of reasoning is influenced by early cultural practices and language in an individual's life. The Cultural Frameworks in Teaching and Learning model (see Table 1.1) was developed and honed from earlier research (see Chávez, Ke, & Herrera, 2012; Ke & Chávez, 2013) and through our ongoing practice and research with faculty as they strove to balance cultural frameworks to teach more

TABLE 1.2
Cultural Frameworks in Teaching and Learning

Individuated		Integrated
In a culturally <u>individuated</u> framework, a private compartmentalized, linear, contextually independent conception of the world is common, assumed, and valued		*In a culturally <u>integrated</u> framework, an interconnected, mutual, reflective, cyclical, contextually dependent conception of the world is common, assumed, and valued*

effectively across cultures. Table 1.2 is an abbreviated piece of the model to generally introduce cultural frameworks.

From Monocultural to Multicultural

All learners would benefit from a wider integration of cultural norms in teaching practice such as shown in the continuum of individuated to integrated cultural norms or worldviews in Table 1.2. Ultimately, balancing across cultural frameworks would mean that we engage the cultural strengths of every student in our teaching practices to enrich student learning overall. Strengths-based approaches are commonly invoked in the fields of positive psychology and business, though they lack a cultural application (Snyder, 2010). Balancing cultural frameworks in teaching would mean that students would be able to apply some of their own natural strengths from ways of learning in their upbringing to their learning in college.

Yet college norms and processes including teaching are currently situated primarily in a cultural framework with origins in Northern European cultures (Ibarra, 2001; Rendón, 2009; Chávez, Ke, & Herrera, 2012). This cultural framework falls on the individuated side of the model in Table 1.2. Within an individuated cultural framework, individual, linear, abstract, mind-based orientations represented on the left side of the model are the norm. Integrated cultural frameworks that are interconnected, circular or seasonal, contextual, and mind/body/spirit/heart-based are much less common—even rare—in academic cultures and in collegiate teaching. Working from any one monocultural orientation privileges populations of learners for whom this cultural framework is natural. Working in only one cultural framework also underserves populations of learners that grow up in another cultural framework. Students of color throughout our studies described feeling outside the norms of teaching and learning practices in college, while Northern European American students in our study usually did not.

I feel like that old song about having to leave my face in a jar by the door when I leave for class. I feel like I have to pretend to be someone else. Someone I don't really know how to be. It all feels so unnatural to me. I was taught that learning is meant to be complex, interconnected, and whole, but my college courses are separated and so focused and abstract that I get lost in spending time learning facts, figures, theory, and equations seemingly without their meaning in engineering or in life.
—Spanish American mechanical engineering student

My educational experiences have always felt really comfortable to me. I learn the same basic way that my teachers and professors teach.
—Scandinavian American math student

A more monocultural basis for teaching makes learning more difficult and unnatural for students whose cultural norms are outside of its specific cultural framework. Difficulty learning happens because a monocultural framework is based on only one or a few sets of cultural norms. For students who have been raised in cultural frameworks outside the dominant individuated one in collegiate learning environments, learning becomes an additional challenge as individuals try to negotiate academics taught through cultural frameworks not their own.

Culturally dissonant teaching exists when those in cultural groups find few of their own cultural norms in learning environments, assignments, course activities, or academic interactions. Students who feel a sense of cultural dissonance in their courses often originate in cultures with norms in cyclical, mind/body/spirit/emotion, and contextual orientations (Chávez, Ke, & Herrera, 2012). In more monocultural learning environments, *all* students miss out on learning through a mixture of cultural frameworks, disadvantaging them in a global society where learning and retooling professional skills and knowledge is now a constant necessity. Learners with origins in the dominant cultural framework are often unconscious of missing anything, yet some describe a sense of something missing in most of their classes. A few describe unique experiences with a specific professor that go outside the bounds of their educational experiences and lead to greater learning.

I have this professor who is always telling stories, giving examples first, and stretching us to do things in class that I haven't done in college. He rarely lectures but instead has us constantly applying concepts and theory to situations going on around us and in our own lives. This was really uncomfortable for me at first because I was so used to coming in, sitting down, and taking notes, then regurgitating facts on a multiple-choice exam. I feel like my mind stretches with this professor. I've never worked so hard, but I am learning like never before.
—German-Danish American psychology student

We believe that one key to effectively teaching across cultures in college is to purposefully redesign and balance pedagogies, interactions, assignments, and evaluations across integrated and individuated cultural frameworks.

The following sections in this chapter as well as subsequent chapters in this book are designed to guide faculty in reimagining and developing teaching toward a balance of individuated and integrated cultural frameworks. We hope you will find this as powerful a practice as we have in our own teaching.

A Model of Cultural Frameworks in College Teaching and Learning

In this section we present the full model of cultural frameworks in college teaching and learning (Table 1.1) derived through empirical research and application to teaching practice. The model highlights eight continua in college teaching and learning across integrated and individuated cultural frameworks. The continua are discussed in relation to transforming teaching over time toward more culturally balanced and inclusive practices. Cultural frameworks are provided as a scaffold and decision-making tool for teaching faculty to develop understanding of how culture plays out in student learning, in reflection on our own cultural manifestations in teaching, and in the transformation of teaching practice.

We incorporate narrative data of faculty and students from empirical studies to illustrate and enhance the meaning of the cultural frameworks and eight continua of teaching and learning. Teaching scenarios and vignettes illustrate the integration of multiple cultural norms in pedagogy, interactions with and among students, and purposeful development of practice. We provide numerous concrete examples of teaching strategies.

In later chapters of this volume, we offer the following:

- Underlying conceptions of culture in teaching
- Ways to engage in cultural introspection of teaching practices and interpretations of students
- Rewards, tips, and hazards of developing a more culturally integrated teaching practice
- Specific guides for many aspects of pedagogical design and facilitation

Development of the Model

The model of Cultural Frameworks in Teaching and Learning (Table 1.1) emerged from two narrative studies of college students at two universities and a narrative national study of faculty who attended a workshop on balancing cultural frameworks in college teaching. It was then honed through application, cultural introspection, consultation, and observation of teaching by 37 faculty in a yearlong culture and teaching faculty development project at two universities. Because most of the current literature on ethnicity in U.S. higher education has been conducted at eastern, western, or southern U.S. colleges and universities, we based our studies and faculty development work in New Mexico and Arizona, states with large populations of Native and Hispano/Latino American students.[2] Many of these peoples have been in the region since before the founding of the United States. We believed that this long history of cultural immersion would assist us in gaining a deeper understanding of how culture manifests in teaching and learning. The following studies were drawn from to develop this model, and narratives throughout this book derive from these studies.

Comparative cultural study of teaching and learning among graduate and professional students. In this study, 26 graduate and professional students were interviewed individually for 90 minutes. Half of the students were domestic or international students of color, and half had ethnic origins in Northern European American cultures. Students were sampled from the graduate school at the University of Arizona as well as the medical and law schools. Students were asked to describe what processes they apply when they need or want to learn something. Students were then asked to compare and contrast these ways of learning with their learning experiences in college as well as with their learning experiences in their families and home communities. From this study emerged a basic cultural frameworks model that served as a precursor to Table 1.1. Student quotes from this study are included throughout this book to illustrate various concepts.

Comparative cultural study of teaching and learning among undergraduate students. In this study, 100 undergraduate students were interviewed individually for 90 minutes. The students were sampled across those with Northern European, Hispanic/Latino, Native, African, and Asian American ethnic origins. The study took place at the University of New Mexico, and students were enrolled in six academic colleges. As in the Arizona study, students were asked to describe what processes they apply when they need or want to learn something. Students were then asked to compare and contrast these ways of learning with their learning experiences in college as well as with their learning experiences in their families and home communities. The Cultural Frameworks in Teaching and Learning model emerged from analysis of this narrative data as well as review of the Arizona study data.

Culture and teaching narrative study among faculty. Thirty faculty who participated in a national workshop on balancing cultural frameworks in college teaching were interviewed six months after the workshop to gain an understanding of how they were balancing cultural frameworks in their teaching as well as what they were noticing in learning among students from varying cultural origins in their courses. Some narratives from this study illustrate various concepts throughout this book.

Culture and Teaching Faculty Development Project. In a collaborative project, we invited teaching development directors at our respective institutions, the University of New Mexico and Northern Arizona University, to work with us to design and implement a yearlong faculty development project focused on engaging in cultural introspection to understand how cultural worldviews influence teaching. Faculty worked on developing a balance of cultural frameworks in their teaching practice. (For a more extensive description of this project, see Chapter 8.) A more sophisticated iteration of the model as well as many teaching scenarios and methods emerged from teaching observations, consultations with faculty, collective brainstorming of pedagogies, and culture and teaching autobiographies written by faculty.

Integrated and Individuated Cultures in Teaching and Learning

Individuated and integrated cultural frameworks of teaching and learning emerged from the studies described previously as well as eight continua within these cultural frameworks. We believe that the entire spectrum of cultural framework is important to student learning and valuable in making unique contributions to the world of teaching. Our hope is that faculty will find value in drawing from this full spectrum of culture to enhance their teaching and student learning.

Integrated Cultures

College students with integrated cultural frameworks interpret the world in a highly contextualized manner, conceptualizing and interacting through interrelational connections and considering everything within an interdependent whole. Learners from highly contextualized cultures are those for whom learning is situated in a wide milieu of environment; nonverbal communication; and auditory, sensory, and visual perception. An integrated learner more naturally wishes to study the entire body, the complete car, or the overall system to get an overview of the whole, and then turn to various parts and their interactions with each other and the whole. Integrated learners often struggle with the common academic norms of

Individuals from integrated origins often learn most naturally when the whole is studied before the parts and collective processing happens before individual study. Time for reflection is important to many integrated learners so that they can process thoughts, especially before sharing. For integrated learners, application precedes drawing out theory so that the whole can be considered, and knowledge is taken in through multiple senses.

studying components of a topic through separate courses; these topics are rarely synthesized within or across courses or across a field of study.

In a culturally *integrated* worldview or epistemology, an interconnected, mutual, reflective, contextually dependent conception of the world is common, assumed, and valued. Learners operating within an integrated cultural worldview grow up in environments where the collective is given precedence and responsibility for others is expected; context, especially relational context, is emphasized. Synergistic connections, including mind/body/spirit/heart connections, are assumed in an integrated worldview. Subjectivity is expected as a natural aspect of comprehension, and self-reflection is considered essential to understanding.

Individuals from integrated origins often learn most naturally when the whole is studied before the parts and collective processing happens before individual study. Time for reflection is important to many integrated learners so that they can process thoughts, especially before sharing. For integrated learners, application precedes drawing out theory so that the whole can be considered, and knowledge is taken in through multiple senses. Most U.S. colleges and universities are not organized in an integrated paradigm, though there is movement toward new forms of teaching that integrate content within and across subjects (e.g., active and collaborative learning, teaching across the curriculum). Some of this movement, however, is more conceptual than broadly applied in practice.

Individuated Cultures

College students with individuated cultural frameworks conceptualize and interact with the world in a more compartmentalized manner and consider first from an individually operating perspective. Learning is focused on separate components with little context and is likely to entail predominantly text-based visual, compartmentalized, and discrete knowledge acquisition, with less attention to the surrounding environment, including its nonverbal messages. An individuated learner more naturally wishes to study parts of the body, the car, or the system first to gain an understanding of the parts separately, then possibly turn to thinking about the whole. Individuated learners often pay significant attention to the parts and focus or specialize to gain an understanding of what is studied.

In a culturally *individuated* worldview or epistemology, a compartmentalized, private, individualized, contextually independent conception of the world is common, assumed, and valued. Learners operating within an individuated worldview grow up in environments where the individual is given primacy. Responsibility for oneself is expected and prioritized within this worldview. Understanding primarily through an objective mind is given precedence, and subjectivity is likely to be considered peripheral to and sometimes distracting from or in contradiction to clear understanding.

Individuals from individuated origins often learn most naturally when individual study precedes collective processing, components are studied individually before the whole, theory is processed before application, the mind is prioritized over the senses, and reflection through discussion is peripheral. Most U.S. college and university instruction and curricula are organized in this kind of individuated paradigm. Academic subjects and degrees are often organized into parts relying on one synthesizing course or culminating project and not emphasizing integration of subjects regularly across a degree or even across the major degree courses.

> Higher education ideally will transform to honor, incorporate, and balance *both* integrated *and* individuated worldviews in teaching and learning so that all learners benefit.

Some learners originate in mixtures of these cultural continua and have some learning traits on one side of the continuum and others on the other side. It is most common, however, for learners to originate more completely from one side of this cultural set of polarities or the other, and much of the world originates from an integrated worldview. This makes it critical for college teaching to transform to incorporate integrated ways of learning, especially with the rapid cultural, ethnic, and racial diversification of students in higher education. Higher education ideally will transform to honor, incorporate, and balance *both* integrated *and* individuated worldviews in teaching and learning so that all learners benefit.

Both-And: A Cultural Key to Learning

An important key to learning in a culturally diverse context is a "both-and"[3] conception and practice of learning and teaching processes. This conception occurs when learners experience *both* the comfort of their own culturally natural framework of learning *and* the challenge of negotiating other cultural frameworks of learning. Students need to see and experience their own most natural ways of learning in our classes. Drawing on both realms creates the balance of comfort and dissonance necessary for complex learning. This balance of challenge and support is essential to learning (Baxter Magolda, 1999; Sanford, 1967). We enrich learning by melding many ways of seeing, understanding, experiencing, processing, reflecting, discussing, and making sense with others.

> An important key to learning in a culturally diverse context is a "both-and" conception and practice of learning and teaching processes.

Individuals learn most complexly when they are able to study *both* the component parts *and* the integration of the whole. Different learners may also start at different ends of a sequence of abstraction and application yet learn best from experience with both. Individuals take in knowledge from many senses, perspectives, and sources and may consider component parts both discretely and within their natural contexts. To learn most complexly, it is critical to study, reflect, and process *both* individually *and* collectively. In essence, a both-and balance and integration cultivates the most complex learning.

We conceptualize integrated and individuated worldviews as *symbiotic polarities* along a continuum, synergistic and essential to each other and the world in ways similar to concepts such as the Taoist *yin-yang* (necessity of opposites; see Figure 1.1); the Maori *ako* (reciprocal learning); the Zulu *ubuntu* (humanism of human beings collectively); and the Lakota *Mitakuye Oyasin* (we are all related)—rather than as dichotomies in opposition to each other, such as good/bad, right/wrong, or even either/or (see the chapter on non-Western perspectives of learning and knowing in Merriam, Caffarella, & Baumgartner, 2007; on Indigenous paradigms of education in Cajete, 1994; and on the Aztec concept of blending thinking and sensing in Rendón, 2009, for helpful discussions).

In symbiotic polarities, seemingly opposite forces are interconnected and interdependent in the natural world and give rise to each other as they interrelate. We believe that just as biodiversity is necessary for the health of all living beings and overall ecosystems (Wilson, 2010), a diversity of teaching

Figure 1.1 Chinese Yin-Yang Symbol

pedagogies, interactions, relationships, and ways of taking in and processing knowledge is necessary to deepen learning among a diversity of individuals in any learning environment. Similarities among learners assist in producing comfort and connection while differences create dissonance that stimulates interest, critical thought, intellectual and personal growth, and multiple lenses with which to ponder and analyze old and new knowledge. Each is essential to and connected with the other, as represented in the circles coming through in the Chinese yin-yang symbol, the interwoven lines of the Tibetan symbol of balance (this symbol appears on the first page of every chapter), and the many circular symbols of balance among Native American tribes. Large studies suggest that diversifying the cultural enrollments of students in college courses increases learning for everyone because natural dissonance and critical inquiry are created within the learning environment (Hurtado, 2007). Developing a culturally both-and practice in teaching further generates a context for rich learning.

A Note About Inequity in Learning

As faculty, we hold the power to create learning environments and experiences that are more or less equitable among students. We may teach in similar ways to how we were taught in college, in our families, or in our home communities and believe that this is the way teaching is done.

Yet, if one student in our classes always experiences those teaching techniques they grew up with and another student rarely or never experiences those teaching techniques they grew up with, we set up a disproportional effect, an inequity of learning, because one student has to negotiate unfamiliar ways of learning in addition to learning new subject matter while the other just has to learn the subject matter.

As we interviewed students in our studies about their own learning processes, this dynamic became clearer. In our discussions with students, we asked them to share with us what they do when they really need or want to learn something. We were fascinated with the variation in their learning processes as well as with their clarity in understanding and articulating. We learned that students start by applying their own areas of strengths and areas that feel very natural to them. As we had students and some faculty describe their learning processes, we discovered some really important considerations for teaching. The main one is that individual learners start with their own strengths whenever possible:

My professor always starts by explaining a theory in only one way, but I do best when I can compare and contrast multiple interpretations. So I ask several students to meet me for coffee before class so we can talk through our own conceptions of the theory. Then when we go to class I compare the way the professor explains the theory with all the other ways we have discussed it and then I usually understand.

—Malaysian law student

I have to chart it out to get it. Doesn't matter what it is: English, chemistry, math, art theory. I draw a flow chart and then I get it.
—Japanese American mathematics undergraduate student

Running is time to think. I let my mind go blank for a while. I listen to my breathing and my footsteps on the trail. Then I focus my thoughts on what I need to learn and thoughts start trickling in, and I process them in a rhythmic way with the sound of my footsteps. Later I return to not thinking, just listening to my breath, my footsteps, the birds, my heartbeat. Usually by the time I finish my run, I understand.
— Hopi medical student

I learn by doing. I'm an "If all else fails, read the directions" sort of guy. So as often as possible I start by putting something into real life, how math relates to a real problem, how a business theory applies to a real business, and then I work out what I would do. If I can actually do something to practice, that is especially helpful.
—Scandinavian American business undergraduate student

All of the students in our classes are more likely to learn if we teach within an epistemology of cultural both-and, incorporating many different techniques from across the integrated-individuated cultural spectrum so that each student can engage some of their own strengths in learning. If we have one student who starts naturally with reflection, another who often begins by visually working something out with a flowchart, and still another who feels most comfortable talking about it first, then our role as teachers is to move among a variety of techniques so that all students are able to find at least a little bit of their own learning strengths in our classes. In this way we can cultivate and provide more equitable and effective learning experiences and environments for all students.

Teaching Within an Epistemology of Cultural Both-And

An engineering professor[4] is socialized in her profession to teach things in an abstract, theory-first manner and expect students to learn applications primarily in lab and fieldwork. She regularly lectures on engineering theories, explaining them the way they were explained in her own engineering courses in college, yet notices that students struggle to understand and students of color seem especially disengaged.

After she has considered both integrated and individuated cultural frameworks in relation to student learning, she decides to try something different. She asks students to gather in threes for a demonstration and discussion, then she brings in some water in a plastic cup and begins her class by asking students to observe. She knocks the cup over and water rushes out, cascades off the table, and creates a small pool on the floor.

This professor then asks students to discuss the movement of water in relation to an engineering principle assigned in the readings for this class session. Later she encourages students to offer their explanations to the larger class and inserts her own perspectives and questions into this sharing and processing. Then she begins to ask how this theory might play out in other situations. She notices that everyone is highly engaged and seems to grasp the highly abstract theory much more easily. After class, she wonders what would have happened if she had also given students a moment or two to reflect before they discussed in groups and decides to try this next time—alternating reflection with immediate discussion to foster understanding in learners with differing learning processes.

This professor engaged a both-and design, blending in cultural continua from integrated and individuated frameworks to more fully engage her students, mix application and theory, and interweave discussion among students with guided processing. She also considered adding reflection time to her next class session. This facilitated incorporation of a number of learning processes, including doing, observing, discussing, applying, making sense of, imagining, and generalizing to new situations (merging facets of Kolb's 1984 experiential learning model, Bonwell & Eison's 1991 active learning models, and Bloom's

1956 Taxonomy of Learning Domains). In essence, she drew from polarities of culture to engage all students in natural and challenging ways, creating a balance of comfort and dissonance that led to deeper learning than previously observed when using primarily one cultural end of the continuum.

By designing carefully with a balanced combination of cultural frameworks, faculty can intersperse activities, assignments, interactions, course materials, and even evaluations from integrated and individuated cultural frameworks to benefit a diversity of learners. The following sections provide a thorough introduction to the cultural frameworks model as well as its general application to balancing cultural frameworks across eight continua of teaching and learning. Each of the eight continua includes a teaching vignette to illustrate a blending across cultural frameworks, examples of pedagogies for consideration, and narrative quotes from students and faculty to assist with deeper understanding.

Applying a Model of Cultural Frameworks to Teaching Practice

A continuum model of integrated and individuated cultural frameworks across eight continua of collegiate teaching and learning (see Table 1.1) was derived from empirical research, enhanced by faculty cultural introspection, and honed through application to practice. Look over the model and take a moment for a reflective interlude (see Box 1.2).

In the upcoming subsections, the eight cultural continua of teaching and learning are presented, described, interpreted, and illustrated across integrated and individuated cultural frameworks. Using a teaching and learning context, each continuum is explained, illustrated with a teaching scenario of practices balanced across individuated and integrated cultural frameworks, and interpreted through student and faculty narratives. Later in each section, pedagogies are offered to assist in balancing across integrated and individuated cultural frameworks for each continua. The model incorporates eight continua showing cultural frameworks of each in a continuum of symbiotic polarities. Cultural continua include purpose of learning, ways of taking in and processing knowledge, interconnectedness of what is being learned, responsibility for learning, time, role of the teacher/control, student interactions, and sequencing.

We encourage teaching faculty to apply this model to analyze the cultural foundations of their own teaching practices and to systematically observe and converse with students about their natural learning processes. Over time this will help transform teaching practices to balance integrated and individuated cultural frameworks across all the continua. The cultural frameworks model (Table 1.1) and the remainder of this book are designed to assist in this transformation.

In our work with faculty, we find that individual faculty members benefit from a variety of contemplative and pragmatic activities over time to transform teaching toward a balanced both-and practice across integrated and individuated cultural frameworks. This allows individual faculty to engage a wide variety of culturally based and other strengths toward enriching student learning. Faculty benefit from deep cultural introspection (Chapter 4) combined with gaining insight and learning perspectives of students from many cultural origins (Chapter 4) and incrementally considering cultural foundations from a variety of teaching aspects including design, interactions, pedagogies, assignments, evaluation, and assessment (Chapters 5 and 6).

Box 1.2: Reflective Interlude

Take a moment for some cultural introspection.

For each of the eight continua in the Cultural Frameworks in Teaching and Learning model (see Table 1.1), place an X along the continuum where you believe you are in how you teach. Then reflect on the following questions:

- Given where you are on each continuum, what are some of your most distinctive values and priorities related to teaching?
- From where in your life and identities do these values and priorities originate?
- How might a student with a cultural framework dissimilar to yours experience your courses in contrast to a student with a similar cultural framework?
- What does this mean for student learning?

We believe that strengths are inherent in every culture and contribute to the full spectrum of cultural frameworks that emerged from our studies of students and faculty. We also believe that all students as well as faculty will benefit from a range of cultural strengths in college teaching and learning. The following sections are designed to help faculty gain an understanding of and learn to purposefully incorporate strengths from across an integrated–individuated cultural continuum. The following tables are represented in order of the continua in Table 1.1. Each continua begins with a table of the framework and its definition, followed by a table of teaching techniques.

TABLE 1.3
Purpose of Learning

Individuated		Integrated
Knowledge, individual competence, to move forward toward goals and the betterment of humanity	⟷	Wisdom, betterment of the lives of those with whom we are connected—family, tribe, and community

Purpose of Learning

To balance across integrated and individuated cultural frameworks in relation to purpose of learning, an accounting professor facilitates case studies with students using a variety of settings, including budgets for a tribal health clinic, a local school, and a corporate initiative. She balances individual goals and collective purpose by asking students to consider both how the case might matter to their future professional lives and how the case outcome might matter to those they serve in the organization and community. She personalizes her interactions by calling students by name in her 75-student class to process calculations and share their perspectives on how various financial commitments are likely to affect the organization and the community. To learn students' names the professor relies on name tents each student created in the first class session and places them on student desks as they arrive.

Purposes of learning range across cultures from learning for knowledge, individual competence, and professional goals—so as to contribute and not become a burden to society (individuated)—to learning for wisdom and the betterment of the lives of those with whom we are connected and responsible (integrated). Values taught by family and community about the purpose of education can differ sharply across cultures. Northern European American students are more likely to highlight educational and professional goals when discussing a collegiate education.

> I don't want to be a burden so I focus hard on educational and work goals and keep my eye on the ball of graduation and getting a good job.
> —German-Danish American undergraduate student

> Learning toward my career is my goal and I make most of my decisions in college with that in mind. My folks often remind me that this is a time in my life to focus on me and my learning and not get distracted by other responsibilities.
> —British American graduate student

Chinese national students, though focused on goals, are also more likely to overtly relate them to family and country.

I work hard in my classes so I can get a degree and a good job to make my family and country proud.

—Chinese national graduate student

In our studies, Native, Hispanic, Middle Eastern, and Southeast Asian American students usually relate education to making a difference in their extended families, home communities, and tribes.

I learn best when the professor starts with real examples from the community and helps us consider larger implications and effects. In my art appreciation class we had a conversation in the first session about how public art like murals and park statues makes us feel and their possible meanings to the community. This made me reflect on public art in my small island home and how when I return I should speak up for this in the community. The professor's emphasis on art in our own communities also made me look more deeply for meaning in art as we progressed through the course.

—Hawaiian undergraduate student

Some populations of students are oriented in an individualized way for the purpose of benefiting self, especially toward a future career, and not burdening others. Some populations of students are oriented in a collective way for the purpose of benefitting communities of origin through work and contributions such as community or political service. Though we understand that there are regional, community, and familial variations and that Indigenous populations in any country are likely to emphasize collective orientations, students from Northern European American and Northern Asian American origins in our studies often described how their families encourage suspension of family and other responsibilities while their children are in college. Students from African, Native, Southeast Asian, and Hispanic populations described being reminded often by parents and other family about their continued responsibilities, especially within their extended families, even while in college. Some faculty also described this distinctive difference. One faculty member shared,

I was really kind of stunned the first time a Hispanic or Native student shared some of their ongoing responsibilities within their extended families or tribes. One of my advisees drives two hours home on Tuesday evenings so he is there to take care of his grandmother every Wednesday. Navajo students in our program often return home for numerous traditional ceremonies each semester. At first I felt irritated because I assumed they didn't care enough about academics. Now I am truly humbled by the dedication these students show to their college educa-tion and to family and tribal responsibilities.

He continued,

Honestly, I cannot imagine if my parents or community had expected me to come home more than at winter break. I was encouraged to focus on me and on college.

Later he discussed how this difference gave him the idea to center his examples, stories, and case studies across these distinctive cultural frame-works.

I was really excited when it came to me that I could offer both. I could some-times create a case study or give an example that I connected directly to future professional work and sometimes create one that was related to serving home communities or tribes. Sometimes I combine the two and I see just about all of my students light up and engage.

On the one hand, an individual orientation is common to some student populations and to many faculty. It is also highly normative in higher educa-tion because U.S. colleges and universities were designed from a framework of English and German cultural norms. On the other hand, a more collective or community orientation is common to many cultures in the United States and in other countries, making community, family, and tribal orientations important factors to incorporate when designing and facilitating learning.

In some countries, values predominant in educational environments may differ in certain ways from those in social and familial contexts. In China, Japan, and India, for example, individual goals and competition are often encouraged at high levels in educational environments even at very young ages. Work environments are likely to expect similar qualities. Yet in these same cultures, a collective orientation is emphasized, especially in social and famil-ial activities (Bennett & Bennett, 1994). Individual competition and goals may be considered detrimental and discouraged in social and familial environ-ments yet encouraged in some aspects of work and educational environments. These cultural orientations may offer us a clue as to why learners from these socially collective cultural populations often do very well academically in the competitive, individuated contexts of U.S. colleges and universities.

The key is to understand that there are distinct variations in ways indi-vidual students interpret the purpose of their learning. As the professor in the previous example did, it is helpful to incorporate these variations into the way we design learning experiences for our students.

Some disciplines receive critical attention for their student demographics and industry expectations. STEM degree programs, for instance, may find it helpful to incorporate a collective orientation more fully when designing programs, services, and teaching practices. Overtly making connections between commonly individuated and abstractly presented science, technology, and engineering knowledge and the clear benefits of this knowledge to communities of origin is likely to serve as a hook to capture and maintain learner interest among students of color. In addition, problematizing and considering beneficial and detrimental aspects of science and technology on human and other life forms, even in beginning coursework, will assist in the development of these fields and the engagement of students from cultural origins embodying integrated, collective, interconnected worldviews. The following example serves to illustrate ways these suggestions specifically played out in a teaching situation.

> *I teach at a university in North Dakota where there are many Native American students, and I found that I was having trouble engaging them in learning about and getting excited about chemistry. After having attended a workshop on culture and teaching and having a conversation with the facilitator, I came up with the idea to create chemistry case studies and team projects based in various communities in the area. It occurred to me that if I could design something that connected chemistry to collectives that matter to students, I might facilitate student learning more effectively across cultures. I created several projects to do so, including a project where students tested soil samples from Indian reservation areas known to have toxic residue from mining, a project chemically comparing air quality in a nearby inner-city area to suburban areas in the same city, and a project testing water quality in rural agricultural farming areas. I asked students to consider the chemical aspects and their probable impact on communities. It made all the difference; not only did the Native students engage with great enthusiasm, all the students were more engaged and excited about the realities of chemistry in their lives.*
>
> —Welsh American chemistry professor

Online learning presents its own challenges to and benefits from teaching across cultural frameworks. In web-based learning environments, designing projects for students that ask them to apply some of what they are learning to local concerns and issues is especially helpful. Application provides activity and critical thinking that may parallel simulated activities in a face-to-face classroom and goes beyond abstraction to apply directly to student lives. The teaching narrative illustrates the following:

> *I teach an online graduate course in instructional development. I wanted to get students more involved in thinking about the learning needs of students in their*

communities. I designed an assignment where students had to identify a learning challenge in a class they currently teach in a school. Then I asked students to interview at least three students from a cultural background different from their own about how they learn best and what process they use to learn something they really want to understand.

Students then had to write a paper about their findings and teaching recommendations and share this paper with the class as a reading for the next learning segment. I was amazed at the outcome. Not only did students really get excited about what they learned from local learners, they were also kind of stunned at what they learned from the writing and analysis of student peers in the class. I think that by involving students in their work environments and communities and not just in theory or abstract assignments, things became more real and present for them. They learned a great deal from not one but two collectives . . . the children they interviewed and their fellow students.

—Diné education professor

To facilitate learning among students raised with differing purposes of learning, faculty can incorporate examples and cases that highlight both individual competence *and* betterment of the lives of others. The more a subject can be connected to the lives of learners, the more it will stay with each learner. Creating case studies specifically from local or regional situations and issues is especially helpful to this balance. Achieving a balance is sometimes portrayed as situating learning in the lives of students (Baxter Magolda, 1999); the balance facilitates student engagement by connecting subject learning to what matters to each individual. This type of technique offers the added benefit of applying a variety of learning processes so that students experience more complex learning and skill development. Professors can take teaching across cultural frameworks a geographic step further by including some activities or assignments that ask students to identify a national or global situation or issue to process.

We encourage making connections between students and subject matter as a culturally responsive approach to encourage associations with individual goals as well as collective values. Encouraging students to consider relationships between academic subject areas and future professional and personal lives will help students think about these connections and consider subject areas more deeply in their lives.

Within the purpose-of-learning continuum, faculty may wish to add pedagogies, interactions, assignments, and evaluation activities from either the integrated or individuated side of the cultural frameworks continuum. Table 1.4 offers a few ideas that might be helpful. Many teaching techniques can be reimagined and then redesigned to facilitate learning in both frameworks.

TABLE 1.4
Teaching Techniques Within Cultural Frameworks: *Purpose of Learning*

Individuated Techniques	*Integrated Techniques*
Connect subject matter to future profession or career realities, practices, expectations, mores	Connect subject matter to needs, realities, challenges, or opportunities in local or student's community, tribe, family
Design individual exams, assignments, class activities	Design paired or group exams, assignments, class activities
Assign optional reading and problem sets	Promote community engagement through action research (e.g., oral history or design to benefit community projects)
Create assignments designed to explore theory without application to a specific situation	Create assignments or activities designed to explore theory in relation to specific situations, especially ones that students can relate to in their own lives
Learning in the course discussed in relation to the subject matter itself	Learning in the course overtly discussed in relation to the context of a major, becoming a better person, professional aspects, or current realities
Facilitate critique of course content on its general quality without relation to its wider impact—for example, scientific discovery for the sake of discovery alone	Facilitate critique of course content in relation to influences on community needs, health, future generations— for example, scientific discovery problematized for its helpful and detrimental qualities
Assigning all students the same situation to process	Assigning students the task of identifying and processing real situations about which they are concerned or interested

Note. Special thanks to the faculty in our Culture and Teaching Faculty Development Project for brainstorming techniques across cultural frameworks for each of the continua of teaching and learning as well as for allowing us the privilege of gathering ideas from observing their teaching.

It is also possible to mix qualities from both sides of the cultural continuum in any pedagogical technique. For example, mixing from the first set of techniques, a professor might connect subject matter to future professional and community needs or, instead, ask students to brainstorm in both areas.

TABLE 1.5
Ways of Taking In and Processing Knowledge

Individuated		*Integrated*
Mind as primary, best, or only funnel of knowledge	⟷	Mind, body, spirit/intuition, reflection, emotions, relationships as important aspects and conduits of knowledge

Ways of Taking in and Processing Knowledge

A landscape architecture professor struggles with students' understanding of special design concepts through design assignments using descriptive, hypothetical instructions alone. She decides to try something that engages more of the students' senses, emotions, and human input, choosing a walkthrough alley near campus and gaining permission to have students collectively improve the space. The professor encourages students to spend time there, taking in the area through all of their senses, talking with those walking through, and trying out design ideas. As a result, she notices that student learners form a very different relationship with the space, understand theoretical concepts more deeply and pragmatically, are more enthusiastic about applying theory to their designs, and come away with much richer learning. Thanks in great part to the project, the alley is now an attractive walking path that students can be proud of and that benefits the community.

Individuals use a variety of ways of taking in and processing knowledge as part of their learning processes. Latino and Native American students as well as many African American, Southeast Asian, and Asian American students in our studies described learning most naturally through the use of a variety of ways of taking in and processing knowledge considering the mind, body, spirit/intuition, emotions, relationships, and reflection essential to understanding and learning.

> *My bio professor is so cool. She is always taking us out on campus or having us meet at a local park or ranch to explore biological concepts. She has us touch, listen, watch, and even taste. She even asks us to describe what our intuition or spirit might be revealing about something. My parents are from South Korea, and we lived there for a while during my high school years. I had teachers who*

often did this kind of exploratory teaching, and somehow even though I was born and raised in the [United States], it makes me feel more at home, in a way like I'm home with my parents exploring something with all my senses. Like I'm learning more. This professor is rare in that quality, though. Most of my classes are really detached and one-dimensional in focusing on the abstract only.
                                    —Korean American computer science student

In contrast, learning and processing through the mind were characterized as the best, primary, or even the only way to learn by many Northern European American students in our studies. Some students from these cultures describe being encouraged to work at keeping other influences from distracting processes of their minds.

I'm usually really comfortable in my classes. I like the way we can immerse ourselves in theories and philosophy of things. It's really straightforward, and I don't really have to worry about the real world. The professor tells us what is critical, and I can keep it in my head, you know? I was always cautioned growing up not to let other things cloud my head or my learning, not to get emotional, not to be subjective, not to personalize. I'm most at home when none of these things are part of the classroom.
                                    —Scandinavian American literature student

Striving toward an abstract and often detached, compartmentalized mind is traditionally at the core of teaching and learning in U.S. higher education. Learning is facilitated through many senses in the very early grades, especially kindergarten, yet U.S. education leaves much sensual learning behind for an increasingly cerebral orientation in teaching techniques. These techniques can be traced back not just to the early U.S. history of separating the mind from the body but further yet to what is often called the Age of Enlightenment in Europe, when certain aspects of Indigenous belief systems were discarded (Takaki, 1993). Yet some learning theory as well as some neurological research in learning suggests that all individuals learn better when a wider variety of learning processes, lenses, techniques, and modes are applied in learning contexts (Medina, 2011; Zull, 2002).

Emotions influence learning; this point is especially important to consider for those emotions that inhibit learning, such as fear of a subject. One faculty member discussed how he works through fear with students to improve their learning in his courses.

I teach all levels of math and learned long ago that many students are really frightened of math and that this is a significant barrier to their learning. I thought about this and realized that this is true for many, so it is something I

need to pay attention to in my teaching. I talked with students and colleagues over time to gain a better understanding. I tried different things and eventually found that the simplest thing helped. In the first class session of every course I ask students to reflect for a moment on how they feel about calculus or algebra or geometry, depending on the course. I ask them then to share with another student and then ask for a few to share with the whole class. Inevitably there is a range of emotion, and many are really terrified. This gives me a chance to lead them in unpacking this, coming up with strategies to cope, and reassuring them that I'll be there. It also gives me an opening to have them brainstorm how this area of math might relate to their lives and be useful in future work. I've come up with many pedagogical techniques to facilitate through these fears, encouraging fun and confidence that lead to learning math.
—English-Welsh American math professor

Many students of color in our studies described a need to learn by doing, sometimes called *kinesthetic learning* or *learning through the body*.

I just don't learn something until I do it, practice it. I could read all the books and talk about it forever but until I do it myself it doesn't sink in. When someone tries to tell me how to do something on a computer or on my phone, I always tell them to wait a moment while I sit down with it and then I ask them to walk me through it, having them pause as I try it myself. I've heard that this sets up a kind of muscle memory in your body and that is certainly true for me.
—African American graduate music student

Many cultures in the world emphasize learning through a wide range of techniques, sensory lenses, and experiences. Teaching processes that include a variety of pedagogies make it more likely that learners will benefit from both those more natural to them and those more challenging. Faculty can develop teaching in the area of taking in and processing knowledge across cultural frameworks by observing ways we engage student minds, bodies, emotions, intuition, and spirit. We enrich learning with a greater variety of ways to engage students with the subject matter through different sensory lenses.

Students are invaluable partners in this endeavor, so asking for their input is useful. It is helpful to ask students how the class might apply various sensory lenses, how they feel about something and follow up with processing through these feelings, what intuition tells them about something, or how they learn best, most naturally, or most easily. Theoretical tools such as the cultural frameworks model in this chapter, Gardner's Multiple Intelligences (2006), Rendón's sensing/thinking pedagogies (2009), Tisdell's framework on spirituality (2003), and the Myers-Briggs introvert/extravert typology (1995) are especially helpful for developing a wider range of pedagogies.

Gardner (2006), in his theories on intelligence, encourages us to consider not a dualistic *whether* learners are intelligent but rather *how* they are intelligent. Eight types of intelligences, or ways of knowing, are suggested within this theory, including verbal, visual/spatial, logical/mathematical, musical/rhythmic, bodily/kinesthetic, naturalist, interpersonal, and intrapersonal. By incorporating activities, assignments, evaluation processes, and interactions based in a variety of intelligences, and across cultural frameworks and personal characteristics, we engage a variety of sensory lenses and strengths of individual students.

In a similar manner, Rendón (2009) urges faculty to incorporate pedagogies that facilitate sensing and thinking ways of knowing and processing. Rendón's research suggests that including both sensing and thinking and alternating between starting with reflection and starting with application is helpful to student learning. The Myers-Briggs introvert/extravert typology is a helpful tool for designing ways of taking in and processing knowledge. Even a moment of reflection often benefits learners who are naturally internal processors (introverts), allowing them to gather their thoughts before discussion. External processors (extraverts) often benefit from starting with discussion as a way of gathering and processing their thoughts. By incorporating a balance of both kinds of techniques, faculty assist learners from cultures whose norms are based primarily in internal processing and those whose norms are based primarily in external processing.

Learning is positively influenced by intuitive, spiritual, and emotional aspects of taking in and processing knowledge (Tisdell, 2004), as confirmed by neurological research that indicates humans learn more deeply and with higher retention when multiple senses and emotions are invoked—particularly those of vision and positive emotion (Mayer, 2001; Medina, 2011; Zull, 2002). The learner's *ontology*, or way of being, influences his or her ways of knowing. Some learners connect all learning to the spiritual aspects of their lives, while others are highly attuned to intuitive urges or gut feelings.

> *My grandfather urged me all of my life to run in the morning to stay in touch with my spirit, and to process everything I am learning through spirit. How does this connect to the larger world? How is it important to who I am and to my community? What is the deeper lesson here? I find it invaluable to stay grounded in spirit as I take my engineering courses.*
> —Zuni engineering student

Faculty can apply simple approaches by validating multiple sensory lenses, including those of spirit and intuition, encouraging students to process knowledge related to the subject area that arises from intuitive leaps or spiritual connections. Many advances in professions arise from such leaps of intuition or spirit as well as through logical and linear means. Acknowledging, encouraging, and facilitating these approaches and lenses deepens learning and encourages complex thinking and processing. At a minimum, faculty can acknowledge sensory lenses and go further to offer examples, tell stories of their own, and encourage multiple sensory lenses in activities, discussions, and assignments.

Encouraging students to reflect in their own ways and through guided assignments and activities provides students with opportunities to access various facets of their natural learning processes. Connecting knowledge construction processes to cultural images, symbols, rituals, and metaphors is an additional way of helping learners develop understanding (Tisdell, 2004). The more abstract a concept, the more helpful it can be to have students brainstorm symbolic, visual, metaphorical, rhythmic, or other examples to represent the concept. The process of making these connections individually and together allows students varied means to understanding. When students share what they come up with in class, understanding is enhanced through both the process of explaining to others and the natural comparisons made across representations of a concept. We often find that students share insights under these circumstances that strengthen their own grasp of a concept and help others to understand.

TABLE 1.6
Teaching Techniques Within Cultural Frameworks: Ways of Taking in and Processing Knowledge

Individuated Techniques	Integrated Techniques
Encourage students to deeply engage their minds in their discovery and understanding of knowledge	Encourage students to listen to and engage their intuition, body, mind, emotions, and spirit as part of their discovery and understanding of knowledge
Encourage focus on thought and abstract processing in assignments and class activities	Include reflective, philosophical, emotional, interrelational, and physical components in assignments and class activities.
Facilitate student objectivity in relation to the subject matter in a course	Facilitate student emotions related to subject matter in a course
Include lectures, memorization, problem sets, derivations, and papers to enhance knowledge	Include multiple means of sharing knowledge such as video, audio, stories, examples, application to specific scenarios, and conversing with those affected or served

TABLE 1.7
Interconnectedness of What Is Being Learned

Individuated		*Integrated*
Compartmentalized and separate; belief that understanding how the parts work separately, abstractly, and in isolation will lead to the greatest understanding	$\longleftrightarrow$	Contextualized and connected, belief that understanding how things affect each other within the whole and within the family and community will facilitate understanding

Interconnectedness of What Is Being Learned

A construction management professor assigns a series of empathy papers in which students must develop, process, and offer rationales for solutions based on five different perspectives of individuals intimately involved in building projects, including the owner, the architect, the safety inspector, a construction worker, and a prospective building resident. The class processes similarities and differences in the needs of these individuals as well as a variety of solutions to challenges and issues that arise during discussion. The professor encourages students to consider win-win outcomes, interconnections, and the best ways to meet varying constituent needs. He facilitates discussions on resolving conflicting needs and perspectives and shares ways that former students resolved the same issues in their papers.

Students from Northern European American cultures in our studies described relatively compartmentalized ways of thinking about teaching and learning. These students described their preference for learning about the parts of something before they consider the whole or the context in which the whole is situated. Many are fascinated with one specific part of a system, wishing to specialize in the study or application of one aspect, whether in medicine, engineering, literature, or education. Some disregard or even avoid connecting the parts to understand the whole, as if this option is not in their minds unless brought specifically to their attention. Others find it helpful to study the components of something deeply to gain a better understanding of the whole later. This stance in learning is consistent with an individuated cultural framework. An individuated thinker may begin with this focus or may resist when asked to consider the components of something, its history, or the context in which it is situated. When queried, these students often explained that these *external* factors serve as distractions from specialization, expertise, or understanding; some students lament a loss of objectivity toward understanding a specific component.

> *It is important to me to understand various parts of something and then put things together as a whole later. In this way I am able to get a sense of smaller things first before tackling the larger picture. Sometimes I actually don't want to hear about the whole because I fear it will sidetrack me from understanding the specific part I am studying.*
>
> —German American radiology student

Students in our study from Middle Eastern, Italian, Hispanic, and Native American cultures often spoke of the benefit from learning processes that start with an overview of the whole and then facilitate connection between the subject of study and the world around them, including history, context, and their own lives. Though these students discussed some interest in the components or parts, they tended toward a greater interest in the whole subject and the connections to its context.

> *I need to understand how things connect and interrelate. What I don't get is how to understand something without thinking about the whole of it first. So many of my classes focus on the components of something first without considering the overall system. Even my degree separates learning into discrete classes that we never interrelate or connect. How can we ever understand the parts or the whole without both? And how can I begin to design the parts without first thinking about and even designing the whole first? Even more than that, it is critical to understand the surrounding context, the place where a building will stand, the community it will serve, the history of architecture in the area, and the land on which it will sit. I relate more to famous architects who started with this than I do those who were so into their own design without much regard for anything else.*
>
> —Malaysian American architecture student

For Native American and other tribally raised students in our study, opportunities to place knowledge in historical context were described as a critical part of learning. Many of these students discussed practices of returning to previous course materials as similar to oral history and learning from often repeated teaching stories within tribal communities. These students expressed relief when professors used web enhancement to make previous lectures, discussions, and other materials available throughout the semester.

Students in our studies, especially those in rural areas, often identified online learning as a way for them to integrate their learning with the world around them. Online courses make it possible for students to stay involved in their home communities, tribes, and families. They said that being able to make local associations helps them understand what they are learning through college courses in deep, pragmatic ways. In sharp contrast to much of the rhetoric about students needing to be on campus for the richest learning experiences, many students in our studies framed remaining in their home communities while in college as directly enabling complex learning through interconnections between collegiate learning and their own lives (Ke & Chávez, 2013).

We believe learning can occur whether students choose to immerse themselves wholly in a collegiate campus environment, remain within their home communities, or adopt some hybrid of the two. We also believe that all students benefit both from study of discrete components *and* study of connections, relationships, context, and history. Indeed, research on gender differences in learning supports interconnected approaches with women, especially in STEM fields (Becker, 1995; Belenky, Clinchy, Goldberger, & Tarule, 1986). Faculty can facilitate learning for all students by purposefully facilitating activities, assignments, and interactions that ask for and promote understanding of components, connections, and whole systems.

Complex learning occurs for both individuated and integrated learners when the parts and the whole, as well as the system and its context and history, are examined. Neurological research suggests that learners benefit from combining deep with broad understandings of topics studied (Medina, 2011). It is helpful to alternate learning experiences that start with the whole and its context and history with learning experiences that start with studying discrete parts in isolation. Faculty can do this by alternating starting activities and assignments that focus on component parts with those that focus on the whole, the context, and the history. It is often helpful for faculty to point out connections as well as facilitate student reflection and discussion of additional components and connections. Curricular movements to integrate and synthesize across courses, programs, and degrees are helpful ways to extend beyond discrete courses.

In various course formats, faculty can help students make connections by providing ways to continually return to course resources, lectures, readings, and visual materials. Many technological sites are available for faculty to provide access to these resources and which allow students to continually return as needed for additional study and connections. Faculty can provide an archive by posting PowerPoints, notes, videos, and summaries of lectures; provide ongoing access to grades, class agendas, handouts, and class activity instructions; and build final papers, case studies, and exams using multiple concepts from the course. By enabling students to return to course materials, faculty facilitate learning for students who find course history helpful.

TABLE 1.8

Teaching Techniques Within Cultural Frameworks: Interconnectedness of What Is Learned

Individuated Techniques	Integrated Techniques
Facilitate class activities and assignments in which students process components and the whole in objective and discrete ways	Facilitate class activities and assignments that promote understanding of component parts, connections among the parts, their relationship and function within the whole, and the relationship to the contextual environment
Ask students to consider a phenomenon	Ask students to consider more than one perspective of the same phenomenon
Discuss course concepts incrementally and discretely	Regularly discuss and ask students to identify connections between concepts across a course, between courses, and across the curriculum
Expect that students will keep notes and refer to past materials on their own	Provide past lectures, notes, online discussions (if applicable), and other materials for students to return to for study. Encourage students to use these materials for their own learning
Offer multiple ways of building on knowledge components and using definitions, classifications, quantitative assessments, and proofs	Offer multiple ways of connecting knowledge, using case study, service-learning, study abroad, group work, and community-based research

Responsibility for Learning

A professor of management information systems encourages learning, collaboration, and responsibility for self and others by designing regular quizzes that encourage all three. Near the end of a class session, she hands out quarter sheets of paper with multiple-choice questions and directs students to gather in trios around the room. She asks students to work together to discuss the questions and then individually fill out the quizzes, add their names, and hand them in before they exit the classroom.

* * *

In a nursing program, professors use an online health community that includes great detail about individual and community health characteristics. One professor designs projects, online discussions, and activities that alternate between collaboration and competition to build both capacities in student learners. Competitive activities are typically designed as fun, game-type activities that increase excitement, positive kinds of tension, and healthy competitive skills without encouraging paraprofessionals to work against each other. Collaborative activities often direct or encourage students to develop the ability to identify strengths in each member of a team toward fulfillment of the project objectives.

TABLE 1.9
Responsibility for Learning

Individuated		*Integrated*
Learning is a private, individual activity; responsible for one's own learning so that family and others are not burdened	⟷	Learning is a collective, shared activity; responsible for one's own as well as others' learning

Conceptions of responsibility for learning differ substantially between integrated and individuated cultural frameworks. Individual self-reliance and responsibility primarily to self in a learning environment characterized most of the Northern European American students in our study. These students considered taking care of oneself and being self-reliant to be important responsibilities in college courses and in a healthy society so that one does not become a burden to others. Some individuated learners also discussed the importance of competition to their learning. Competing for time to share thoughts in class, competing to give the best presentation, and striving for the highest grade are important motivators for many of these students. Working together with other students is usually seen as a distraction, a threat to one's grade, or a waste of time by students with individuated cultural frameworks. Resistance is often less to collaborative efforts that are ungraded or classroom-based than to graded or outside-of-class efforts.

> *My classes are really intense and competitive, which works well for me. I get revved up by the need to compete with other students. This often helps me to discover what I believe about the work. I look out for myself, and they look out for themselves. The profession and the world benefit from this kind of competition.*
>
> —English American medical student

It's really important for me to be self-reliant. When I graduate I'm going to be on my own and I have to practice those skills now. So I study on my own and try to avoid classes with group assignments. I really want to be able to take care of myself and think for myself so I don't become a burden on anyone else.
— Danish-Austrian American business student

For individuated learners, providing a balance of individual class activities and assignments is helpful to develop skills in the area of self-reliance and, for some students, to develop sharper individual perspectives and interpretations. Healthy competitive activities can increase energy in a class and provide motivation to some kinds of learners.

In contrast, a sense of responsibility for peers and peer learning was described by many Native American, Pacific Islander, Latino/Hispano, African American, Middle Eastern, and Southeast Asian students in our study. Integrated learners are often raised in learning environments where understanding and clarity are facilitated by comparing and contrasting multiple interpretations and perspectives as well as assisting everyone to learn for the common good.

In my family and community we are taught from a very young age to take care of each other out there, away from home especially, and to help everyone to be their best for the good of the community. For me that translates to a sense of responsibility for others in a class. I tend to form study groups, offer assistance to those who are struggling, and suggest ways we can all do well. It is good for everyone if we all do well. I also find that I learn best when I can compare and contrast my ideas to others. This assists me to home in on and develop my own perspectives while also considering others'.
— Spanish American communications student

Guided interactions in class discussions online or in face-to-face classes are helpful to those with an integrated orientation to learning. Reciprocity and mutuality are important within integrated cultures, and students from these origins often feel a sense of responsibility for helping their student peers to learn and be successful, believing that success for all will benefit everyone. Because teaching another person is one of the more helpful pathways to learning, designing with this kind of process is helpful to everyone.

Some students from integrated cultures discussed their discomfort with competitive activities in relation to learning and college courses by explaining that competition is helpful to some activities such as sports and games but can be hurtful to relationships in a learning or working environment.

I really hate it when a professor has us debate or sets up an assignment as a competition. I find that not only does it break down relationships between teams and individuals, it causes problems within teams because some people in my classes are more motivated by winning than by maintaining relationships with peers. At home on the Rez we are careful not to bring competition into education or into work and family situations. Competition is fun in sports and in playing games, but in my experience it can be really hurtful to relationships in other activities, including learning.

—Acoma Pueblo finance student

Having both individually and collectively oriented learners in the same course can be a challenge. One faculty member discusses the challenge of differing senses of responsibility for learning among students.

It hadn't occurred to me that students might think about learning together so differently until I attended a preconference on culture and teaching. Then I started to talk with and observe students. I noticed almost right away that some students would go out of their way to assist others to learn, and when asked they shared that they felt responsible for others' learning. I noticed that this was almost all the students of color. Some students stay more to themselves, instead believing in competition for air time in class, with grades, etc. and putting your energy into your own learning as best for improving the world. I realized that both have merit, and so I started working on pedagogies that drew from and encouraged both.

—Jewish American professor

Group assignments, however, may have markedly different implications than group discussions and other forms of learning responsibility in courses. The added burden of group assignments outside of class time can become overwhelming, especially for those with children, tribal commitments, extended family obligations, or full-time work responsibilities. Miscommunications, power struggles, differing expectations for responsibility and trust, and varied abilities all make group assignments difficult for some learners. In many cases, collective learning in classes combined with individual assignments provides a helpful balance for students. However, group assignments can be developed intentionally in ways that are equitable, helpful to learning, and not so overwhelming. We suggest consulting the literature in this area for those who are interested specifically in improving group assignments.

Teaching across varying senses of responsibility for learning is a thought-provoking challenge for faculty when they design interactions, activities, and assignments. It requires paying attention to immediate dynamics within a class session, to interactions among students, and to the ways students respond to each other and to activities and assignments.

In relation to classroom activities, it is helpful to vary individual and collective activities and styles of interactions throughout each class session. Varying activities allows students to benefit from some time learning in their own natural orientations and some time learning in orientations not as comfortable. It is also helpful to vary collaborative and competitive activities. Competition is most helpful in the form of games such as ungraded activities, where less is at stake. Competitive activities must be monitored carefully to minimize unhelpful or hurtful forms of competition or interaction detrimental to learning and learning relationships. Faculty should be ready to step in and reframe or mediate when necessary. Collaboration is most helpful when it is designed and monitored for individual strengths to come to the fore as well as for equalizing forms of evaluation to minimize an unfair burden on some individuals. Facilitating students in identifying specific skills they bring to a project or activity can help both individuals and groups engage and appreciate the role of varying abilities in learning and accomplishing a task. Power dynamics are also a consideration in collaborative activities, especially when the stakes are high, such as in presentations, because of their public nature, and in graded group assignments.

In relation to classroom discussions, students from individuated cultures may interpret discussion in classes as an opportunity and believe that "important learning" will rise to the top through this form of opportunity or competition. This perspective can become problematic, as is often the case, when only the ideas and perspectives of a few individuals are regularly shared with the class. When faculty shift thinking away from encouraging opportunism toward seeing it as their role to draw out many ideas from the whole class, learning is enhanced. Many collective activities provide a turn-taking approach to glean insights from all students. This also helps students develop important listening, supporting, and speaking skills. Students from some cultures expect discussion to be a time when each person is individually invited to share for the good of everyone's learning. This type of learner is likely to wait respectfully until invited to share and may seem confused and a bit lost when professors do not reach out regularly or use only opportunistic techniques to elicit responses, such as asking those who wish to speak to raise their hands. Students tied heavily to opportunistic forms of speaking may become angry when they suddenly experience a class with different expectations. In addition, students who are used to remaining quiet may be intimidated at first by this kind of expectation. We find that students tend to step up when discussions are consistently and fairly facilitated.

TABLE 1.10

Teaching Techniques Within Cultural Frameworks: Responsibility for Learning

Individuated Techniques	Integrated Techniques
Incorporate opportunity-based discussions among pairs, trios, and small groups in class sessions	Incorporate turn-taking discussions among pairs, trios, and small groups in class sessions
Facilitate consideration of what each individual brings to a particular individual assignment or activity	Facilitate consideration of what strengths each student brings to a particular group activity or assignment and discuss how each might benefit the task at hand
Design competitive activities, exams, and assignments	Design collaborative activities, exams, and assignments
Employ opportunity-based questions from the professor to the whole class	Employ turn-taking and invitation-based questions from the professor to each individual in the class
Ask for volunteers to write insights gleaned from the readings or an activity on the board for processing by the student or professor	Have all students write insights they gleaned from the readings or an activity on the board for processing by the whole class
Offer clear objectives and goals for each learner to succeed in class; give regular updates on course progress and class grades	Use peer review, incorporating detailed, positive feedback; assign shifting roles to students—facilitator, participant, leader

Box 1.3: Academic Disciplines . . .

Take a moment for some cultural reflection on academics.

For each of the four constructs in the previous sections, place an X along the continuum where you believe your academic discipline is generally in relation to teaching and learning. Then reflect on the following questions:

- Given this reflection, what are some of the most distinctive qualities of your academic discipline in relation to teaching and learning?
- Do the cultural norms of your academic discipline center primarily in an integrated, individuated, or balanced framework?
- How might students from different cultural frameworks experience your academic discipline?
- How might your own teaching within your academic discipline evolve toward a more balanced foundation of cultural frameworks?

TABLE 1.11
Time

Individuated		*Integrated*
Linear, task oriented, can be measured and used; to be on time shows respect	⟷	Circular, seasonal, process oriented, dependent on relationships; to allow for enough time shows respect

Time

In a web-based course, an art professor uses a variety of interactions throughout the semester, including twice monthly online class sessions in which she facilitates synchronous spoken discussion and weeklong written interactions in which students log in any time, read peer postings, then post their own comments. She finds that individuated students engage more deeply in peer interactions, with which they are most comfortable at first, and by the end of the semester, they engage more equally in each type of peer interaction as they gain confidence, practice, comfort, and skill. She designs class interactions alternating synchronous classes (all able to listen and speak online together) with asynchronous (students able to write their thoughts when they are ready), because she believes it is important to engage students in a variety of ways and facilitate new interactive skills that will be beneficial in the art profession. Alternating kinds of interactions has the added benefit of offering some learning activities in which students react in the moment and others in which there is time to think before discussion.

Time and the conception of time are important components of teaching and learning across cultures. In a traditional 50- to 75-minute class session, time is highly bounded, and most faculty use every minute to share knowledge with students through lectures (Rendón, 2009). Students are expected to be on time to class and to submit assignments. It is often acceptable for students to leave early, presumably to make it to another important engagement. The business of the class session usually starts right away, and time for questions and interactions is usually left until the end of class, if such time is available at all.

In online courses, students have time to reflect between most learning activities. For example, in asynchronous written discussions there is time enough for everyone to contribute because students can post comments anytime 24 hours a day before instructor deadlines. This approach also allows students to work when they do academics best and within busy schedules. Deadlines are still in play, and some instructors mark down for late work or do not accept it at all. In most U.S. academic environments, being on time is expected, and lateness is usually interpreted as a sign of disrespect or irre-sponsibility. Timed, bounded exams are usually expected and are often the only form of evaluation in a specific course.

Yet different cultures have different conceptions of time and responsibility. This student from our studies explains:

> It took me a while in college and work to understand about differences in time. At home on the Rez, it is important to stay somewhere as long as it takes because that is what is important to our relationships and to the needs of the People. Gatherings and ceremonies start once everyone is gathered. But in college and other situations off the Rez, I notice that folks get really upset if I'm not there at a certain time. I notice also that at home we start with social stuff so folks can arrive as they need to and the other purposes of a gathering take place later. Here in my campus job and classes the "business" comes right away and social happens during the breaks, and most of the time it doesn't matter much if people leave early. At home, we stay as long as we are needed, and people really notice if someone leaves early before activities are completed.
>
> —Santa Clara Pueblo biology student

Students we interviewed who were raised in integrated cultures that are highly relational and contextual—such as those originating in Africa, southern Europe, the Middle East, and Latin-based countries, as well as Native American students—often experience incongruence between time orientations in traditional classes and their own sense of time. These students described growing up with time based in relationships, less structured definitions of *time*, and the freedom to take the time needed to complete something instead of using only the time assigned. For many of these students, time to allow for internal processing through reflection, dreams, and prayer is considered essential to deeper levels of learning. For Hispanic American students, time is often highly relational and comparatively less bounded, and these students often described time needed to process with others. Most of these time norms are not accounted for in the design of academic learning.

For Northern European American students in our study, time was often conceptualized as bounded and divided between activities. This is in sync with the ways most academic realms operate, especially in face-to-face classes. Specific starting and ending times, a schedule that allows only short amounts of time between activities, class sessions filled with specific activities, and timed exams meet the common expectations of most students and faculty from Northern European cultures. For some, online courses allow for the flexibility helpful to busy, constantly changing life schedules. For others, online courses are too intrusive into their time, too unbounded. These perspectives are often influenced by levels of responsibility to work and family.

> *It drives me crazy when professors or students come in late to class or if we don't get down to it right away. My time is valuable, and I don't want someone else to waste it.*
>
> —Czechoslovakian American geology student

For faculty raised in Northern European cultural frameworks with a sense of time as bounded and related to tasks, and in which *being on time* is a sign of respect, working with learners from cultures in which time is instead shaped by relationships and cycles can be a confusing challenge. Faculty can easily misinterpret student behavior as a lack of respect for someone else's time or as irresponsibility instead of as a difference in time orientations. The following example illustrates this:

> *I spoke up kind of complaining to the culture and teaching facilitator about the Mexican students in my classes: how they always seem to walk in after my class starts and how I think they are not committed to learning. Right away she brought me up short by asking me when I did the question-and-answer portion of my classes. I said that if I did this at all it was at the end of class. She then asked me if these same students ever stayed after class, and I looked at her with amazement because they do and they usually stay to talk with me about the class and often invite me to have coffee and keep talking.*
>
> *The facilitator then explained that in some cultures and countries, it is considered respectful to stay with people until things conclude naturally and not so important to be on time. She suggested that their staying after class so often showed that these students seemed very dedicated to learning. She then suggested that I try placing a question-and-answer time at the beginning of class and see what happened. I did, and these students started coming early. I e-mailed the facilitator to ask why, and she explained that some students come from very relational or collective cultures and so are often highly motivated by class activities that are more relational, like discussions and Q&A. I really learned something about the assumptions I was making in my perceptions of students and in my teaching.*
>
> —Swiss-Polish American literature teacher

If we learn to frame the realities of time differences as an opportunity to innovate teaching techniques across culturally divergent interpretations of time, we can develop ways to work with all students and reframe our judgments about students.

To teach effectively across differing cultural conceptions of time, it is helpful to alternate pedagogical activities, sometimes starting with those that are more interactive and relational and sometimes starting with those that are more task oriented. This approach helps student learners benefit from sometimes prioritizing their own natural sense of time and sometimes prioritizing a not-so-familiar sense of time. Faculty can do this easily in face-to-face courses by moving question-and-answer and discussion time around among the beginning, middle, and end of class. This variation has the added benefit of mixing up activities, which helps students stay engaged. In an online course, alternating asynchronous interactions and discussions, which allow large amounts of time for student reflection and response, with synchronous discussions and interactions, which are more in the moment and trigger immediate thinking and response skills, is a good strategy for including a variety of time orientations. Having both approaches communicates to students that relationships and tasks are important to learning, to the subject area, to other students, and to the professor.

Additional pedagogies highly influenced by cultural orientations of time are exams and quizzes. Most examinations in collegiate courses are timed and conducted in class, which typically privileges learners who are raised in individuated contexts where time is often bounded. Professors can balance time orientations of exams by including some that are timed and in class with some that are done outside of class and untimed. In this way, learners benefit from both kinds of time orientations in their learning. Alternating time orientations has the added benefit of offering students practice with multiple kinds of deadlines and varying the pressures to produce, realities that will be present in future professional and other responsibilities.

TABLE 1.12
Teaching Techniques Within Cultural Frameworks: Time

Individuated Techniques	Integrated Techniques
Administering timed exams and quizzes either in class or online	Administering take-home exams and untimed exams online
Facilitating learning activities in class that focus students on a specific task	Facilitating learning activities that focus students on both the task and relationships with other students
Designing timed activities that remain within the class period	Designing activities that include both time within a class period and time outside
Synchronous written discussions during a bounded online class session	Asynchronous written discussions over a weeklong period
Assignments with firm deadlines; option for submitting late work with penalty; no revision option	Assignments with negotiable deadlines; options for revision and late submission without penalty
Class time bounded by beginning and end of class session	Class time extends to discussion after class, in groups or one-on-one
Exams serve as culminating activity and closure	Exams followed by discussion of results and reflection on learning

TABLE 1.13
Role of the Teacher

Individuated		*Integrated*
Provider and evaluator of knowledge—best perspectives and ways of learning, predetermined or bounded learning; communication primarily between teacher and students	⟷	Facilitator of learning experiences—multiple perspectives and ways of learning, emergent-constructivist; wide variety of interactions among students and between teacher and students

Role of the Teacher

A 20-year teacher and engineering full professor tries every kind of engaging lecture technique that she can think of and that she learns in teaching workshops. She then shares her conclusion that lecture doesn't engage student minds enough, even when she uses metaphors, examples, visuals, stories, and even some interactive queries in class sessions. She concludes from her experiences that she must move from being a provider of knowledge to becoming a facilitator of student learning experiences. She plans to observe faculty who teach in collaborative learning classrooms, especially other faculty in fields where students need to learn complex calculations and theory. She has been reading about active learning, multiple intelligences, and some aspects of culture and learning and is looking forward to recreating her courses to more fully engage student learning.

Students across cultural groups applaud faculty who facilitate activity that enhances their learning; share personal experiences; have a confident, enthusiastic, positive presence in classes; and provide tutorial support promptly in person, through e-mails, and in web conferencing sessions. Students often drift off, skip class, or learn only for the test in classes containing mostly lecture, even with some question-and-answer time. This is true even when faculty are highly engaging lecturers. Although more facilitative faculty often believe that making instructional content fluid and not predetermined is helpful for active learning, most students also want well-structured and predetermined content with clear guidelines on assignments to help them remain on the right track. So, once again, effective teaching design includes a balance—in this case, a balance of structure, faculty knowledge, active forms of interaction, and engagement with the course content, the faculty member, and student peers.

Higher education pedagogy entails two predominant course instructional approaches. An individuated *content+support* approach is more instructivist and highly structured, with predetermined course content and tutorial support (Ke & Chávez, 2013). The learning process comprises reading; comprehending written, video, or class lectures; and completing assignments or taking tests to evaluate knowledge. Peer interactions represent little to no class time, whether the course structure is face-to-face, online, or hybrid. In this approach, the professor is the main conduit of knowledge, and students act primarily in a receiving role, what is often referred to as a *banking* teaching philosophy (Freire, 1993). The banking approach does not tend to engage students at any great level nor facilitate complex or lasting learning. One student said,

> *I can't remember a time when I wasn't sitting in a class with the professor or teacher talking to us, telling us, showing us. My whole education has been filled with this kind of lecture-based teaching. Mostly I show up and sit there but I'm not really learning much that I couldn't just get by reading the text myself. I have friends who are able to skip most of their classes, come in for the tests, and get straight As. So what is the use of this kind of teaching?*
> —Indian American nutrition student

A professor in earth sciences recounted the following from a Native American student: *"Please don't reteach yourself by standing at the front of the room reinforcing what you already know."*

On the other end of the continuum, a *social constructivist* or *active learning* approach requires immediate engagement with the course content to figure things out, usually with peer interaction at the heart of class activity. In this approach the course content is more fluid and less structured. Social constructivist course design comprises reading, interactive discussions for content comprehension, interactive activities for content application, and assignments completed collaboratively or with peer consultations and support (e.g., peer review or collaborative work). In this approach, the professor is a designer and facilitator of engagement with course content rather than purely a source of knowledge. A student describes the experience of such a history class using this approach:

> *My History of the Americas class is unlike anything I've ever experienced. Usually I just hate history because it is just a recitation of dates and events, so unconnected to my life. But this professor engages us in history by having us write our own histories, read and discuss first-person narratives about real*

people's experiences of important historical events, and even draw timelines of critical developments in communities around us. I show up for class and in a blink it is over because we are so engrossed, so involved. Our professor is constantly challenging us, offering additional questions to consider, teasing us to go further in our thinking.

—African computer science student

Students vary in their preferences, but most are accustomed to the first approach with faculty acting as the primary bearer and evaluator of knowledge. The second, more constructivist or active approach engages students across cultures especially when other elements of course design are balanced as noted throughout this chapter. In a more active or constructivist approach, students still see the professor as having expertise yet want to be a part of learning within the whole group. Student learning is deeply enhanced when the professor's role is more of a facilitator of learning than a disseminator of knowledge.

Balancing across content and process is a matter of designing a wide variety of ways to engage with subject matter and each other. Professors can interweave mini-lectures, or lecturettes, with more interactive and applicative activities. This constant mixing of intake and active processing draws from the best of both frameworks to deepen student learning. Mixing kinds of assignments, forms of engagement with each other and the professor, and types of evaluation offers a complexity of interaction with subject matter that enhances learning. Faculty integrate short lecture, processing and application of content by students, a variety of means to assess student learning, and many other processes to create a complex, multifaceted, and engaging learning environment. Many media and other sources of content are available to mix things up, and faculty who teach in this way tend to include many visual, audio, and interactive resources and activities. One hallmark of this engaged teaching is a focus on designing ways for students to figure things out together in class combined with individual work, reading, and preparation, usually out of class. Some professors also assign, encourage, or provide extra credit for students' out-of-class work together.

Professors and students both have a hard time getting accustomed to a more balanced approach to the role of the teacher. Discomfort and even fear may be present, especially at the beginning of class. It can be helpful to discuss the way class will operate and periodically provide *road maps* for students. Road mapping, also referred to as *sharing the metaconversation*, is when professors explain where the learning is going; what the learning objectives are; why the subject matter is important within the profession, the discipline, society, or student lives; and how the class will reach its objectives through various learning activities and assignments. Road mapping brings learning and the learning process into the consciousness of students, which assists with understanding. It can also help faculty more purposefully reflect on, design, and facilitate effective learning approaches. But it is important not to become rigid in following a plan set for a particular class session or online learning module. Students and their learning benefit when professors also pay attention to student learning and modify or change activities and focus when needed to facilitate student learning over time. Because each class group is unique, asking for student feedback informally early on and throughout a course can assist a professor in modifying approaches along the way.

Engaging students in the teaching process is also helpful, yet it can be uncomfortable at first for everyone. Faculty we worked with often found that as they did more of this, they also gained new ideas and learned from content that students found on their own.

An English literature professor experimented with asking students to facilitate sections of class conversation on reading topics. Even though discussion is more constructivist than content oriented, this professor found that giving up control of facilitation was challenging. Inevitably, students facilitated in very different ways from the instructor, who found that even after she had presumably given up control of content, giving up control of facilitation was another challenge altogether. However, by doing so, students took more responsibility for their learning, as well as for their environment and their peers' learning. This professor also began to learn new techniques from the many ways students facilitated, over time incorporating many of these techniques into her own teaching.

Student Interactions

A geology professor encourages revisions on assignments and exams after consultation among students. He provides a grade and feedback to students, and they can either accept the grade or choose to revise and resubmit the assignment within a week. When asked, this professor discusses his dedication to student learning rather than student evaluation, explaining that his whole perspective changed when he realized that his earlier teaching was not really focused on ensuring learning among students. He explains,

> I realized that I was focused more on evaluation and testing and that if I really wanted to facilitate complex student learning, I needed to find ways to have them help each other, and allow me to assist them, too. The competitive, timed, pressure-oriented nature of exams and quizzes was more about testing than about learning, and those are completely different things. It actually got in the way of learning. So I began to think about how I could have students help each other; how I could relieve the pressure of assignments, quizzes, and exams; and how I could make everything more about learning. Encouraging students to assist each other through revision is one of the most effective ways I've found.

TABLE 1.14

Teaching Techniques Within Cultural Frameworks: Role of the Teacher/Control

Individuated Techniques	Integrated Techniques
Connect subject matter to future profession or career realities, practices, expectations	Connect subject matter to needs, realities, challenges, or opportunities in local or student's community, tribe, family
Offer learning outcomes, course objectives, assignments as assessment of learning outcomes, and grading rubric in syllabus	Road-map for students regularly to share where learning is going and how we will get there
Request student evaluations at the end of the course and sometimes also at midpoint; incorporate into future courses	Request student suggestions, ideas, feedback regularly; incorporate into current course
Require students to process specific theories or concepts chosen by the professor	Ask students to choose what theories and insights to process and apply in assignments and exams
Teacher as expert keeper and disseminator of knowledge	Teacher as colearner, transparently sharing shifting and evolving thinking with students
Teacher constructs learning objectives	Students coconstruct learning objectives

TABLE 1.15
Student Interactions

Individuated		Integrated
Others' perspectives are optional for learning. Primarily rely on verbal messages; individuals are paramount, predominantly verbal in both written and oral communications	⟷	Others' perspectives and interpretations are important, even essential to learning. High use of nonverbals, collective as paramount, and multiple streams of communication

Even with something as sacrosanct as tests, faculty may find ways to balance cultural norms. When learning is at the center of thinking, teaching design, and course facilitation, professors provide activities for learners who need individual processing time and for learners who need collective processing time. This approach facilitates varying ways for students to help each other learn.

Individuals from integrated cultures are often raised in environments where learning includes a great deal of collective interaction for comparison and contrast. One student in our studies said,

> It helps me to hear others' interpretations and sense making, and I constantly compare this to my own. This helps me to clarify my own thinking as I compare it to other ideas. Over time, I become really sure of what I think or believe and I'm able to explain how this differs and how it is similar to someone else's interpretation.
>
> —Puerto Rican undergraduate biology student

Individuated learners, however, are usually raised in environments where learning includes a great deal of individual study. An English American philosophy professor said,

> It was all about individual, often isolated study for me growing up, both at home and in school. It is to the point that I have trouble thinking when I'm around others, so I still isolate myself when I need to really learn something. It has been tough for me to go beyond this to design learning experiences for those who benefit from more interactive processes. Yet when I face my own discomfort to apply a wider variety of techniques across individual and shared processes, I observe students truly learning.

Different cultures are normed around more internal or external processing, which influences how learning takes place in early educational and familial environments. At the individual level, internal processors (introverts) who describe themselves as needing time to think before discussing often favor reflection and prep time before discussions whether in online or face-to-face courses. External processors (extraverts) who need to chat to figure out what they think are likely to favor live class sessions during which immediate input, feedback, and interaction enhance their thinking. Faculty can balance both needs by sometimes offering time for reflection before discussion and sometimes offering time for discussion immediately. Offering both also means that introverts will benefit from practice with external processing and extroverts will develop in their abilities to process internally.

Native American students from many tribes often prefer having more time for internal processing and being invited individually into conversations by the professor or interacting with other students in small groups or pairs. This is often because of the commonality of this kind of learning and interrelating process in the upbringing of Indigenous peoples. Many Native American students in our studies said that storytelling or discussing subjects in connection with personal experiences was more possible in web-based courses because of the time available before discussions and the prevalence of written asynchronous discussion formats. A Navajo student reflected,

> *I can always count on time to reflect with other students over written discussions in my online courses. This is time I benefit from to reflect, read, reread, discuss with others, even sleep and dream. I did have one professor in a face-to-face class who often gave us time to reflect or draw or jot down notes before discussions, sometimes in pairs or small groups and sometimes on our own. She would often give us a thought question at the end of class that we would start with the next class. This was great and really in line with my kind of learning.*

Storytelling is an important way of making sense of learning in many cultures. In African American communities, families, neighborhoods, and churches, through song, rhythm, and narrative, often serve as common story-sharing entities. In many Hispanic families, everyone from the youngest to the oldest is encouraged to tell stories. For Native American students, childhood learning is often in the form of storytelling, especially by Elders. Among Northern European students, storytelling also plays an important role, though in contemporary contexts may be more focused on entertaining than on learning life lessons. Yet many students find that when they can connect stories to their own lives, they learn more deeply and complexly.

Providing a balance of individual and collective learning experiences is beneficial across the spectrum of integrated to individuated learners. Designing individual and collective time for reflection is a critical aspect of learning for some. Internal processors benefit from even as little as 30 seconds to collect their thoughts, jot down a note or two, or draw their conception of something before they have to enter a discussion with peers or offer insights to the professor and the class as a whole. External processors benefit most from being able to turn to a peer and discuss something before having to share thoughts with the professor or the whole class. There are many activities that assist those with varying perspectives on the role of student interactions.

Promoting interactions among students and with the professor is helped by creating in-class activities, such as discussions of course materials; question-and-answer periods; pair, trio, and whole class problem solving of case studies; shared lab work; quizzes with whole or partial collective processing; academic games; interactive video and media; and sharing and then processing student insights or problem solving on the board.

Discussion can be as simple as posing a question and asking students to discuss it in pairs, then inviting a few brave volunteers to share insights from their discussions. It can also be very complex, as when instructors use the Socratic method to probe and pose increasingly detailed questions as students respond. Or discussion can be a sophisticated step-by-step interaction among students to collectively figure out a complex task or apply theory. This variation offers a guiding influence to lead students toward increasingly complex sense making or understanding. Inviting specific students to share their thoughts (even encouraging half-formed thoughts) is helpful to all students and is common in some cultures in which learners wait respectfully to offer input only after a teacher has invited them individually.

Alternatively, when dialogue is structured in simple, individual, rote ways, discussions stay on the surface, and students often compete to see who can say the right answer first. In our work with faculty, many acknowledge that it is almost always the same three or four students who volunteer. Yet when professors offer deeper critical thinking questions, expectations of interaction and comment, and support this through positive facilitation and class norms that motivate students in these directions, such as turn taking or grading rubrics for discussion, conversations deepen and increase in their learning value. Instructors make a difference in student learning experiences through the quality of student interaction.

> *I used to assume that it was the smart or engaged students who volunteered when I asked a question in class. Now I understand that it can be any number of reasons, including self-promotion, a need to talk, or a real interest in the topic. What has been important for me to learn is that the other students also have much to offer, and it is my job to invite them into discussion through turn*

TABLE 1.16
Teaching Techniques Within Cultural Frameworks: Student Interactions

Individuated Techniques	Integrated Techniques
Assign individual assignments, exams, and quizzes	Assign collaborative assignments, quizzes, and exams
Use techniques that are taken in and processed by individual students, such as lectures, individual lab work	Use teaching techniques that require students to interact in classes, such as discussions, case studies, shared lab work
Teacher does not expect students to support one another; may encourage competition to increase student motivation	Teacher encourages peer/cohort groups to gather outside of class; overtly expresses expectation of active support among students
Students not expected to interact in or outside of class	What students learn from one another is regularly incorporated into class discussion
Students assessed on individual work	Students assessed on quality of their work as well as support and feedback to one another

taking, inviting, and other means. I am a bit embarrassed to say that by doing this I have found great intelligence in students I previously thought were not very smart or didn't care. I was blinded by not only my own assumptions but by my teaching practices.

—Norwegian American physics professor

Partially or fully collectively graded projects, assignments, presentations, and even quizzes or exams are also highly beneficial to learning and to promoting key interrelational skills necessary in most professions. The challenge involved in collective work serves to enhance synthesis skills as learners are prompted naturally by others' input to incorporate multiple ideas, perspectives, and insights into the whole. Completing individually graded projects, assignments, and presentations and taking quizzes or exams develops other skills, such as the ability to struggle with complex issues through one's own independent insights and interpretations.

Sequencing

Balancing sequencing of learning steps is critical in different ways to learners. Students from families and cultures that teach young learners by

A mathematics professor realizes that she always starts her classes with applications of mathematics using problems and scenarios that students can relate to in their current lives. She notices that some of her students often seem confused when she talks with them; one explains that he has always learned by solving math equations and is having trouble starting with real-life situations and translating them to equations. The professor decides to mix it up by sometimes starting with the equations and theory and at other times starting with everyday scenarios. As a consequence, this student and other more individuated students seem to perk up in her classes and enjoy math once again.

TABLE 1.17
Sequencing

Individuated		*Integrated*
Learning by mastering abstract theory first, followed by testing; unlikely to include application, experience, or doing in real life	↔	Learning by doing, listening to others' experiences; imagining or experiencing first, then drawing out abstract theory

showing or having them try something before they verbally process how it works often described a marked preference for learning by doing first in our studies.

> *My parents hardly talked when they were teaching me something. My dad would show me how to do something and then gesture for me to try. My mom often placed my hands in the needed position and then would gently nudge them to assist me as I tried. There are so many words in higher education, and we are rarely shown something or helped to do anything. I find this disconcerting, and I struggle to adjust. I remind myself of this when I'm working with those I teach.*
>
> —Taos Pueblo undergraduate education major

Students in our studies who were raised in families and cultures who teach young learners first by verbal or written description often display a marked preference for learning first by more abstract means such as reflection, listening, or reading. These are often sequentially individuated learners.

These individuals often learn difficult theoretical distinctions best by working independently to figure things out and by having to argue for principles or theories in which they do not believe (McDermott, Rosenquist, & Van Zee, 1983).

> *I disappear into my head a lot. My boyfriend teases me that I stew, but really I'm just thinking—about what I'm learning, about what I read yesterday, about what is coming up next in my classes. I like to have lots of time to study something on my own so I can understand.*
> —Finnish-Irish-American Latin American studies student

All types of learners benefit from experiencing some of each way of sequencing learning steps. The support of our own natural, comfortable ways of learning combined with the challenge of new ways of learning develops cognitive complexity and ability.

Integrated learners learn most comfortably when faculty approach abstract concepts from a place of "doing" first by having students conduct a laboratory experiment, explore a case study, listen to an example, or watch a simulation video before they draw out theory. Individuated learners benefit from a more common Cartesian method of teaching theory and then applying it in the laboratory. A likely use of less contextual, applied, and more abstract pedagogical techniques by a largely Northern European American pool of professors may be less culturally congruent for integrated learners who benefit from starting with contextual stories, examples, case studies, lab work, and simulations followed by processing related theory.

Balancing sequencing across integrated and individuated learning needs is mostly a matter of alternating the focus of the beginning of learning processes. Professors can sometimes start by introducing a contextual situation or example to students through the use of story, case study, applied lab work, or demonstration or by coaching students to imagine or identify a situation. It is helpful to follow this approach by asking students to draw out the theory from this situation or example or by demonstrating this process for students.

At other times professors can start with theory, through perhaps the sequential steps in the theory, offered via a PowerPoint, handout, or writing on the board. Then they may gradually apply the theory or have students apply it in lab work or a case study. A key to learning is to alternate the sequencing of the learning process with students and to include both kinds of processing as often as possible.

TABLE 1.18
Teaching Techniques Within Cultural Frameworks: Sequencing

Individuated Techniques	Integrated Techniques
Start with explaining theory to students; may or may not be followed by application or processing by students	Start with an example, story, autobiography, case study, or lab work and then follow up with having either the students or the teacher draw out theory
Have students write about or answer test questions about theory	Have students process a case study in assignments or tests, including processing of theory
Ask students to describe and explain the components of a theory	Facilitate students in developing their own case study, example, project, or story to illustrate a theory
Present theory using stages (e.g., 1–5), derivations, chronologies, and graphic organizers	Present theory using stories about the context of the era in which theory was derived, including autobiography of theory authors
Start with writing of theory authors/experts, then extend to application in current era	Start with student experiences, concerns, and questions, and then pull back to broader context/theory

Taking It From Here to Enrich Learning Over Time

To enrich learning and success across many student cultures we encourage faculty to do the following:

- Balance instructional activities, assignments, and interaction from both individuated and integrated frameworks.
- Assess our own cultural frameworks of teaching and learning using the cultural frameworks model in this chapter (Table 1.1).
- Systematically observe how our own cultural frameworks play out in current pedagogy, relational dynamics with and expectations of students, and application to the classroom climate.
- Alternate sequencing of learning activities between integrated and individuated epistemologies so that sometimes we start with one and sometimes with the other.
- Interchange starting with reflection or discussion to promote student interaction and balance the needs of internal and external processors.
- Develop ways for students to learn from and with other students.

Take some time to brainstorm pedagogies with the guide in Box 1.4.

Box 1.4: Brainstorming Pedagogies . . .

Take a moment for some cultural introspection.

Choose one of the eight continua of teaching and learning you've just read about. Take a piece of paper or pull up a blank document on your computer. Write the name of the cultural continuum you've chosen at the top. Now create two columns and label one "Individuated" and the other "Integrated." If it would be helpful, write in the description of the integrated cultural framework on one side and the individuated cultural framework on the other side from (see Table 1.1).

Brainstorm as many pedagogical activities as you can think of for each of the columns.

- How do the two columns compare? Does one have more activities? What does this mean to you? How might this matter to facilitating student learning across cultures?
- What can you do to balance the two? Who can you talk to, learn from, and brainstorm with?

Our Continued Learning

There is rich opportunity for our own continued growth and development in the area of teaching and learning across cultures, including the following:

- Developing a deeper understanding of learning processes common to students from specific cultures
- Crafting ways to interact across cultures in relation to course subjects
- Exploring and analyzing how our own cultural identity relates to course design, pedagogy, facilitation, and evaluation
- Learning from and collaborating with faculty who are working to balance cultural continua in their teaching
- Incorporating facilitation that promotes deeper relationships and sharing among students
- Learning how varying ways of reflecting and discussing influence overall student success and learning
- Gaining insights about how student peer work influences student overall learning, satisfaction, and success across cultures
- Seeking ideas, insights, and understanding of students over time

All these ideas can be explored and learned over time when we purposefully experiment with a variety of techniques, pay attention to our own reactions and those of students, and discuss and collaborate with students and colleagues to develop our teaching practice.

The Journey Forward

Many college students, especially domestic and international students of color, reside firmly within an integrated cultural paradigm as they approach learning. It is likely the result of the Germanic and English origins of higher education and the high prevalence of faculty from cultures based within individuated cultural frameworks that many domestic and international students of color are experiencing a disconnect between their cultural ways of learning and their learning experiences in college courses. In addition, students from individuated learning origins may well be missing out on the complexity possible in their learning through more integrated cultural pedagogies and dynamics. By learning to balance across individuated and integrated forms of teaching and interaction, we can craft learning environments that draw from strengths across cultures to enhance learning and benefit everyone.

Notes

1. All narrative quotes are from interviews with students and faculty. Some identifying information has been modified to protect the anonymity of participants.

2. *Hispano* is a common term used in New Mexico for individuals whose Spanish American origins date to families who immigrated to this area from Spain in the mid-1500s. The term is a derivative from the Spanish term for Spain, *España*, and is preferred by many in the area to the term *Hispanic* or the more general term *Latino*, which also includes Cuban, Puerto Rican, Mexican, South American, and technically, though not usually, Italian, French, Portuguese, and other Latin-based cultural origins with different immigration patterns.

3. The phrase "both/and" in relation to diversity in higher education was originally coined by Hazel Symonette, University of Wisconsin–Madison. She says that it was inspired while she was doing community action work in the Fillmore District of San Francisco in 1969–1970 by a jazz club of that name (H. Symonette, personal communication, November 5, 2013). Though she tied this more generally to diversity in higher education and not specifically to teaching and learning, it is an important characterization of the essential and necessary balance and equality of polarities to working effectively with diverse populations. We decided to use a tilde symbol (~) to further emphasize a synergistic polarity rather than a dualistic oppositionality. For application of both~and to leadership and research in higher education, see Symonette's 2006 and 2008 works.

4. Teaching examples are compilations of teaching observations and discussions with faculty, pedagogical brainstorming with faculty cohorts, and our own teaching practices. Identifying information is modified to protect the anonymity of participants.

2

Culture in
College Teaching

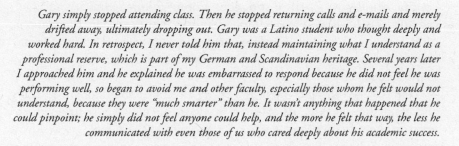

Gary simply stopped attending class. Then he stopped returning calls and e-mails and merely drifted away, ultimately dropping out. Gary was a Latino student who thought deeply and worked hard. In retrospect, I never told him that, instead maintaining what I understand as a professional reserve, which is part of my German and Scandinavian heritage. Several years later I approached him and he explained he was embarrassed to respond because he did not feel he was performing well, so began to avoid me and other faculty, especially those whom he felt would not understand, because they were "much smarter" than he. It wasn't anything that happened that he could pinpoint; he simply did not feel anyone could help, and the more he felt that way, the less he communicated with even those of us who cared deeply about his academic success.

I fear we sometimes fail to extend sufficient compassion or understanding to reach students soon enough to encourage their staying—just a few more semesters, just a little longer to make it over the finish line. I know they drift away, perhaps never telling a sole faculty member about their sense of inadequacy or anger at institutions that could not fully invite them into the experience of college life and learning.

—Susan Diana Longerbeam

The previous quote[1] illustrates one of the primary reasons paying attention to culture in learning is critical to students and one of the common consequences of *not* paying attention. When students do not find something familiar or empowering in their learning experiences in college, they may become disengaged. Empowerment and support from faculty are especially important for students from cultural frameworks that, as the norm, reinforce students' sense that they are capable, smart, and needed in the world. Support from Elders, teachers, and faculty is a human need, but it is more overtly expressed in some cultural frameworks than in others. When students from some cultural frameworks come to college, they begin experiencing a constant sense of a loss of the supportive engagement to which they had been accustomed in previous educational contexts. Balancing integrated and individuated cultural frameworks in our teaching assists us in engaging students for learning, success, and retention through college. By placing ourselves in cultural frameworks outside our own, we have a greater opportunity to connect with a wider diversity of students and to incorporate teaching techniques that are natural for a wider variety of learners. By balancing our own cultural frameworks of behavior with those of others, we create learning contexts conducive to a wider diversity of students as learners.

In this chapter we discuss demographic shifts and disparities among students and faculty; provide some theoretical underpinnings related to cultural worldviews; clarify distinctions among culture, ethnicity, and race; provide a synopsis of some cultural strengths within specific populations; offer teaching examples from integrated and individuated cultural frameworks; and connect some of our work to a basic understanding of learning neuroscience.

On college campuses there is a rising urgency about student learning and graduation rates across cultures. Students of color report struggling to learn in their courses, and retention rates among them have risen slowly, from about 20 to 30 percent in the past 50 years. Specifically, retention rates for Native populations have not exceeded 30 percent, and for Latino and African American populations, they are only about 40 percent (United States Department of Education, 2012b). With less than half of these students graduating, compared to about 50 percent graduation rates for all cultural groups of students in college, we have a long way to go to reach equity in learning and retention across student ethnic groups. Indeed, with only at best a 50 percent graduation rate for all students, we are a far cry from where we should be for at least half our students. Strengthening learning by working with students from whom they are is an important consideration for us as teachers and mentors. Doing so culturally is the focus of this book.

As faculty we can contribute to higher graduation rates because we have an opportunity to transform our teaching to incorporate and build on the cultural and other learning and living strengths of our students. And focusing on strengths is more likely to produce positive learning outcomes (Snyder, 2010). We can learn more about our students as learners, about the deep influences of culture in learning and teaching, and about our own cultural influences on our teaching. We choose to resist justifying our own frustrations by blaming students' lack of academic readiness, insufficient motivation, or some other deficit. We seek to avoid misinterpreting behavior across cultures as a result of assuming something about our students on the basis of our own cultural frameworks. Instead, as we learn gradually about our students and ourselves culturally, we build our capacity to transform our teaching practices to be more effective in facilitating learning across cultures.

Through our research and work with faculty and students across cultures, we discovered two critical insights. First, faculty need to become proficient in developing a culturally balanced teaching practice that incorporates learning constructs from across cultures (Chávez, Ke, & Herrera, 2012; Ke & Chávez, 2013; Ibarra, 2001; Rendón, 2009). For example, over time, teaching in cultural balance brings with it a greater understanding of how culture influences student learning and behavior in learning environments. We offered the Cultural Frameworks in Teaching and Learning model to assist you with this in Chapter 1 (Table 1.1). Second, as faculty, it is helpful to examine our own cultures and the ways our cultures of origin manifest in our teaching and our work with students. In doing this, we become more aware of how culture influences our teaching practice and also more cognizant and empathetic to how culture, including our own, influences student learning.

Theoretical Underpinnings of Our Work

Though the cultural frameworks model in Chapter 1 (Table 1.1) is drawn from empirical data rather than theory, we are influenced in our thinking by scholars who theorized about culture and learning before us. We are primarily influenced by Edward Hall on cultural contexts, Laura Rendón on *sentipensante*, and Robert Ibarra on cultural contextuality, though we acknowledge the very early work of Lev Vygotsky on the influence of culture on cognitive development. Each wrote about the importance of cultural influences on the natural ways that students learn and the criticality of balancing teaching to draw upon multiple cultural approaches to learning. These theorists suggested implications for pedagogy consistent with balancing across cultural frameworks. The following section outlines each theory and then provides some of the theorists' suggestions for higher education pedagogical practice.

Lev Vygotsky (1978) was a Russian psychologist known for his assertions in the early 1900s concerning the effect of culture in shaping cognitive development; most of his works were published after his death. Though the translations of Vygotsky's work have come under scrutiny, he is the earliest recorded individual to suggest the foundational role of differentiated cognitive development based on cultural influences. Hall (1981) theorized several decades ago that learning is inherently cultural when he wrote that humans learn how to learn differently depending upon their cultures of origin. Hall identified three dimensions of learning—formal, informal, and technical—and he said that all three dimensions are influenced by culture because culture is primarily rooted in the subconscious—in the old mammalian brain.

Hall (1981) was concerned that U.S. education institutionalized learning and fragmented knowledge into increasingly linear, compartmentalized pieces. This concern drove his claim that educators needed to understand better how humans learn in order to develop the tools to teach more effectively. Hall (1981) called for more research on the science of learning in the 1980s—and since that time, research on learning neuroscience has become plentiful. Neuroscience knowledge now supports Hall's concern about compartmentalized learning. We now know, for example, that humans learn primarily through identifying patterns.

Ibarra (2001) studied cultural context and *bicognition*, or the ability to think in dual cultures, dependent upon cultural context, as a means to understand Latino graduate student success. He discovered the students in his study were challenged most by "chronic cultural dissonance" (Ibarra, 2001, p. 44)—and the students were largely more concerned about higher education cultural values that did not align with theirs than they were about overt racism. Dissonant academic cultural values were the challenge to their success. Those who were successful adopted bicognition, adopting academic community values while retaining their Latino cultural values. Multicontextual students are those who can interact selectively across cultural styles and cultural contexts. It is easier, Ibarra (2001) claimed, to incorporate a range of cultural values in higher education than to change culture. He suggested that faculty need to adopt both high- and low-context teaching styles to meet the learning styles of both high- and low-context students. Ibarra (2001) seeks to reframe the cultural context of higher education to illuminate and alleviate its barriers.

Rendón (2009) studied the concept of and developed a model for *sentipensante*—the balance of thinking and sensing processes entailed in learning. Rendón (2009), like both Hall and Ibarra, called on higher education to balance cultural approaches to teaching and learning. She called for reconciling dualism by adopting a full pedagogical range of intellect and intuition, content and contemplation, individual and community, and learning and personal development outcomes. To reconcile dualism, she drew on the Aztec concept of *difrasismo*, which transforms two dualistic concepts into a third option. Rendón (2009) suggests that the implications for higher education are to encompass the whole student in order to improve both teaching and learning.

In our work, we chose to explore how college students from a diversity of cultural origins describe their own learning processes. Distinct cultural frameworks emerged from these studies that paralleled some of the cultural theory of Hall, Ibarra, and Rendón. We then took what we learned from students and worked for over a year with faculty, guiding them to balance pedagogy, facilitation, and interaction with students across these cultural frameworks. We also engaged faculty in cultural introspection about their own origins and manifestations in their teaching practice. This led to both a honing of the Cultural Frameworks in Teaching and Learning model (Table 1.1) as well as a deep well of ideas for balancing teaching across cultural frameworks.

A Note on Essentializing and Intersectionality

We address here the common concern that arises in addressing culture: essentializing individuals. Our work is in no way intended to overlook or minimize individual differences. On the contrary, our aim is to make more complex our understanding both of culture and of individual learners. The alternative to addressing culture is to avoid the topic in teaching and learning, an alternative that would not serve to move culturally inclusive pedagogy forward.

> We acknowledge the constant dualistic tension between individual and cultural variance, yet the need to address culture remains.

We have noticed that concerns about essentializing sometimes arise out of personal discomfort with addressing culture. Unfortunately, the claim of essentializing can dampen research about the cultural influences on teaching and learning as well as developing teaching practice that is more balanced across cultural frameworks. We acknowledge the constant dualistic tension between individual and cultural variance, yet the need to address culture remains. Challenges usually exist in discussing cultures, and one of those challenges is that each individual student life experience is influenced by a composite of intersecting identities, including mixed heritages and cultures, and also gender, socioeconomic class, religion, sexual orientation, geographic origin, age, citizenship status, and other identities. For the purposes of our work on culture and learning, we acknowledge intersectionality and encourage continual study of both culture and the ways that culture and other elements of identity manifest and influence learning in each individual student.

We must look outward to understand our students and the influence of culture in their learning. We also need to look inward to reflect on our own cultural, educational, and familial influences and understand from whence our values, priorities, beliefs, assumptions, and behaviors came. Then we must consider how these cultural norms influence our teaching and student learning across cultures. This ongoing purposeful reflection assists us in transforming our teaching over time to include teaching practices from across cultural frameworks.

The Changing Student Body Alongside the Relatively Unchanging Faculty

The rapidly increasing ethnic diversity of college students is well documented and has an influence on learning. Ethnic diversity in classrooms exerts an empirically significant influence on student learning (Chang, Denson, Sáenz, & Misa, 2006; Hu & Kuh, 2003; Hurtado, 1992; Milem, 2003). Classrooms with greater ethnic diversity consistently exhibit greater learning across cultures (Gurin, Dey, Hurtado, & Gurin, 2002; Milem, 2003) because students from different cultures hold distinct learning frameworks, conceptions, and needs (Chávez & Ke, 2013; Chávez, Ke, & Herrera, 2012; Ibarra, 2001; Merriam, Caffarella, & Baumgartner, 2007; Rendón, 2009; Tisdell, 2003) and contribute differently to the learning of all students in classes. Students also benefit from the differing ways in which faculty teach, which points to a need for increased diversification of pedagogical strategies.

Currently pedagogical strategies do not align with cultural learning frameworks of many students of color, especially those with Indigenous, African, Latino, Native, Middle Eastern, and Southeast Asian cultural origins (Cajete, 1994; Chávez, 2007; Pai, 1990; Shade, Kelly, & Oberg, 1997; Tisdell, 2003; Tuohy, 1999). Lack of cultural alignment in the classroom may be one of the reasons that out-of-classroom strategies to increase retention did improve U.S. college retention rates to some extent but those rates leveled out at a point at which we are still not graduating and retaining students at equitable rates across cultures.

Faculty ethnic composition is not changing significantly in U.S. colleges and universities; faculty are still predominantly of Northern European American heritage. In part this composition has changed very little because faculty are not retiring quickly (Jaschik, 2013) and in part because the hiring and retention priorities and practices of colleges and universities have not successfully led to an ethnic diversification of faculty.

The disproportion of faculty compared with student demographics is striking. According to the National Center for Education Statistics (United States Department of Education, 2012b), the total student enrollment for 2011 was 38.8 percent students of color and 61.2 percent White students.

Among 2011 full-time instructional faculty (United States Department of Education, 2012a), 74 percent were White and 26 percent were faculty of color (the lowest percentages were 4 percent Latino and .05 percent Native). The discrepancy is larger for tenured faculty. Among professor and associate professor ranks, 19.9 percent were faculty of color and 80.1 percent were White (the lowest percentages were 3.4 percent Latino and .04 percent Native). Students as a group are much more ethnically diverse than are faculty.

Despite these demographic disparities, faculty can reach all students when we understand the influence of culture in teaching and learning, our own cultures of origin, and the impact of our origins on our teaching. Education research is limited by work focused generally on the cultural identity of students, as well as some more specifically on culture in learning and teaching. With some important exceptions noted earlier, there has been little focus among collegiate educators and researchers on the influence of culture on teaching practices and on student learning. Nor is there enough focus on how faculty cultures of origin influence preferred styles of teaching and working with students. The cultural disconnection between faculty and students matters because the relationship with faculty influences student learning and completion (Chickering & Gamson, 1987; Kuh, Kinzie, Schuh, & Whitt, 2010).

Student Completion Rates

Completion rates inch up slowly, often appearing not to budge at all. The rates for completing a four-year degree within six years hover at around 50 percent for all U.S. students. Student completion rates are often calculated using a six-year time span because many students complete their degrees after they have stopped out or transferred and because four-year rates, hovering around 20 to 35 percent, look worse still. For the 2005 entering cohort, six-year completion rates at all four-year institutions by ethnicity were 62.1 percent White, 51.0 percent Latino, 39.9 percent African American, and 39.8 percent Native (United States Department of Education, 2012b).

Though higher education initiatives exist to reduce student failure, we as educators need a more intensive approach to improving success rates and student learning across cultures. Educators have done extensive work on course design and redesign, course evaluations that have greater reliability and validity, grade inflation, tutors and peer advisers, and early-alert systems using complex algorithms to predict student challenges and successes. Now is the time for more in-depth human approaches, especially within college courses; we hope the pendulum is shifting away from targeted initiatives and toward a whole-person approach to education, encompassing mind, body, spirit, emotion, and culture. To achieve this whole-person approach, we think faculty connection is a key element. We applaud the emerging work in active learning, service-learning, and interdisciplinary learning in higher education, and our hope is that this work on cultural strengths in college teaching offers an additional approach to enhance student learning across cultures.

Faculty Matter

Faculty are unique relative to other employees on a college campus because we alone offer students the badge of academic legitimacy and learning. We hold the keys to course credits, transcripts, and diplomas. We provide the foundational aspects of what students come to college to gain. We are usually the professionals who spend time most regularly with students. We also facilitate what they most consciously come to college to do: To learn and obtain a degree, certificate, or specific skills. Faculty assist students in remaining connected to their learning process and to staying with challenging course content through to successful completion of their degrees. Faculty matter to students.

A trend in public higher education is to fund graduation rather than or in addition to enrollment—and these new funding structures are spurring support for student success initiatives. These initiatives highlight the need for new kinds of faculty involvement in and out of the classroom. For instance, the downside of initiatives focused on graduation is an increasing pressure on students to graduate within four years, a time frame not always sensitive to, or relevant for, all students or all cultures. Native American students, for example, routinely approach their educational careers by stopping out and starting again, sometimes multiple times. Native students generally did not believe graduating within a predetermined time frame (i.e., four to six years) was important. For Native students, education is often approached as a cyclical rather than a linear path (Jackson, Smith, & Hill, 2003). Stopping out is a critical strategy when one is required by cultural norms, family, and tribal obligations to attend ceremonies and family occasions during seasonal cycles that do not correspond with academic calendars. One way faculty can support these cycles is to build greater flexibility into course deadlines. We can also offer incompletes rather than poor grades and continue to work with students beyond the traditional semester calendar. Additionally, we can reframe learning in our conversations with students as a lifelong endeavor rather than using language that implies timelines. Finally, we can advise Native and other students in ways that help them achieve their own personal, educational, and professional sense of purpose and develop our pedagogies in ways that are flexible to both individuated and integrated learning processes.

By learning about influences of culture on teaching, learning, and student success, faculty can transform academic practices to serve a diversity of students more effectively.

While increased funding for student affairs and student success initiatives is helpful in supporting student learning, we need to preserve a focus on the important faculty role in student learning. Caring relationships with faculty are a key dimension of student learning in college and beyond (Kuh et al. 2010). Faculty not only develop relationships in the classroom but also advise, mentor, design pedagogy, and deliver content—all of which are influenced by culture. To navigate successfully through the college experience, students must ultimately succeed in coursework, and faculty remain almost exclusively in control in the course domain. Faculty have an influential potential to contribute to student learning in courses, through an understanding of and a willingness to engage culture, one of the most powerful approaches to reach and connect with students.

Culture Matters

Culture is powerful because of a reach that is much broader than other elements of identity such as ethnicity or race. Culture, ethnicity, and race are related but distinct concepts. Culture underlies ways people teach and learn. "Cultures are created over time as people convene regularly, talk, and do things over and over again" (Kuh & Hall, 1993, p. 9). Cultures include values, beliefs, assumptions, and norms and involve shared beliefs. Cultural traditions are capable of eliciting strong emotion. Cultural references create a sense of belonging and include cognitive and emotional conjoining that has an influence on our identities, thoughts, feelings, and cognitive processes (Deal & Peterson, 2009). Culture infiltrates our psyches, as culture is the language through which mothers speak to their babies and professionals speak to their colleagues. It is also evident in the language we speak to our students, the priorities we set, the values we demand, and the assumptions we make. Culture underlies everything we do in a learning environment and everything we and our students bring with us to the learning experience.

Definitions of *culture* endure; they are old and yet still relevant. According to Boas (1911), culture is

> the totality of the mental and physical reactions and activities that characterize the behavior of the individuals composing a social group collectively and individually in relation to their natural environment, to other groups, to members of the group itself, and of each individual to himself. (p. 149)

In a contemporary definition, *culture*

> refers to the cumulative deposit of knowledge, experience, beliefs, values, attitudes, meanings, hierarchies, religion, notions of time, roles, spatial relations, concepts of the universe, and material objects and possessions acquired by a group of people in the course of generations through individual and group striving. . . . A culture is a way of life of a group of people—the behaviors, beliefs, values, and symbols that they accept, *generally without thinking about them*, and that are passed along by communication and imitation from one generation to the next. (Choudhury, n.d., emphasis added)

Elements of Culture

We prefer complex definitions of *culture* in higher education such as this one:

> Culture is viewed as the collective, mutually shaping patterns of institutional history, missions, physical settings, norms, traditions, values, practices, beliefs and *assumptions* which guide the behaviors of individuals and groups in an institution of higher education and which provide frames of reference for interpreting the meaning of events on and off campus. (Kuh & Hall, 1993, p. 2, emphasis added)

We find each of the major elements of culture (see Figure 2.1) helpful for transforming teaching practice, including visible artifacts and behaviors, beliefs, values, norms, and underlying assumptions.

Visible Behaviors and Artifacts

Visible behaviors and artifacts are the most obvious and conscious elements of culture. Examples of behaviors include the fleeting look of disappointment that crosses our face when students don't understand something right away; or whether we greet students with a hug, a nod, a handshake, or not at all; or the complex pedagogies we facilitate in class. Our behaviors influence how students learn, how they feel in our class, and whether they connect with us or with the course content. Unexamined behaviors often derive from uninspected values, assumptions, and beliefs originating in the ways we were raised . . . in our cultural origins.

Visible artifacts are another easily seen, though not always inspected, aspect of culture. The structure of a course into semesters or quarters, the syllabus as a symbolic and practical contract with students, a chalkboard, a PowerPoint presentation, the home page of an online course, the way classrooms are set up, and even the words we choose to address students are all artifacts of teaching and learning. For instance, in our teaching observations, greetings and parting words struck us—the initial and concluding words faculty spoke to their class. The parting words "I am going to turn the lights up and I do

Figure 2.1 Elements of Culture

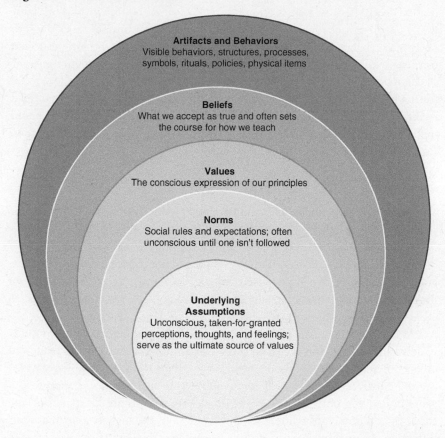

not want you to hurt your eyes" versus "Get out of here" were remarkable in their distinct difference in effect upon the students as they left the classroom.

Beliefs

Our beliefs derive from our assumptions about the world. They are what we accept as true, often with unquestioning confidence. They denote

> how we comprehend and deal with the world around us. . . . Beliefs rest on faith rather than evidence . . . and are established based on history and its interpretation. . . . Beliefs are powerful in schools [and colleges] because they represent core understandings about student capacity (immutable or alterable), teacher responsibility for learning (little or a lot), expert sources of teacher knowledge (experience, research, or intuition), collaboration (useless idea or core principle), and the direct or incidental link between teaching and learning. (Deal & Peterson, 2009, p. 66)

Our beliefs about students and about learning are likely to set the path for how we teach. Because beliefs often rest on faith and on our own and our families' interpretations of the world, they can be seen as immutable and tough to resist or challenge. Beliefs about teaching and learning often go unquestioned until something provides a catalyst for introspection. "It is a student's responsibility to learn" and "It is my responsibility to make sure students learn" are fundamentally different belief systems about teaching. Each is likely to lead to different choices in how we work with students. Developing a wider, more inclusive set of beliefs about both teaching and learning is crucial if we are to teach across cultures effectively.

Values

Values are the conscious expression of principles by which we live our lives. "Values define a standard of goodness, quality, or excellence that undergirds behavior and decision making and influences what people care about" (Deal & Peterson, 2009, p. 66). Individuals often assume that their own values are good or right and that others' may not be. In a learning environment, we may expect students automatically to hold similar values about things such as education, respect, responsibility, time, excellence, and work ethic.

What can trip us up is that the same values may be expressed through widely varying behaviors across cultures. For example, some cultures make eye contact to show respect and openness, while others show respect by not making eye contact, especially with someone new. In this manner, respect is the value underlying both behaviors, yet misinterpretations are likely across cultures. In addition, vastly different values may hold the highest esteem among different cultural groups. The more we learn about the many ways we and students show values in daily academic behavior, the more likely we are to value our students and develop teaching practices that are effective across cultures. Try reflecting on your own expectations of students using the guide in Box 2.1.

Box 2.1: Expectations...

Expectations we have of others are often based on our values. Take a moment to reflect on one strong expectation you experienced growing up and that you now apply in your teaching.

In what ways do you hold your students to this expectation?
How is this expectation helpful to their learning?
How might this expectation be a barrier to their learning?

Norms

Norms are "unstated tokens and taboos governing behavior, dress, and language. These mores or informal rules become 'behavioral blueprints' that people are obliged to follow" (Deal & Peterson, 2009, p. 67). Norms often become obvious when we go against them. Others' reactions to our behavior indicate that we have stepped outside expected behavioral norms.

In an academic setting, norms often influence how things are done and what is expected of teachers and learners. Once again, reflecting on and then questioning current classroom norms is an important aspect of diversifying our teaching practices to include those normative to a wider cultural world of teachers and learners. Continuing with transformed practices can be difficult in part because we may need to sustain them through social pressure from those around us to return to accepted or common academic norms. For example, timed exams may be expected as a primary evaluation tool in a specific academic department. As we gain understanding of the roles of time and place in student learning across cultures, we may decide to provide a more varied set of evaluations in our courses, perhaps having one timed exam and one take-home exam. This may or may not meet with approval from colleagues or even students because of expected norms in our discipline. Sustaining through pressures to conform may be necessary to transforming to a balance of cultural frameworks in our evaluation systems.

Underlying Assumptions

Assumptions most deeply and usually unconsciously influence all other aspects of culture. We find assumptions fascinating and sometimes troubling because they are often unacknowledged and influence all other dimensions of culture. Uncovering beliefs through watchful introspection and observation is critical to identifying assumptions we have about teaching, learning, our expectations of students, and to identifying our judgments, especially those that are negative. We can then choose to enhance assumptions that contribute positively to our teaching effectiveness across cultures. Similarly, we can challenge assumptions that negatively influence the way we see and work with students across cultures. Doing both allows us to consider and find strength in a wider variety of ways of being among learners and in transforming teaching practices accordingly.

Culture is often invisible, particularly when it is not contested. Culture matters especially when it is not seen. Choudhury (n.d.) refers to "ways of life without thinking," while Kuh (1993) refers to assumptions. Indeed, culture is often most powerful when it is invisible. Power engenders its most insidious influences when it is not seen because it goes unchallenged and unchanged. Cultural assumptions, beliefs, values, behaviors, and norms most familiar to us in academe often go unexamined and so carry with them the most power.

Whitt (1993), an educational anthropologist, urges us to "make the familiar strange" by purposefully studying underlying cultural influences of everyday phenomena in college environs. Transforming the familiar to the strange could occur through examining teaching practices, assumptions we make about students, or the knowledge we consider essential in our field. By studying ourselves, our teaching, and our students as though we are entering a foreign country for the first time, we become able to deeply explore and gain understanding of the what and why of our underlying values, assumptions, behaviors, and beliefs in learning environments. For instance, when we walk in a classroom, what is our first greeting? Reflection on our first words to students and throughout our student encounters will assist us in transforming the ways we think about our work and our practice as teachers. Try reflecting on this with the guide in Box 2.2.

Box 2.2: Making the Familiar Strange . . .

Next time you are in your classroom or online in a course, notice some of your behaviors or assumptions that you are making.

Try problematizing this behavior or assumption. What is helpful about it? What is problematic about it in relation to student learning?

How are students responding to you in this situation? Is this the way you want students to respond? Are there differences in how individual students are responding? Are there differing responses among specific populations of students?

What does this mean for your teaching, and how might you develop further in this area?

Ethnicity and Race

Ethnicity is related to culture but is not the same as and not equivalent to culture. Often associated with national origin, ethnicity encompasses both national origin and ancestry. *Ethnicity* is a marker of origins sometimes similar to race yet specific to national populations, such as Italian, Irish, Nigerian, or Spanish. Culture is related to ethnicity but is deeper, and often mostly unconscious. Culture is learned, passed down through those who raise us, and encompasses values, beliefs, assumptions, and ways of thinking and learning.

Race, on the other hand, is a term that generally reflects groupings of people—in the United States into five populations: Black, Latino, White, Asian, and Native. The construct is not biological, but social; that is, there are more biological differences within these groups than across them. The groupings are drawn from social and historical contexts in the United States. Culture is influenced by race as populations adapt cultural elements to changing social influences, including treatment by others based on racial factors (Sue & Sue, 2013).

U.S. Higher Education Heritage and the Invisibility of Monoculturalism

Many people in a U.S. democracy may want to believe in a postracial/post-cultural world; a global world; and an equal, meritocratic ideal (Sue, 2004). For example, we think that we are neutral when we are expressing a cultural worldview or that our cultural norms, including our teaching norms, are the standard ones in a global society. Many in the United States now think that we are without culture or that there is only an American culture or there should be only an American culture. Yet, whether culture is spoken about, conscious, seen, or not, it is still strongly present in everything we are and do. Faculty and students both bring culture to learning environments and experiences, whether consciously or not. When leading with verbal instructions on course expectations, without corresponding nonverbal instruction such as visual aids, we are assuming learners will absorb auditory information. Including visual diagrams through follow-up on course websites, which supports learners who are not primarily auditory information processors.

What is most challenging about the illusion of cultural neutrality is that neutrality is difficult to uncover because it looks benign, at least to those whose cultural norms are common practice. Yet when one's culture is not present in the learning environment, the learner experiences an additional struggle to learn. Inequitable collegiate learning environments occur when some learners comfortably experience their own culturally natural ways of learning, while others experience learning norms far from those in which they were raised. For example, a student who is from a more collective or tribal cultural origin will likely grow up experiencing many group learning activities in which discussion and comparison/contrast are commonly used to facilitate learning. If this individual then enters a college learning environment where the norm is listening to lectures and individual questions to the professor are common or even exclusive, the learner is out of his or her culturally normative or natural learning process and will struggle more to learn than individuals raised with listening and individual interactions. Usually those raised outside of the dominant culture of an organization become hyperaware of these differences because of their recurring experiences negotiating cultural norms that are not their own. The following is one such case.

On my first day of teaching, I facilitated my beginning graduate class session in a way that felt natural to me. I introduced myself describing some of my background, Mestiza cultures, and reasons for teaching in our field; assisted students to get to know each other with a sharing activity related to the topic of the class; and gave out the syllabus and discussed it as a living document. Next, I facilitated an activity for us to add student ideas for readings, assignments, and focus, and used techniques to allow everyone a turn at contributing. I worked to create a safe yet challenging learning environment for everyone, inviting quiet individuals to share their wisdom with us and teasing those who monopolized conversation to create room for everyone. With certain necessary modifications, these were all techniques I used previously in very large classes.

After class, a group of seven students approached me to talk. One of the students shared that they were all from Jewish origins and that they wanted to ask me how it was possible that I taught so like their aunts, mothers, and grandmothers when I was from a Native and Spanish heritage. They explained that in all their years of college, they had never experienced a professor who felt familiar in teaching style to the ways their families taught them or the rhythms of their cultural communities.

In this way, an awareness began to arise in me that my teaching was somehow not the cultural norm in academe. It became commonplace for me to have domestic and international students of color remark on this and share their relief at finding a professor who taught in familiar ways. It also became commonplace for some students to resist my teaching, usually putting it down in some way as being less than academic even while noting that my courses were some of their most challenging. It was this contrasting feedback in many ways that called me to balance my teaching across cultural norms, to strive to learn to add pedagogies that were less comfortable for me so that all students would find themselves culturally in my classes, and that led me to this research and work with faculty in their teaching.

—Alicia Fedelina Chávez

In contrast, those raised within the particular dominant culture of higher education are largely unconscious of its cultured nature or of specific cultured teaching practices. This happens in great part in the United States because so many people, especially those from Northern European cultural origins, do not see themselves as manifesting culture. Sue (2004) called the postracial cultural myth *ethnocentric monoculturalism*. Northern European Americans, or individuated people (see Chapter 1 for a discussion of individuated cultures), usually have a hard time seeing culture, including all of its values and assumptions, and its relevance *within ourselves* to learning (Sue, 2004). Because the entire environment is formed within their own cultural norms, things seem the way they should. This is what is meant by being a part of the dominant culture. Things around just seem like *the way things are*. Thus, many do not understand how individuals and cultures of color are denied and minimized by the absence of their own cultural norms within institutions such as colleges and universities. Those who are in dominant cultures might assume normality, yet in a diverse world, there is no universal normal. In the Lee Mun Wah film *The Color of Fear*, the character Victor famously expressed the frustration of uncovering assumed dominance.

> That's part of what it means to be American to me. That you have all these things you can do if you want to and you don't have to do if you don't want to, and there is a way in which American and White and human become synonyms. "Why can't we all just treat each other as human beings" to me when I hear it from a White person means, "Why can't we all just pretend to be White people? I'll pretend you're a White person and you can pretend to be White." (Lee, 1994)

Takaki (1993) outlined the origins of this cultural norming, dominance, and division in the earliest history of the United States. Dualities include the civilized (Northern European middle-class Protestants) and the savage (generally Native and African populations—not considered Americans until the twentieth century, yet also Irish populations at one time). Caliban, a character in Shakespeare's *The Tempest*, written in the early 1600s, represented the spirit, emotion, sexuality, violence, the animal, and all things primitive. From the perspective of the dominant culture, his Black character existed in contradistinction to all that was at the highest level of human—that is, of the mind. Mind was separated from spirit, emotion, body, and heart. We differentiated some aspects of human experience as superior—in particular, the mind—at an important point in history.

The Tempest was written about the time English colonizers were beginning to rapidly populate what was to become the United States (Takaki, 1993). European settlers found advantage in positioning Indigenous and later

Latino, Irish, Jewish, Italian, Asian, and Black peoples as problematic, making it more comfortable and even morally right to dismiss them, take from them, pay them less, and even enslave or kill them. To do this required positioning cultural frameworks from these populations as less than, bad, or wrong. Positioning some cultural norms as good and right and others as bad and wrong remains embedded in many current societal norms and expectations (Takaki, 1993), including those related to teaching and learning (Fried, 1995). If we instead learn to establish a wider variety of cultural norms as legitimate and good, we begin to reverse this history and embrace a more diverse range of cultural worldviews and practices in academe.

The specific duality between mind and all other aspects of being human was reinforced by Cartesian notions of the mind/body split. "I think therefore I am"—the Descartes philosophical tenet of the 1600s—guided Germanic higher education, from which the United States borrowed heavily. The United States completed this separation and compartmentalization on college campuses, drawing from the Germanic higher education model (Fried, 1995). Higher education teaching in the United States continues to reflect the thinking that the mind is separate from other aspects of human beings. Thus, the dualities of *savage/civilized* and *body/mind* became paired and reified in the higher education context. Uncovering these histories is important because they are largely invisible to many of us, operating at an unconscious level (Sue, 2004). Cultural values made invisible but usually uncontested include individualism, materialism, Protestantism, linearity, future time orientation, and oral and written teaching and learning. Cultural values that often get minimized include cooperation, spirit, emotion, present and past time orientation, allegorical story, and visual teaching and learning (Fried, 1995).

An example from educational psychology illustrates this (Corey, 1996). The counseling professions value individualistic separateness and teach these values to students. Because these cultural values are mostly unacknowledged, they are expressed in uncritical stances. For instance, boundaries are generally good (because they keep clear separations), and enmeshment is generally bad (because people should not be too entwined with one another). The following experience demonstrates this dilemma:

> While I served as dean of students at the University of Wisconsin–Madison, I became highly aware of my own discomfort with the restrictions of privacy expectations and policies when assisting individual students through crisis situations. Within my Native and Spanish American upbringing, the first thing you do is let many people know that someone is in crisis so we can each engage our abilities to assist that person.

This is limited within the laws of individual privacy for an academic institution; yet, I wanted to make sure students were receiving the essential support they needed from not only university professionals but also those more personal in their lives. So I came up with a technique to balance the two. As part of my work with individual students, I would ask them who they felt safe with and supported by in their lives, and when they named specific family, friends, and/or Elders, I encouraged them to consider letting some of these folks know their situation and request their support. In some cases I offered to have them practice with me to feel more comfortable sharing; students often called from my office so they had my supportive presence while going through this often uncomfortable initial conversation. It was important to me that I draw from across the strengths of both collective and individual cultural practices, honoring each with a blending of both.

—Alicia Fedelina Chávez

Likewise, in current collegiate teaching, much is centered on individual work, accomplishment, and evaluation; subtle forms of competition; dualistic framing; and linear processing. These pedagogical and culturally derived norms often alienate students from cultures centered in collective work, accomplishment, and evaluation; forms of collaborative learning; relativistic framing; dual or multiple relational roles; and circular processing. Students from integrated cultures and ways of learning are thus likely to face collegiate learning contexts and experiences that are less natural to their learning and so are presented with additional burdens.

Cultural Strengths

Little is written on cultural strengths relative to the writing on cultural deficits. We use the term *cultural strengths* to refer to abilities in students that derive at least partly from their cultures. These strengths range from psychosocial to intellectual to spiritual assets. Faculty and other higher education professionals who possess some awareness of these strengths may be best able to notice them and perhaps build upon them when they interact with students and design teaching and learning experiences for them. We outline some very broad cultural strengths from the five broad categories of U.S. socially constructed racial groups described earlier in this chapter. In this broad outline, we do not intend to deny the vast variation in individual students. Instead, our aim is to offer some general cultural strengths so that we have a shared language with which to notice and communicate about these strengths. Identifying and communicating strengths may serve to advance students' success (Seligman, 2002).

Our choice of groups is based in the Sue and Sue (2013) U.S. racial and ethnic group populations. Because this book is based primarily on U.S. populations, we leave out many worldwide cultural groups, and because our focus is on ethnic cultures, we do not address here cultures related to religion, gender, sexual orientation, national origin, socioeconomic status, and age.

Our discussion of cultural strengths and a strengths-based approach to teaching and learning is one way we offer prompts to thinking about students and their cultures. We find it helpful to think of these strengths as possibilities that we might find and be able to connect with to enhance student learning. By no means is this broad outline of cultural strengths meant to substitute for learning about each student as an individual. Once we know students as individuals, some of these cultural strengths may or may not continue as relevant or applicable. Knowing something about cultural strengths is only one avenue to understanding individual students; basic knowledge of these strengths may serve to prompt our recall of the possibility for tapping into these strengths in our pedagogical design, teaching, and mentoring of students. We introduce overall strengths identified in studies and then provide autobiographical quotes from students demonstrating those strengths.

Latina and Latino American

Some strengths of people in Latino cultures include perseverance, interpersonal/emotional intelligence, affection and loyalty, respect for elders, commitment to family, spirituality and faith, and bilingualism (Rendón, Nora, & Kanagala, 2014; Yosso, 2005). The following Spanish American student shares one of the ways he learned as he grew up:

> *Comparing and contrasting with other students is often how I learn best. I have friends who are not from my cultural origins who get distracted by this and want to first be sure of their own ideas, but I find my ideas firming up the more I can contrast them with others'. This I think is something that comes from being raised with a lot of group learning techniques. That is what I am used to, and so that is what helps me to learn.*

The following Mexican American and Navajo student expresses perseverance and interpersonal and emotional intelligence.

I think that as an adviser and a teacher you have to treat your job more than just a job. You have to treat it as if it's precious to you—that was it, if there was no advice or no genuine caring and love in their words, I wouldn't probably go see them again. I think that if the person is really genuine and really cares about you, they try to take their time to help you. I pick up on that. Whereas I can pick up on people who kind of shun you and just like, "This is what you need to do, this is how you get your help." (Longerbeam, in press)

Native American

Some strengths of people in Native cultures include values of honor; respect; generosity; cooperation; noninterference; spirit, body, and mind interconnection; listening; extended family; environmental respect; mindfulness (present orientation); and generativity (Gilgun, 2002; Sue & Sue, 2007). The following student (tribe unidentified) is one who is honored and in turn extends respect to a professor:

I think once I realized that professors are so willing to help you, you're much more willing to go in and say, "I need help with this." I think just establishing your relationship with your professor and, I mean, my adviser, I've had a few classes from him—it's always, he's always kept an open door with me. I can go in and ask him for help. And that's been nice—establishing a relationship with my adviser and my professors. (Jackson et al., 2003, p. 554)

A Jicarilla Apache student discusses the foundational importance of spirituality in her learning and among some of her friends who are also Native American:

The other day, I was in the Native Cultural Center having coffee with a bunch of other students. We were comparing our experiences in college with how we grew up. One student said, "I notice that I seem to compare everything to spirituality or to nature. It is kind of my go-to for understanding." Then we all started sharing stories of how we each do this as we talk, as we write. Many of us draw our ideas and a lot of us run in the morning to connect with Spirit and to ask for understanding as we learn.

Northern European American

Some strengths of people in Northern European American cultures are rooted in individuality. Individualism is often expressed in individual striving, goal and future orientation, a competitive spirit, a focus on advancing in education to advance in a career, a focus on intellect, and individual accountability for one's success (Katz, 1985). Building upon these cultural strengths may entail accessing existing educational opportunities in historically and contemporarily predominantly White institutions. The following illustrates the sense of independence and competitiveness that served as inspiration for this Northern European American student when challenged by the professor.

> And when he would grade my papers, he would be so critical of them and tear them apart and just dissect them. And I was like, I looked at it as he's not trying to tear me apart because I suck, he tears me apart because he took the time out of his own personal life to tear me apart because he feels possibly I have something to give back? And he would say that in class, like you guys are the future. You know, and started talking, he just inspired me and he didn't treat me as though I was a student or less than him. He treated me as though I was smart and intelligent and I just needed to be educated. And that helps and that kind of led me to have the confidence to talk to my professors. (Longerbeam, in press)

A German American student discussed her initial distrust of feelings in her learning processes.

> *Every now and then I have a professor who wants us to talk about our feelings. My math professor started our class by asking us to share how we felt about math. At first all my warnings kicked in and it was as if my parents and early teachers were in the room warning me about not getting distracted by the subjectivity of my feelings. But then something interesting happened. I started to hear how other students were afraid, and that made me feel less alone. This professor then asked us to brainstorm how we dealt with these fears and then offered some great strategies of his own. He shared a story of his own fears when he took his first math course in college and how he laughs that he is now a math professor. Everyone seemed to calm down, and I found that I was actually feeling more able to learn.*

Asian American

Some strengths of people in Asian cultures include commitment to extended family and family goals, respect for elders, interpersonal harmony, ritual, emotional self-control, honor, and humility (Sue & Sue, 2013; Kim, Atkinson, & Yang, 1999). A Pakistani American student voices the strength of her respect for elders, humility, honor, and commitment to family.

> I know that I must face certain pressures from my parents while living up to the expectations I have set for myself. I know that my parents have sacrificed their youth and adulthood to ensure that their children will realize the American dream, and I feel a sense of duty and honor in returning the favor. I know they want me to return home to Houston after graduation.

Yet, having physical distance from my parents during college has actually helped bring me closer to them. I would like to continue to strengthen this tie. (Hassanali, 2007, p. 184)

A Japanese American student discusses the importance of ritual to her success in college.

Each morning I get up at 5 a.m. and make tea, do some stretches, and then study for several hours before I walk to my first class. I don't deviate from this because ritual helps me to do what I need to learn and be successful in college. I draw from what my parents taught me to do—what I need to do.

African American

Some strengths of people in African American cultures include extended family support and cohesion, spiritual and religious devotion, commitment to life balance, flexible gender roles, survival skills, and ethnic pride (Parham, White, & Ajamu, 1999). This African American student expresses the resilience and ethnic pride she gained from her mother:

Then my mother turned to me and said, "Remember this if you don't remember anything else, Chantal. You have to be twice as good as any White person to get the same recognition! None of them will expect you to succeed, but you do it in spite of them." . . . Thinking back on this incident helps me realize that one of the many characteristics my parents instilled in me was racial pride. (Chantal, 1999, p. 189)

The following African American student expresses perseverance to continue pursuit of a college degree.

When I'm backed against the wall, I can do it. I said, "You know what—if it doesn't work, you stay at SWU and you stick it out. Do what you need to do to get it done." It was pretty much a promise I made to myself. I wasn't gonna sit around and whine about it anymore. I was gonna get it done. (Longerbeam, in press)

As a part of ongoing learning about cultural strengths, and to hear more voices of college students, we encourage readers to consult the many ethnographic and autobiographical works that feature their voices. Andrew Garrod edited several books of college student narratives, including African American, Muslim, Latino, Native, mixed-race, international, and Asian American students. Schoem (1991) edited a collection including voices of Jewish, Black, and Latino students. Prince-Hughes (2002) wrote a collection of stories by students with autism, and Howard and Stevens (2000) edited a book of stories by LGBT students.

Culture Matters to Learning

Many underlying and often unconscious influences in faculty teaching and student learning are related to culture and its values. We encourage increasing the visibility and consciousness about culture among faculty as well as students. When we examine cultural influences on our understanding of learning, we might better meet students in their own worlds, or at least move halfway toward them, not by becoming actors on a stage or performing for students, but by authentically attending to varying cultural ways of knowing. Transforming our teaching toward a full balance of cultural frameworks might then support all students in achieving optimal learning. The following provides a narrative illustration:

> I am of Danish, Swedish, German, and English cultures, and there are aspects of my cultures of origin that I especially enjoy. As a child, my parents consistently taught me that I could reach my goals as an individual—and this individualism allowed me to relish in the confidence that I would not only reach my goals but have agency in choosing them. I was an earnest student. I felt a sense of mastery; I loved learning and I knew I would achieve success.
>
> I tell students that they can achieve success in life, too. I believe in them because my parents believed in me. But I recognize perils for some Northern European American students who share my earnestness about success. In Joan's case, her striving was leading to an undue emphasis on grades, résumés, and degrees, to the detriment of her learning. With unconditional positive regard, and honest feedback, I extended myself beyond what my Scandinavian and German heritage taught me. I felt like I was being intrusively caring when I explained to Joan what matters is who you are humanly, not your credentials. I emphasized the importance of integrity and of relationships with faculty and peers. I shared that ethics and relationships are at the heart of success. I implored her to focus on taking risks, rather than on her GPA. My concern arose with Joan because I knew that her cultural tradition encouraged material success, but I wanted her to reach beyond herself, to experience transformative learning and development. I wanted more for her.
> —Susan Diana Longerbeam

Accessing the whole person for learning is a core philosophy in collegiate teaching literature (American Council on Education, 1937, 1949; Joint Task

Force on Student Learning, 1998). Meeting students in their cultural worlds is encouraged in philosophy to teach students where they are developmentally (American College Personnel Association, 1975). However, higher education is moving ever more quickly toward a business model in which outcomes must be measured in quantitative terms—measurements and assessments that focus on cognitive knowledge but fail to measure wisdom or learning, and that do not predict success, purpose, or fulfillment in life. Alternatively, faculty might develop a focus on engaged learning, or what Fried (2012) calls *transformative learning,* through deep engagement. Transformative learning is made possible through teaching using a full balance of cultural frameworks.

While the teaching and faculty development literature focuses on teaching practices, it often stops at teaching technique. For example, those techniques include aligning learning objectives with learning assessment (Biggs, 1999). The assumption is that when assessment includes verbs such as *relate*, *analyze*, and *solve*, students take a critical approach to learning. Ironically, even contemporary pedagogical approaches such as deep/active/service/cooperative learning themselves risk becoming reductionist, the very embodiment of surface approaches to learning. By separating teaching into the component parts of learning objectives and assessment, we lose the spirit of reaching students through accessing their own meaning making.

Our goal in this book is to unmoor the approaches to teaching and learning from their mechanistic applications and to extend our reach to the broader influence of culture in teaching and learning. When faculty balance cultural frameworks in college teaching, meaning making and learning are deepened through the symbiotic relationship of comfort and dissonance; the melding of knowledge through heart, mind, body, and spirit; the interface of contemplation and discussion; and the weaving of circular and linear patterns of processing.

The Expanding Nature of Learning Environments

A focus on student learning entails just one of the many contemporary pedagogical approaches in higher education. In recent years, higher education has experienced an explosion of new learning contexts, technologies, pedagogies, and environments; web-based learning, including online courses and programs, massive open online courses (MOOCs), correspondence courses, and other forms of technology-based learning contexts, are multiplying quickly and offering learners a wide variety of choices. Weekend, evening, monthly, and other alternative formats of face-to-face courses are rapidly expanding to serve growing numbers of learners of nontraditional ages and circumstances.

Course redesign, cognitive behavioral approaches, peer programs, and other kinds of initiatives are also changing collegiate learning approaches and contexts. In addition, many colleges and universities are building new forms of classrooms more conducive to group and interactive learning. We understand that these add to the already diverse contexts within which faculty teach, including a variety of class sizes, labs, and studios, and clinical and independent study modes of teaching. Current learning contexts and coming evolutions create many opportunities for diverse learners to find more culturally natural ways to learn.

These evolutions present challenges and opportunities for faculty as teachers. In the busy professional lives of faculty, incremental, slow changes in teaching are understandable and usual. Though transformation toward more culturally balanced teaching may take longer in this widened learning context, evolving our teaching practices incrementally over time is conducive to ongoing development. We encourage faculty to begin developing a balance of cultural elements in teaching regardless of teaching context, student demographics in a course, and our own cultural origins. In subsequent chapters of this book, we offer pointers, examples, strategies, and suggestions in a wide variety of teaching and learning contexts and environments to assist you as you develop your own teaching methods.

Neuroscience Supports Balancing Cultural Frameworks

> Learning is enhanced when a full range of learning processes is activated, such as those represented by teaching across cultural frameworks.

Balancing cultural frameworks in teaching practice (discussed in detail in Chapter 1) is supported by the neuroscience of learning. Learning is enhanced when a full range of learning processes is activated, such as those represented by teaching across cultural frameworks (see Table 1.1). The process of learning incorporates emotion and the senses. The Descartes model of intellect alone is not the consummate learning model for humans (Mortiboys, 2012). Student narratives from studies upon which the model of cultural frameworks is based and our work with faculty suggest that teaching is most effective when we draw upon the full range of individuated to integrated learning. Learning is sometimes particularly challenging, such as for some with abstract or technical concepts and for others with learning human behavior or artistic concepts. During challenging times, students are more likely to consider rather than avoid the challenge when our teaching approach matches the learning process most comfortable and natural for them. As well, it is also important to learn through ways that are not as natural. To maximize and deepen learning, learners need to experience both some learning processes that are culturally natural and some that are culturally new. Faculty can facilitate learning by culturally balancing a variety of teaching pedagogies, interactions, and learning projects in any one course.

We are motivated to learn when we are both excited and comfortable. Humans naturally want to learn; a useful theory for explaining our natural motivation when we are taught in ways comfortable for our culture is a theory for intrinsic motivation. Ginsberg and Wlodkowski (2009) argue that we cannot expect students to simply be motivated; instead, we need to foster intrinsic motivation, which occurs when we as educators address the best motivating conditions for each student. Motivating conditions are establishing inclusion, developing attitude, engendering competence, and enhancing meaning (Ginsberg & Wlodkowski, 2009). So when educators focus on teaching across cultural frameworks, we are more likely to tap into each student's sense of inclusion, fostering an approach rather than avoidance attitude toward learning, thus enabling students to feel competent and create meaningful applications.

A Brief Summary of Learning Neuroscience

The need for teaching across cultures is reinforced by the neuroscience of learning (Zull, 2002). For learning to occur, learners must be able to attach new information to current structures in their brains—to something they already know. Students also need a way to file new information, to attach new learning to existing structures, and to give some order to their brains (Zull, 2002). Because students must have an existing folder in which to save new information, we need to find ways to reach students with that which they already relate, especially something visceral and important. In other words, we need the new information to attach to something they care about. All of this is more likely when at least some educational processes are within students' own culturally natural modes of learning and frames of reference.

To best gather new information, humans rely on using senses. Once students have places in their brains for new information, they need to use the new information in order to retain it. Another way of looking at this process is to start with pictures and stories, which are like maps we use to attach ideas to existing structures or prior knowledge. Learners conduct the learning process by reflecting, creating, and actively using sensory, associative, and motor functions. Exercising these functions in different parts of the brain creates recallable, permanent physical connections. Thus students gather using senses, connect to existing information, and recall. Through a cyclical process that evolves toward greater complexity, students may again use senses, file, apply to new situations, and ultimately create ever expanding structures. However, the human learning process is complex, and the order of learning may vary by individual (Zull, 2002).

Reflection integrates the information into existing structures, and for many, reflection best occurs in solitude. It is about a search for connections, and for some, reflection works best when distractions are diminished—that is, not by using continuous partial attention, such as the kind of attention increasingly in use when multiple technologies (cell phones, the Internet) are competing for our attention (Stone, 2008). Within other familial and cultural traditions, individuals are encouraged to still themselves and open all senses at once to let them flow through and form interconnected understandings.

> *All through my childhood, my father would take my siblings and me out into the mountains or the desert, sit us in a sheltered spot, and guide us in opening all our senses to the world. We were encouraged to just let what we heard and saw and felt flow through us, to let it all coalesce so we could understand our place in the world and the beauty of interconnections all around. He taught us to still our bodies and minds so we could listen with our other senses. My mother did this in different ways, leading us outside and having us absorb for a moment to capture not only the visual but also the sound, the feel, the spirit before painting with clay on the river boulders near our home.*
> —Alicia Fedelina Chávez

When we allow sufficient reflection, we gain insights—or we experience the familiar "click" that signals wonderful aha moments—when emotion, intuition, and intellect come together. When given sufficient time between new content, without too much information to interrupt the process, we may achieve these learning moments.

Concrete teaching applications of these neuroscience concepts, using a blend of individuated and integrated approaches, include structuring class so that after complex topics have been introduced, we might introduce a reflective activity to integrate and contextualize the learning, completed alone. We might then follow with interpretations and perspectives from peers (individuated to integrated). Aother technique might include asking students in a partnered or individual assignment to identify a real-world challenge or opportunity, observe or reflect on the issues involved, and then apply theory from the course to make meaning of it (integrated to individuated). Sometimes we can also reverse these same techniques, perhaps starting with the reflective activity as a way to introduce a complex topic. In this way, as discussed previously, when we balance techniques across cultural frameworks, sometimes learning is in one group of students' natural learning processes and sometimes in others'.

I balance across cultural frameworks differently in a face-to-face and an online course. In a face-to-face classroom, I alternate sometimes starting with my own natural rhythm of telling a story in relation to the focus topic or having students reflect on something in relation to it. In the same class session, or in the next class section, I might go outside my own natural rhythm and start by explaining theory and then follow with a case study so students can apply the theory. Because of my integrated cultural nature, I always explain through professional and personal examples and stories, yet I alternate where I start to meet the natural and cultural learning processes of different students in the class.

In an online course, things are a bit different. I choose to offer everything at once, and then students are able to start where they feel most comfortable. Because I have interviewed so many students now and also ask students in my courses to describe to me how they learn most naturally and to offer me suggestions about how I can teach to their learning processes, I know that they start in very different components of my learning module online. Some go straight to any lecturette I may provide, others will read first, still others will head for the online discussion to find out how their peers are speaking, and still others will reflect privately or in written online discussions to start by processing their thoughts with others.

In both learning contexts I find it critical to be as inclusive and balanced as I can across cultural frameworks of teaching and learning.

—Alicia Fedelina Chávez

Once students reflect on new knowledge and integrate it into existing structures, they are more readily able to create new knowledge for themselves. The full prefrontal cortex is now involved, busy at work creating new relationships and new meaning, and developing new language— in one's own language, which is the measure of how one knows the new knowledge is lodged in the brain. Writing, for example, is a good way to incorporate knowledge into one's own language. For students to find their own language, we need to encourage them to find their voice; they must think it themselves for it to nestle into places in their brains. Marcia Baxter Magolda (2001) refers to this as *self-authorship* and describes it as essential to learning that sustains itself, in contrast to learning that only lasts until the next exam.

Learners must create their own knowledge and work with it in their own words, images, time, and senses. Learners need agency for this process: they need to be able to see, feel, and remember stories and images, integrate them, use them, work with them, re-create them, handle them, communicate them to someone, and rest. They need time for reflection (generally with full, not partial attention). They need to recall stories. Finally, they learn best when they communicate the new knowledge by explaining, drawing, or writing about the concepts or stories—and finally when they use the new knowledge again in another context, perhaps with higher complexity (Hender-Giller, 2011; Medina, 2011; Zull, 2002).

The best way to remember higher complexity, or bigger chunks of, information is with visual images. Our brains are hardwired for the visual (Medina, 2011; Zull, 2002). Processing information through visual forms is powerful because light delivers more information more quickly to our brains than do other sensory modes, such as touch or hearing. We can facilitate learning using visual images and creation of knowledge, but as faculty we cannot create these events for students. We can offer the general environment, structure for the process, and facilitation through processes. But each brain is unique and will attach and use knowledge differently. Though neuroscience is not specifically focused on the cultural, it has many implications for understanding and attending to cultural elements.

The following illustrates the process of how we as instructors might teach this discussion on the neuroscience of learning using the two cultural frameworks: one with an individuated example and another with an integrated example (the cultural framework language from Table 1.1 [p. 8] is in *italics*). The learning outcome for each lesson is to understand how the human brain learns. Unlike the example earlier, each of the following examples is centered primarily on one side of the cultural framework continuum to illustrate each in teaching practice.

Individuated Teaching Example

We teach with *theory first* in a lecture on the following *linear* stages in the neuroscience of learning. In teaching aligned with individuated culture, we begin with mind and text. Each step is a *separate* stage of individual parts. The learning process is a *private*, individual one. To measure progress, we might attach a rubric and assess outcomes for *individual competence*. Communication occurs primarily from teacher to student. We draw upon mostly verbal transmission—using a lot of words. We want students to get the theory of neuroscience first, test the theory later, and finally apply it. For example, we might provide a *linear* outline of the neuroscience of learning:

1. **Gather**
   a. Provide theory
   b. Read
   c. Listen
   d. Sort
   e. File in folders

2. **Create**
   a. Read
   b. Talk
   c. Explain
   d. Test
   e. Search
   f. Recall

3. **Recall**
   a. Communicate
   b. Write
   c. Demonstrate (individual competence)
   d. Act

4. **Closure**
   a. Finished product (paper, experiment, course) to assess *individual competence*
   b. Repeat cycle at increasing complexity

Next, we might give a quiz on these steps. Finally, we ask students to apply the theory to a hypothetical situation, verbally in the same class, and call upon students who raise their hands to offer their theoretical applications.

This individuated lesson focuses on linear stages in the neuroscience of learning. For students who are accustomed to processing information in linear stages, these sequential steps may help by offering a linear map for memory storage and later recall. This example avoids the application of story, which some students find distracting.

Integrated Teaching Example

In integrated forms of teaching, we weave together many elements in a variety of ways based on the students, the context, how they are thinking and feeling that day, and other important factors that arise as depicted in Figure 2.2, starting with the whole and often communicating through story.

Figure 2.2 An Integrated Example of Teaching

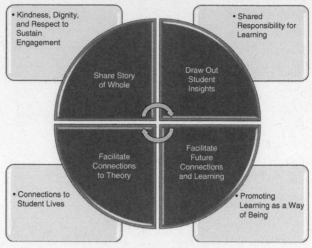

Share a story of the whole idea. Within an integrated framework of teaching, we might share a brief story to embody the process of information connecting to experience (perhaps sharing our own experience of seeing the white van news report on television; see Box 2.3). The white van story was salient to those living in the Washington, DC, area just after the events of 9/11 and aptly depicted attribution error, or the ways our brain makes false assumptions owing to the power of pattern making, a key neuroscience concept. This story is often one that students are likely to relate to in some way and may also be a story from our own personal or professional experience. We might ask students to *reflect* on and then *share* with a partner a story of when some piece of information they were learning *connected* to their own *experiences*.

Box 2.3: The White Van

We are in Washington, DC, in October 2002 and discussing the sniper, who is still at large. We have just learned the sniper is not driving a white van as earlier reported. I ask the class, "How many of us have been seeing a lot of white vans in the past two days?" The class opens up with acknowledgments and affirmative nods. (The information about

white vans connects to their immediate lived experience—they will not
forget the example of—see?) An Austrian-German American student
then shares he used to think African American students always crossed
the street without looking—then he went home for the holidays and
noticed he and his high school buddies did a lot of crossing the street
without looking—and he connected this story to finding white vans
everywhere. "We find what we are looking for," he wisely concluded.

Draw out student insights. We invite students to share their insights about
this process with the class. This can be done in a number of ways, and we
alternate between methods of facilitation, sometimes having students work
in groups to develop insights and later share these visually or verbally with
the class, sometimes inviting individual students to share insights either by
turn taking or raising their hands when they are ready, and sometimes by
asking all students to write one insight on the board. We may encourage
the sharing of *emotions* related to stories or connect to future professional
practice. Each of these activities is designed to encourage individual and
collective responsibility for learning as well as connections to the lives of
students.

   Facilitate connections between stories and larger concepts such as theory.
We point out some of the connections students have already made with
their lay language insights and stories to larger concepts and related theory. This includes positive feedback about student insights as well as gentle
redirections when helpful. This is done with a priority of retaining each
individual's dignity within the collective, honoring each contribution, sustaining engagement with each student in a long-term learning community.
We begin to make connections between student language and sense making and theoretical language and sense making about the neuroscience of
learning. This also involves pointing out connections among the insights of
various students.

   Connect current learning to future learning. We provide students with
some responsibilities for the next class including writing a short paragraph to
summarize the theory just studied in a way that explains it for their student
peers in the class, stating that each summary will be posted on the board at
the beginning of class, and we'll identify larger ideas and patterns from across
all the summaries together. We also let students know that they will have an
opportunity to apply this theory and others to the next assignment, further
connecting current learning to future learning.

Summarize Learning by Sharing Metaknowledge

Regardless of our pedagogical approach, learning occurs when we add or connect new knowledge to existing knowledge, especially when we use patterns, visual sensing, emotional reaction, active engagement, reflection, communication of new knowledge, and finally application of new knowledge in new contexts (Medina, 2011; Zull, 2002). By explicitly sharing this process with students, we are sharing the metaknowledge that helps them make meaning of their learning.

When we teach using a melding of both the integrated and the individuated (e.g., selecting some of both approaches from the previous example), we maximize student learning. Melding both strategies allows us to teach to students' natural ways of learning, which enhances their comfort levels in the classroom, and provides some learning experiences outside of their natural ways of learning, which in turn offers newly challenging modes of learning to students' experiences.

According to current neuroscience research on learning, in the most effective learning contexts faculty act as facilitators of student learning, applying the knowledge of neuroscience to help students make meaning of learning. In other words, faculty can initiate the metaconversation with learners so they realize why understanding how we learn is important, and the meaning behind how we learn, so that they can practice it. In this role we are more facilitator than evaluator. We acknowledge that teaching communities of learners, such as in a classroom, can be challenging because everyone's network of knowledge is different, and though neuroscience is presented in a linear way, the process may vary and is contextually dependent.

New learning is more difficult without prior neural networks, without connections to existing cultural processes, and with massive access to knowledge. But with no attention to the cultural processes involved in learning, it is difficult to know which information is important; sorting is challenging. If we do not know what is important, we think we have to retain everything, and we simply cannot. Theory and story are helpful because they connect with prior knowledge, and the prior knowledge can vary widely—stories remain useful. As teachers, our role is to facilitate students connecting old knowledge with new and the big picture with smaller pictures. The Cultural Frameworks in Teaching and Learning model in Chapter 1 (Table 1.1) serves as a kind of balancing tool or decision-making model: "Do I have some of this, as well as some of that in that class session? In this syllabus? In this assignment?"

Learning Carries Hazards

The learning environment we create is important because the human brain is sensitive to hazards. When the environment is familiar, comforting, and natural, our brains go into an approach state, and we become emotionally engaged and learn quickly (Hender-Giller, 2011). Unfortunately, sometimes the overwhelming amount of modern information in an unfamiliar environment carries hazards to learning because too much negative emotion is aroused. Because emotion and cognition are not neatly divided, our cognition will not engage well when emotion is one of threat. The potential for cognitive and emotional disengagement is why it can be helpful sometimes to process emotions in the classroom . . . especially when the subject is naturally intimidating to many students or the new learning process used is unfamiliar or uncomfortable.

Learning is ideal when conditions contain cognitive challenge and positive emotion—a balance of challenge and support (Sanford, 1966). Our brains are highly attuned to threat. We want learners (and their brains) to approach new material, not resist it. To create approach states for people's brains, we need a positive amount of emotional engagement, in a welcoming environment.

> Some studies have found that it is easier to trigger an avoid response and harder to create an approach response because the avoid response creates far more arousal in the emotional networks of the brain (Baumeister, Bratslavsky, & Vohs, 2001). The implications for learning are powerful. Learners are constantly and subconsciously monitoring their learning environments and are naturally wary of lurking threats. Openness to learn is greatly diminished when there is a perception of threat or when learners sense a potential for loss of control. (Hender-Giller, 2011, p. 9)

The neuroscience of learning thus lends support to the importance of attending to cultural frameworks of student learning. When we create opportunities for comfortable and natural ways of learning, we create approach states for the brain and heighten environments for learning. Designing pedagogies that are attuned to known and emerging concerns, emotions, and hazards is fundamental to deepening learning because we are then meeting students where they are developmentally and guiding them onward from there.

Full engagement in the learning process, one that is inclusive of both integrated and individuated cultural ways of learning, offers students the best opportunity for learning.

Engaged Learning Leads to Boundary Crossing

This is what I'm thinking now about my individuated approach to teaching. I want to use my strength and comfort on the individuated side of the model, by sharing all the parts of learning. I want to share with graduate students the abstract metaknowledge about my own thinking on thinking and learning. I want to share; this is why I structure my class this way. Theory is a story. That is why I ask you to use theory to journal about undergraduate students [with whom they work]. Tell me their story. Now give me examples connected to theory. Now reflect, think through. Tell us in class. Tell your conversation partner. Now write in your reflection paper, each week and summatively.

There are also elements on the integrated end of the continuum that I want to improve. Because I am naturally an individuated learner, I lead with theory but I lack visual cues in my teaching. I want to use more video/photo/blogs and more of what students work with: for example, Facebook and online news stories. My goal is to inspire their hearts and brains, to encourage their firing synapses. I want courses to be more dynamic, with more online posts/reflection/writing—and I want to model dynamic learning for them. I will ask students to tell me about their networks of learning. Who are they thinking with? How do they draw their insights?

—Susan Diana Longerbeam

When we use our current knowledge repeatedly in experiential settings and we experience an emotional connection, learning is engaged and recallable. Though the traditional learning paradigm entails enumeration, there are limits to the scientific paradigm, limits to what can be understood through quantitative assessment. People learn as individuals in complex and holistic ways within an environmental, cultural, and educational context (Fried, 2012). A full continuum, full range, and balance of cultural frameworks in teaching allows learning to happen through engaging the world, practicing the learning through "noticing, inquiring, acting, and evaluating" (Fried, 2012, p. 116). We learn best when we have human interaction with cognition *and* emotion within a cultural context. The need for full engagement in learning is why culture matters and what culture influences. Full engagement in the learning process, one that is inclusive of both integrated and individuated cultural ways of learning, offers students the best opportunity for learning.

Note

1. In this chapter, we use narrative from our own writings, discussions, and reflections to share with readers some of how we make sense of integrating the strengths of our own cultural frameworks in our teaching as well as some of the challenges and joys we face in balancing across cultural frameworks.

3

Rewards, Dilemmas, and Challenges of Teaching Across Cultural Frameworks

I find incredible challenge and reward in getting to know a student from a background unfamiliar to me. I am jazzed with embracing the challenge of understanding how they see the world and perhaps needing to develop some new pedagogies to meet their learning needs. I find that whatever these pedagogies are, they assist other students, too. I've always been concerned about reaching every student because I think of student learning as mostly my responsibility [, and]. . . that if I can't gain their trust or interest, encourage their curiosity and engagement, find a way to facilitate their understanding, then I need to keep trying new ways to teach and learn more about students. I know I have other hang-ups about students, but these are not them. Did you know that most tribal colleges have no grade of failure; how can anyone fail in the lifelong activity of learning? If a student is not learning, which is in essence what a grade of F would signify, then the teachers, college, tribe, family, and community are not doing our jobs. . . . So how can we assign failure to one individual . . . to one student?

—Native American–Spanish education professor

We begin this chapter with some core principles for teaching across cultural frameworks. Applying these core principles will strengthen your opportunity to achieve rewards discussed in this chapter. As teaching is itself a challenging and sometimes risky endeavor, no matter the pedagogical approach, we consider some common dilemmas and hazards you may encounter when balancing integrated and individuated cultural frameworks in your teaching.

Core Principles

Teaching across cultural frameworks and continua is a challenge. We find it helpful to keep in mind some key principles drawn from our studies as we work to balance integrated and individuated cultural frameworks systematically across pedagogies and facilitate interactions with and among students.

Blend Pedagogical Approaches Across Cultural Frameworks

Integrating a variety of cultural *mores* or ways of being in every aspect of the course is the central message of this book. Blending approaches leads to learning because students will more likely find a way to engage with the material when their own natural ways of learning are present in the learning context. Part of the challenge in this approach is the need to hold the tension of opposites—for instance, small-group problem solving led by students, followed by the professor lecturing and presenting a visual and linear outline of content or blending different kinds of learning processes in an assignment. The blending and alternating of approaches across cultural continua encourages a lively, engaged classroom.

An accounting professor in the span of one class session in a large lecture hall drew upon a remarkable array of cultural continua. She offered a balance of individuated and integrated cultural frameworks and related teaching approaches. The professor used a variety of instructional aids, including paper, laptops, and overhead projection. She asked each student to vote on a question by raising a sheet of paper indicating their answer and then asked for hand gestures from each student to offer answers to posed questions. Another method the professor used was to ask each student to write an answer on a piece of paper, get out of their seat, and walk down to show her. This method has several advantages: Each student is allowed some one-on-one conversation with the instructor, however brief; showing the answer privately removes the risk of voicing wrong answers; and getting out of the chair and walking breaks up the monotony of sitting and increases the energy in the group. Finally, each student was required to walk to the front of the room to sign up for a spot for a future presentation. The professor also asked students to work in pairs with students in adjacent seats on problem solutions. Each of these pedagogical methods set up an expectation of participation by every student and gave them many opportunities to engage with the material and with the professor and other students.

Share Responsibility for Learning and College Success With Students

When students do poorly, the temptation is often to blame them for not applying themselves. But when we share the burden for engagement, we pause to ask ourselves how we might facilitate learning processes in ways that reach all students more effectively. This shifts our teaching processes toward facilitating *until* we are sure students have learned something. When students succeed, we can rest in the knowledge that we constructed the course in ways that worked for them.

Suspend Judgment About Students, Particularly About Level of Effort and Commitment to Learning

The faculty in our study gave us a clear message about student effort: We cannot know what leads students to underperform, and we cannot assume the intensity of their commitment to learning. Too many variables operate in the whole picture of student lives and learning. In addition, our own cultural values and norms operate to influence how we interpret student behaviors—at times incorrectly. Sometimes, when we find the way to earn student confidence, they will show up and "give us the moon" (J. Martin, personal communication, n.d.). We find it helpful to purposefully notice when we are judging a student and use this as an indicator that it is time for us to gain new understanding by engaging students in conversation to learn what is going on with them.

Be Personable and Accessible

Many students prefer to know us as partners along their learning journey. Students who lean toward an integrated approach to the role of the teacher may prefer a variety of interactions with the instructor, including personable and informal as well as formal interactions. Students who lean toward an individuated approach to the role of the teacher may simply want to know that the teacher is accessible to them, and not too far removed. For students who are first-generation college students, talking with professors is often intimidating; a personal and informal approach can alleviate the anxiety of talking with someone they are likely to perceive as smarter than they.

Share Yourself; Embrace Vulnerability

The teaching and learning journey inherently creates vulnerability in both teacher and learner. Vulnerability is especially noticeable when we work to balance individuated and integrated cultural frameworks in our teaching. We learned from faculty participants that humility and vulnerability are intertwined; the more they embraced humility in regard to students and their role as teachers, the more they became aware of their vulnerability. When the fullness of our humanity emerges, the learning and the learning partnership with students deepens.

Walk as a Learning Partner on the Journey

Sharing in the learning journey requires faculty to be courageous. Sometimes redesigning assignments that do not seem to be working opens up the potential to stumble, but sharing in the risks of learning creates more opportunity for student connections to learning. Reaching out to converse with and partner with students by asking them how they learn, requesting their ideas about teaching, and checking in with them about where they are in their learning are all important and effective forms of partnering.

Look for Student Strengths Rooted in Culture

Focusing on culture as a source of strength initiates many routes to learning. Drawing upon the full range of each student's humanity allows for the continuum of cultural frameworks and continua: interconnected and private concepts; wisdom and individual competence; mind and spirit and emotion as complementary as well as mind as primary, contextualized and compartmentalized knowing; learning as collective and learning as private; time as seasonal and time as linear; teacher as facilitator and teacher as expert; peers as integral and peers as optional; and learning by doing and learning through abstract theory.

Find the Positives of Cultural Balance in Teaching and Learning

We know that classrooms are enriched by diverse cultures, and students learn more, with greater cognitive complexity, when classrooms include the voices of students of diverse cultural backgrounds (Milem, 2003). By extension, when teaching includes a multitude of cultural continua, learning is enhanced. The learning advantage is the greatest positive in teaching and learning with cultural balance. Additional positives include the joy and the rewards of engaged teaching and engaged students.

Engage in Cultural Introspection on an Ongoing Basis; Know Self Culturally Over Time

Cultural introspection is not a single event but a life journey. Reflecting on our teaching with attention toward cultural influences opens up windows into what seems natural about teaching practice and what feels like a leap of faith. Remaining cognizant of one's cultural self may steady our awareness while balancing the natural with the seemingly risky, which can occur when adopting a wide range of cultural continua.

Strive to Know Students Culturally Over Time

Part of the great reward with teaching and culture is the constantly changing nature of students: each unique individual, each presenting group cohort and class, and each embryonic adult generation as well as the older returning student offers riches in challenges and rewards. The constant change is an opportunity to continually learn about culture. Whether through direct relationship with students, individual study, or workshops on culture, knowing students over time is a continual and rewarding journey.

Design With a Consciousness of Body, Mind, Spirit, and Heart

Most teaching practice in the West follows a mind-based learning motif. Accordingly, designing with a full range of human knowledge sources needs to be a constant reminder for most of us educated in the West. We can have students process the emotions evoked by something we are learning or ask them to discuss how they feel about the subject overall to help them develop strategies to negotiate feelings. We can ask students to pay attention to what their intuition or gut feelings tell them. And we can facilitate their physical engagement in learning by doing. By designing our courses with the full range of taking in and processing knowledge, we are more likely to teach the entire course within a balance of learning continua.

Believe in Students and Tell Them They Can Do It

The best of our teaching observations elicited a style we came to understand as a "constant positive narrative"—continual encouragement, particularly in active learning classrooms, murmured by the instructor. They pushed and teased and asked questions, constantly inspiring students. The master teachers called upon students; showed belief in them; told them they were getting close to answers; encouraged them to ask one another; and kept up a continual, gentle prodding to reach deeper in their learning. The constant positive narrative varied in style, but whether it was jocular, quiet, passionate, or insistent, underlying the narrative was a firm belief in students. We saw students respond to this positive narrative by becoming more present and engaged in their own learning: they sat up, looked up, became alert, laughed, spoke, and responded.

Locate Learning in Student Lives

Locating learning means finding ways to connect the content of one's discipline with what is important in students' lives. Located learning is one of the best ways to increase student commitment to graduation and completion. When the learning is clearly applied to current interests and future professional goals, students are more likely to remain engaged all the way through to degree completion. Located learning may mean attending to current events in one's profession, to current events in the media, or to world events that do not reach large media outlets. It may mean focusing student attention on realities and strengths in their own families, tribes, or communities.

Opportunities and Rewards of Culturally Engaged Teaching

The potential rewards of teaching effectively across cultures are immense. Great joy awaits when we see students respond, grow, share, show up, come around more often, connect to the discipline, find and see meaning in what we are doing together, or perhaps pursue a career or professional life in the discipline. Excitement ensues when a student is suddenly kicking in and beginning to apply their gifts to learning, when they become active in questioning, examining, creating, and challenging the world.

When learning is a shared responsibility between student and teacher and between students, active participation becomes the norm. When students are encouraged to apply their individual ways of being to deepen their learning, they begin questioning, thinking critically, applying knowledge, comparing, contrasting, challenging, and discerning—all elements of deep and active learning (Biggs, 1999). Active learning, using experiential scenarios, better prepares students for the future when they create and contribute to the world (Weimer, 2002).

When we teach across the full range of continua, balancing cultural frameworks, we encourage our own ongoing learning. Teaching using concrete application of knowledge, visual representation, and active approaches enhances not only student learning but also our own. This learning with greater opportunity for recall conforms to the neuroscience of learning (Zull, 2002). Using the framework of culturally integrated and individuated approaches to teaching and learning subscribes to the neuroscience principles of engagement, scaffolding, and recall. When we invest in our own learning through partnering with students across cultures, we and they are more likely to stay engaged.

Investing in our own learning is the focus of faculty development programs, now gaining in prominence throughout the United States. Though still largely focused on techniques devoid of cultural considerations, and on largely quantitative assessment of those techniques (often driven by accreditation associations requiring learning outcomes assessment), faculty development is shifting increasingly toward broader perspectives using the neuroscience of learning, best practices in college teaching, and some movement toward adding qualitative assessment techniques. Faculty development is likely to continue expanding, given funding models that reward institutions for student learning and graduation rather than just enrollment.

Working and connecting well with all students—including students of color and first-generation students (those who are the first in their families to attend college)—has particular rewards. Intrinsic joy awaits those faculty who mentor students to go far and find potential to make a difference in their communities and beyond. Additionally, when we are working with students in collectivist cultures, our influence is more likely to extend in waves to communities beyond the individual student. Our influence often goes well beyond the individual to ripple out into their families, tribes, and communities in positive ways. This is the nature of collectivism that when we touch one, we are likely to touch many through that one.

Part of the reward of attention to our culture in the classroom is the opportunity to continually be aware of (and in some cases be reminded of) our own early cultural influences. Continually unearthing the connections between our culture and our commitment to education, our profession, our discipline, and our students can serve to remind us of what drives us in our work and enrich the meaning we make of our work.

Though some students indeed may be uncomfortable with varying teaching approaches, others will love when we surprise them, when we share of ourselves. Students form impressions of us as we do of them, and countering their initial impressions of us sometimes delights them. Often, they enjoy seeing our humanity and knowing our own journeys and discoveries through our disciplines and our professional lives. In addition, students often engage more deeply when we purposefully connect them and what they are learning to the world around them and to their own futures.

A further reward of teaching across the full range of cultural continua is embracing a spirit of discovery we often reserve for research or other inquiry. Some refer to teaching inquiry as the scholarship of teaching, when we apply a systematic study and analysis to our teaching, to understanding our students, and to assessing student learning. There is great joy in facilitating student engagement with our academic discipline. Applying cultural analysis systematically to our own teaching and learning allows us to do so. We have the opportunity to experience more fun in teaching, deeper connections with students, greater success for us, greater success for students, and an enlivened academic community, drawing from the full range of human tradition to enrich our organizations. The alternative is faculty malaise. We sense and know when students fail, and their failure disrupts our spirits too. Alternatively, we sustain our spirits through facilitating learning among all students, especially when we engage those we have not previously been able to engage effectively.

But perhaps most of all, we in turn can access broader learning through embracing the varying learning modalities of human culture. We then engage in the core higher education mission of contributing to human knowledge. Newer ways of looking at old problems could influence our own thinking in our scholarship and allow us access to new results.

When we continually look at how to apply cultural continua, we are more likely to apply this knowledge to our own work, our lives, and current events. Using these approaches will serve to keep our teaching new and innovative. Teaching across cultural continua helps us to stay excited by and engaged in our work.

Vulnerability of Culturally Engaged Teaching

Though rewards accrue when faculty teach to a range of learning processes, the effort is not without challenges. For instance, we are asking that faculty examine our own cultures of origin, to become vulnerable in the service of student learning. One faculty member of European American and Mexican ancestry spoke about the vulnerability in examining our own cultures:

> *Initially, I was thinking, you know I was hearing all these weird stories from people in our group . . . and I was really equating it more with ethnicity than culture, and I think that is completely a little bit of a projection from me, because I grew up feeling like I didn't know where I fit. . . . So I had this sense of, "Well, I have no culture," which is ridiculous, because if you live around human beings in the world, you have a culture! And I know that intellectually, but I think that awareness went smashing into some aspect of my own upbringing that I had really not thought about in a long time.*

Being vulnerable is not necessarily comfortable. Perry, a leading theorist on college student development, shared a wistful story about his own vulnerability, when a graduating student spoke to him like this:

> "Then it came to me that these days with you are numbered, too. Like, there comes a time when you have to move over and make room for others who need the time more." And then I thought of her as an older sister

with her four younger sisters. And I said, "Well, gee, yeh, I know. And I've been thinking how I'll *miss* you." And she said, "Oh, really? Have you been thinking that way, too?" And so she just kept looking at me. It was one of those silences that went on for about fifteen minutes. About every five minutes or so she said softly, "Yes." Now I realized that she was a bright person and was putting things together. One of the things she was looking at was a guy whose days also were numbered, and by a lot smaller number than hers, and she looked me right in the eye for a long time. After a long time we got up. (Perry, 1978, p. 273)

Perhaps it is time for us to be vulnerable enough to examine our own cultural background influences on our teaching. Inviting colleagues to conduct teaching observations with a cultural balancing focus perhaps using the Cultural Frameworks in Teaching and Learning model in Chapter 1 (Table 1.1) is one way to open ourselves up to improving culturally engaged practice.

These are all questions about teaching that point to our respective cultural frameworks. By purposefully asking ourselves and perhaps each other these kinds of questions, we begin to develop a deeper understanding of our teaching and consider ways we might include a wider diversity of frameworks and pedagogies. Examining our teaching will, over time, assist us in facilitating learning for a wider diversity of learners in our courses.

> *Alicia asked me, after observing one of my class sessions, "Why do you need to cover every single stage of stage theory?" Why indeed, I asked myself. This is the tyranny of content over process. And why do I allow some students to remain silent, rather than gently inviting them into the conversation? Where does this come from? Why do I continue to rely on text alone? Why not mix up text with other avenues to learning, from the great panoply of choices? Why don't I share personal stories more with students?*
>
> —Susan D. Longerbeam

Design Dilemmas

Balancing teaching across cultural frameworks and continua brings with it some unique design dilemmas, such as the following:

Tension of Opposites

Working across cultural frameworks at times creates a natural tension of opposites. Some cultural modes of thinking and operating are actually in direct contrast to or even in opposition to others. Alternating often between cultural ends of a teaching and learning continuum, letting students know what you are doing and its purpose, and developing skill in facilitating through students' and our own discomfort will assist in balancing these tensions over time.

Educational Relativism

Addressing culture may feel like it challenges relativistic thinking; what appear to be oppositional cultural frameworks and learning styles are actually on a relative continuum, though they sometimes seem dualistic. Challenging ourselves to observe, identify, and reflect purposefully on cultural differences and their manifestations in teaching and learning will assist us in developing even deeper levels of cultural and educational relativism. It can also feel like we are making assumptions about an entire population of people. It is helpful to understand that cultural frameworks are underlying epistemologies that are common within populations yet not all encompassing of individuals. Because we as humans engender a great deal of choice even within the most oppressive of contexts, individuality arises amid larger cultural frameworks. We find it especially helpful to know that these are likely possibilities across the students in any one course and that balancing across cultural frameworks in our teaching will assist us in engaging every student over time.

Personalization of Pedagogies

As we apply more collective and personalizing pedagogical designs, students might become uncomfortable with our humanity or with sharing their own in a learning environment. While we may intend to be more personal in our teaching and to share a more personally oriented student-teacher relationship, students may misinterpret our intent. They might respect us less or assume we have come down from a lofty academic position (this assumption may be especially attributed to faculty of color and faculty who are women). Students may become skeptical and assume that we are turning what should be academic content into a focus upon the personal, perhaps interpreting this from a dualistic either/or perspective. Alternatively, some students will feel more comfortable in the learning environment, and those who start out uncomfortable may begin to gain a wider experience of learning that will benefit them in future situations.

There are joys and there are also hazards to making deeper connections with students. We may feel a greater sense of responsibility to them, which requires more emotional energy and time. As we embrace a range of teaching continua, we may experience a greater moral obligation to facilitate learning rather than to deliver teaching. Although the pressures to make the shift from teaching to learning have been present in the academy for many years, balancing cultural frameworks is riskier than continuing the Western cultural heritage nature of most pedagogical strategies. This transformation can bring discomfort initially yet brings many rewards and enriches learning among students. Comfort tends to develop along the way as well.

As experts in our field within the academy, it is not within institutional culture to be too personal. We are supposed to be expert, to maintain boundaries, and not to upset traditional ways of teaching. In getting closer to students, we sometimes fear emotional wounding, or even increasing risk of physical harm and safety issues. Yet the rewards of connecting with students more deeply remain greater than the potential risks.

Pushback

Students may become uncomfortable with a wider cultural framework of teaching and learning that deviates from a norm to which they are accustomed. They may become frightened and push back against the discomfort of learning in new ways. Learning entails risk, although sharing our thinking about our teaching (the metaconversation in our heads) and about varying teaching and learning styles could alleviate students' discomfort. Openly discussing a variety of ways students learn and sharing your dedication to their learning and success are likely to calm, reassure, and reengage students who are showing these reactions. Asking students to reflect on and then share with each other some of their learning processes is helpful as well, perhaps showing them the cultural frameworks model in Chapter 1 (Table 1.1) and asking them to locate their learning on each continuum as part of this process. Some faculty choose to help students by addressing their fears and other emotions that are causing pushback.

Personal Challenges of Culturally Engaged Teaching

The following are a few of the challenges of transforming our teaching to facilitate learning across cultures. The challenges of teaching across cultures are partly rooted in the whole enterprise—in the discomfort of learning about culture; designing, teaching, and interacting across cultures; learning to practice in different ways; and then continually trying new approaches.

Working Through Emotion and Discomfort

As faculty, we are accustomed to feeling knowledgeable, and addressing cultural differences sometimes makes us feel ignorant or embarrassed about what we previously did not know. When we are able to reframe this as part of our continual learning and professional development as teachers, we are likely to alleviate much of this feeling and move forward toward greater culturally engaged and adept teaching. Teaching with an eye to culture sometimes raises negative emotions for faculty and students; learning theorists report that negative emotion has a great causal influence on cognitive and affective avoidant behavior (Hender-Giller, 2011). To prevent this avoidance, which is a deterrent to learning, faculty can increase the level of support they offer students. Faculty can also reach out to supportive colleagues to process these emotions and to strategize collaboratively. Keep in mind that examining emotions, whether positive or negative, can be a powerful tool to enhance understanding and begin moving in more effective directions with our teaching.

Cultural Assumptions and Stereotypes

As we reflect on culture and teaching and learn more about our students, we might become uncomfortable with our unexamined assumptions about them, including the coded language sometimes used (e.g., "coddling," "not college material," "entitled millennials," "underprepared"). Engaging in an ongoing process of systematically examining and understanding our assumptions about students can not only feel freeing, but also allow us to see how these assumptions affect our teaching and student learning. Then we can purposefully make choices to continue or transform various teaching practices and develop in our work with students. Working more insightfully with students who annoy us, for example, may uncover long-held assumptions and stereotypes about cultural others, an often painful discovery. Like the previous challenge, this kind of observation, identification, and reflection allows us to make purposeful choices to face and confront these assumptions and stereotypes.

The Work and Risk of Change

Moving out of our comfort zones, especially when we are already overwhelmed with work, is not easy. The tyranny of the academic workload is such that changing a syllabus that seems to work can upset the delicate balance in our challenging schedules. In already overloaded schedules, we do not need more work. The risk of changing something that seems to be working is that we may adopt teaching strategies that end up failing. Yet the risk also presents opportunities for trying new things and enhancing student learning. New pedagogies may be uncomfortable for students who are used to feeling at ease in academic environments, and we may receive critique from students as they resist new forms of learning. Learning takes work, yet with peer and instructor involvement in class, the most difficult part of learning—learning for understanding—can be achieved in collaboration with others. Students do better adopting new styles along with us when they have their own buy-in for new learning processes (Smith, 2008). Over time and with purposeful sharing of learning road maps with our students, conditions improve, yet the beginning can be difficult especially for those with less experience using relational skills.

The risk of trying new pedagogies varies for each faculty. With increasing stratification among faculty, there exist varying levels of security to take risks (depending upon whether faculty are tenure-track, instructor, or adjunct, and in more—or less—vulnerable academic disciplines). Paradoxically, we also acknowledge that some of the greatest risk takers are those without tenure security. We believe that it does take a form of academic courage for many to engage in the cultural transformation of teaching, yet courage is necessary if we truly are to facilitate learning among all students.

Diversifying Instead of Essentializing

A dilemma of balancing our teaching between integrated and individuated sides of the continua to reach specific students is worrying about or being suspected of essentializing students, a concern that sometimes arises in relation to culture. However, essentializing occurs when we apply assumptions about a population to an individual or a group of individuals without considering the possibilities of differences in each individual. Balancing across a range of cultural frameworks in teaching offers a wider variety of learning opportunities and experiences to all students, which is not the same as essentializing. Diversifying teaching allows each individual to learn within a diversity of pedagogies, learning experiences, interactions, and relationships, hopefully finding their own natural learning processes somewhere in the mix. Paradoxically, the very acts of addressing culture and varying cultural preferences could instigate concerns about cultural insensitivity and may be perceived as forms of microaggressions (Sue, 2010). In some cases we may realize that we are actually engaging in cultural microaggressions and find it helpful to analyze and address these in our own teaching and through conversations with colleagues.

Support and Connection

Though some colleagues may show enthusiasm, interest, and connection to a wider cultural framework of teaching and learning, some are likely to confer criticism. We may be demeaned or may meet with disapproval in our disciplines. We may meet with indifference or feel alone in our endeavors. Going against the culture of common modes of college teaching may be as uncomfortable for colleagues as it is for students. Worse still, our deepened, more connected teaching approaches may be misinterpreted as too familiar, less rigorous, or not conforming to current expectations. Reaching out to like-minded colleagues across campus and nationally within your discipline and through conferences on teaching and learning offers support and company along the way. Noticing the positive influences on our students and their learning over time will also make us feel more comfortable in our choices to balance across cultural frameworks in our teaching.

Identities and Transformed Teaching

Cultural identities of faculty can influence how we are perceived and treated by students and colleagues, especially when we try transformed teaching techniques with students. Faculty from cultural groups more common in higher education, primarily Northern European cultures, are typically deferred to by students, especially if male (Stanley, 2006; Viernes Turner, 1994). For these faculty, students will more likely go along with or at least not actively resist or complain about new techniques in a learning environment.

Faculty who are women or who have integrated cultural origins are more likely to experience active resistance or complaints from students when they apply teaching pedagogies less common in collegiate learning environments. We found in our work with faculty that these groups faced some challenges related to their cultural origins and gender. Finding our own individual ways to authentically incorporate new pedagogies and relational dynamics with students and reaching out for discussion with and support from like-minded colleagues can be very helpful with these challenges.

Conclusion

Teaching with a balance of cultural frameworks while maintaining an awareness of the rewards and hazards is more likely to result in our long-term transformation through cultural balance in teaching. Knowing the rewards will help us maintain the long-term commitment to engaging culturally with students while awareness of hazards prepares us to expect some resistance and plan accordingly. Overall, we believe the rewards far outweigh the hazards, that students will learn more and succeed at greater rates, and that we will be greatly rewarded both personally and professionally when we engage culture in college teaching.

4

Applying Cultural Introspection to Teaching and Learning

I never realized I was judging students who were quiet in my classes. I made all kinds of negative assumptions about them because of my own upbringing. I assumed that if someone was quiet in class they either didn't care or were unwilling to engage with others. After some reflection and discussions with some of my quieter students, I understand that students are often quiet because they are respectfully or intently listening, because they feel too intimidated or shy to speak up, or even because they don't believe that what they have to say is important enough to share. Understanding this took self-reflection on my own cultural values as well as reaching out to students to ask what made them quiet in my classes. This understanding helps me to develop my teaching so I can create a more inviting, turn-taking, safe environment for students to share. Everyone's learning benefits when we learn from everyone.

— Australian American design professor

Asking students about the way they experience life, the meaning of their behaviors, and their perspectives on how they learn most naturally is an effective technique to gain greater understanding. Similarly, self-reflection or introspection is a powerful tool for gaining a deeper sense of how we bring personal values from our cultural, familial, and community upbringing into our teaching practice. Combining the two helps us as teachers to understand our students and ourselves more fully, enabling us to purposefully challenge our own assumptions, consider other ways of doing things among our students, and then design and facilitate pedagogies that engage students more fully from where they are and who they are culturally.

This chapter is designed to guide faculty through introspection on cultural norms and their intersection with teaching practice. We offer a variety of techniques to understand students over time in relation to their learning. Introspection can be a helpful process for faculty to identify ways that cultural norms, beliefs, values, and assumptions manifest in our teaching and in student learning. Introspection enables faculty to develop a more balanced and integrated teaching practice across cultural norms. We find it helpful to develop pedagogies both within and outside our own cultural norms to teach across cultures most effectively.

Going Inward: Knowing Ourselves Culturally as Faculty

Knowing ourselves culturally as faculty is helpful for understanding some of the reasons behind our interpretations of students and the choices we make in our teaching practices. The following are a variety of daily introspection techniques to assist with developing a deeper understanding of cultural influences.

Day-to-Day Introspection

There are many ways to incorporate ongoing introspection, observation, and analysis into our daily teaching practice. In the busy lives of faculty it can be challenging to carve out time for reflection. The following are a few cultural introspection methods you might find helpful to apply over time in your daily practice. We encourage you to find methods that are comfortable and also to stretch into some that are less comfortable.

Keep a teaching journal. Starting and keeping a teaching journal over time can be very helpful to the development of your teaching in general. You might add a regular reflection on culture by noting observations about yourself, students, interactions, and readings. You might also note pedagogy you are trying in your teaching practice as well as students' reactions to it. A journal can assist in processing emotions, jotting down new ideas to try in classes, and noting reactions and outcomes among students. You could reflect over time on values of your own that you notice are manifesting in your teaching and on how these might each affect student learners from integrated as well as individuated cultural frameworks. You might notice over time which students you are drawn to, those you often do not notice, and those who irritate you or by whom you are repelled. You could mention the name of a student you wish to contact for deeper conversations about teaching, learning, and culture. You could reflect incrementally using the Cultural Frameworks in Teaching and Learning model in Chapter 1 (Table 1.1) or some other model or theory you find helpful. For some, just the act of writing something down sets it in mind, while others find it helpful to revisit their journal for ideas or to gain insight after some time has passed.

You could take time to reflect on how physical and technological aspects of your teaching and the learning environment influence student engagement and learning, trying new techniques to most effectively use the physical and virtual classroom, as well as teaching technology. We find it helpful to reflect often on how technology may or may not be assisting us to relate more or less with students.

Purposefully observe one behavior in our own teaching. A helpful introspective technique that requires little preparation is to purposefully observe one behavior in our own teaching during a class or classes. For example, you might notice that you are making eye contact with only certain students (perhaps only with those who make eye contact with you or those on one side of the room), and you could reflect later on what this means, how you can work to gain eye contact with others, and whether you interpret students who make eye contact more positively than others.

You could then learn more about varied meanings of eye contact by asking a student who does not make contact and one who does what this means to them. Or you could read about eye contact across cultures, even doing a quick web search on "eye contact, cultural meaning" to see what you find. Then purposefully consider and try different ways to connect with students who are not making eye contact and reframe your thinking about students who do or do not make eye contact.

Request colleague teaching observations. Culture and cultural interpretations can be elusive, hard to identify, and difficult to interpret beyond our own experiences. Whether we know little or are deeply conscious about our own cultural origins, we may not think about culture in relation to our teaching or to student learning. Sometimes asking a trusted colleague to observe specific aspects of our teaching or to converse with us about how we are interpreting students and how students are responding to us can be very helpful in developing our understanding and practice in relation to culture. A variety of observations from colleagues across cultures and disciplines over time is especially helpful. We also find it helpful to ask colleagues who teach very differently than us or have very different personalities to observe us and then meet over lunch or coffee to discuss. Engaging in discussions especially during informal time such as over a meal encourages thinking outside the box and sharing even more uncomfortable observations and interpretations.

One instructor who is from an integrated cultural background grew very confused with some of the student feedback she was receiving early in her teaching about a lack of organization in her courses. She increased overt organization of the course, yet nothing she did to address student concerns seemed to change student feedback until she asked both an anthropology graduate student and a faculty colleague to observe her teaching with this specific student feedback in mind. The graduate student asked the students privately what the feedback meant and was able to share their responses with the instructor. The students were confusing organizing course materials with collaborative development of learning goals and outcomes, assuming that the professor must not be *able* to come up with learning outcomes for the course on her own because of a lack of organization. This faculty member was trying to coconstruct the course focus with students, but some of the students interpreted this as a lack of organization rather than attempts to collaborate and empower.

The faculty colleague who, like many of the students, was from an individuated cultural background was able to help this instructor interpret these explanations and find a helpful balance of individuated and integrated pedagogical techniques. Her colleague shared her interpretation that students at this level are developmentally prepared to share in some decision making about course activities, deadlines, content, and assignments but are often not ready to also collaborate on choosing larger learning outcomes and goals for the overall course. The instructor decided to limit her collaborative decision making with students to content and activities within the process of the course. As a result, the instructor stopped receiving that feedback and felt better about her ability to teach in a predominantly individuated cultural context as well as more able to consider new ways to explore coconstructing knowledge and content with students. It took the combined observations, interpretations, and shared discussions of several individuals with differing cultural backgrounds to figure out what was going on and find ways to balance across cultural frameworks in this professor's teaching.

Reflect using the Cultural Frameworks in Teaching and Learning model. Many of the faculty we worked with applied the Cultural Frameworks in Teaching and Learning model in Chapter 1 (Table 1.1) to their introspective processes. Some found it very helpful to better understand intersections between their own culture(s) and their teaching practices. Others found it helpful to their self-observations and systematic analyses of themselves while teaching. Still others found it helpful to their observations and conversations with students, especially those from cultural origins different from their own.

This model can be a useful way to imagine other cultural frameworks as well as to ponder how our own cultural frameworks influence our behaviors and interpretations. Spending time reflecting and observing, then imagining new interpretations different from our usual ones can be very helpful to developing deeper understandings and more inclusive teaching practices. Finally, some faculty used the model over time to systematically analyze everything about their courses, from syllabi to evaluations, finding it a helpful tool in considering and transforming teaching practices in their courses.

Observe our student connections.

> *I noticed after purposefully observing myself for a while that I was much more comfortable and warm with certain students, so I watched even more carefully, paying attention to what made me comfortable with them. Then over the next few class periods, I purposefully made myself approach students I hadn't spent time with, and it was remarkable. These students I thought were not interested suddenly sat up and began to participate. I feel badly that all these years my assumptions and actions may have been causing students to disengage . . . or at least not to engage. Even a smile, or making eye contact, or walking closer to a student when I am speaking seems to engage them. I do it all the time now, moving around and working hard to speak individually with each student as early as possible in a course. The more a student is quiet or reclusive, the more I am likely now to seek them out. I believe these are often the students who need me most.*
>
> — Swedish Lithuanian business professor

Those with whom we connect can be signposts of culture as well as personalities, identities other than culture, or similarities in educational journeys. By observing which students we seem to be reaching or connecting with as well as those we are not, we can get a sense of our own cultural values and the people with whom we feel comfortable. Then we can purposefully reach out to specific students in new ways.

We can also try new pedagogies and observe if previously disengaged students begin to respond. Student nonverbals are often helpful with observation; when students slouch, look anywhere but at the focus of teaching, or even show negative nonverbals like texting, yawning, or going to sleep, we can usually ascertain they are not engaged. On the other hand, when something we present, do, or facilitate prompts students to pay greater attention, sit forward, take notes, or ask questions, we know we are reaching them.

Though we are focused here on connection, learning is one important outcome of greater connection. Learning is, of course, more challenging to discern than is our connection with students. Learning techniques including those discussed in this book as well as inclusion of pedagogies aligned with both ends of the cultural frameworks in Chapter 1 are likely to increase our connections and the potential for greater learning among a wider variety of students.

Write a culture and teaching autobiography.

> *The autobiography has influenced how I am with students. I used to get frustrated with them. Now I reflect; they have different values, lenses. Now I try to see it like they do, and I'm building bridges.*
> — Turkish American engineering professor

A culture and teaching autobiography is a writing exercise that faculty can employ to gain a deeper understanding of how our own cultural norms, values, assumptions, beliefs, and behaviors manifest in our teaching practice. Faculty in our Culture and Teaching Faculty Development Project wrote a culture and teaching autobiography during the year we worked with them. We are publishing a collection of these essays (Longerbeam & Chávez, in press). A culture and teaching autobiography tool can also be used to delve more deeply into understanding how our culturally influenced values and norms affect how we teach. We can then take this a step further using the Cultural Frameworks in Teaching and Learning model in Chapter 1 (Table 1.1), our own observations of students, and our conversations with students and colleagues to consider how our cultural norms may influence student learning. Over time we can develop a more culturally inclusive teaching practice.

There are many ways to write reflectively on culture and teaching. We provide one guide to writing a culture and teaching autobiography in Appendix A of this book.

Getting started. We posed the following question to faculty in our culture and teaching cohort after they had completed their autobiographies; thus, their answers were given in hindsight:

What was your process of writing? How did you get to it?
 Read my old journals
 Talked with parents, siblings, cousins, grandparents, friends, aunts, and uncles
 For very early childhood: dreaming/meditating/remembering

Some looked up personality traits of their ethnicity, particularly when this exploration was new to them (generally the case for Northern European Americans). For example, one German American participant found a description of his cultural heritage while reading and that resonated and prepared him for his culture and teaching autobiography. More examples of autobiography prompts are as follows:

> Read my own student papers and transcripts from undergraduate and graduate work
>
> Started by drawing a pictorial timeline of important events in my life
>
> Looked up mentors on Internet
>
> Contacted and spoke with mentors
>
> Drew images to represent each of my main values and important traits
>
> Used Ancestry.com and other genealogical and genographic resources
>
> Listed my greatest values, then put them in order of priority
>
> Thought of a metaphor for each important value in my teaching
>
> Wrote out a short story of teaching events that were wonderful or upsetting
>
> Talked with a good friend about what they saw as my primary ways of being
>
> Acknowledged the centrality of our vulnerability as teachers
>
> Charted out key values in my teaching and in my life
>
> Recognized the novelty in academia of critically reflecting on and writing about our cultural backgrounds

Not all faculty used these techniques. Most, however, used some combination of personal reflection and conversation with family members to elicit and uncover childhood memories related to culture and learning.

Developing Our Teaching Through Cultural Introspection

A major key in using cultural introspection to assist us in teaching more effectively across cultures is to consider how we interpret, judge, and react to students who come from ways of being that are different from or even oppose our own. We might ask ourselves: How do I work effectively with a student who was taught that to stay in the class late rather than to be on time is considered respectful? How do I reflect on my own values, to still honor them yet to also consider and respect other ways of being? How do I then observe how these manifest in my teaching, how that affects students, and how I might expand my repertoire of teaching to encompass both my own values and the values of my students?

Consider the following narratives from faculty autobiographies. How might each be helpful to some students' learning and a barrier to other students' learning? See some guiding questions in Box 4.1. Some faculty in our cohorts fell pretty clearly into an integrated side of the cultural continuum, while others fell into an individuated side; these core cultural values manifested in their teaching. The following are some passages from faculty autobiographies, under two core themes: forefronting connection and community and forefronting individual effort.

Forefronting Connection and Community

> When I am in front of students, as I am setting up for class and powering up the computer, I do an exercise I came to develop over the years. I casually look at the class, smile at them, and in my inner voice I repeat a few times: "Forgive me, I am sorry, I love you, thank you." With "I am sorry" I mean to apologize for my shortcomings as a teacher, human being, and the role-model role I am being thrust into by standing in front of them. Also, I am asking for their forgiveness, which is related to, but not the same as apologizing.
>
> By expressing my love for them, I am shifting the center of my being away from my mind, toward my heart. I have seen many people do good things, while being without love, being tense, unhappy, and in their minds. I don't want to be that person. Finally, I thank them for being there. I think the precursor for this mantra-exercise was watching Padre Pablo, at the beginning of Mass, praying for God to use him to give a good Mass and sermon. Regardless, the exercise calms me down, makes me smile, and slows me down to allow me to acknowledge my students' presence.
>
> —Argentinean American economics professor

> This spirit of building relationships and community is evident throughout my academic and professional life. The assumptions and beliefs that underlie this value are that a community is important for an individual to be strong. Relationships and community are at the heart of who we are as a Native and tribal person, and if we don't have that or are not connected to that we start to lose sight of the values and vision of our ancestors that have been imbedded in us.
>
> It is important when I am going into a class to understand the student's experiences and connections to what it is that we are going to learn. Once I understand that, I can highlight those experiences and incorporate [them] into the discussions and assignments we are doing for class. Although I am acknowledged as the teacher I also acknowledge I can learn from the students and that as a community within the classroom, valuing each person as a community member is essential.
>
> —Nez Perce Kiowa education and ethnic studies professor

These faculty led with their connection to students and to their communities, and they sometimes followed with comments about student effort. Though nearly all faculty in our study spoke about the importance of community, they did not all lead with it. Instead, those who identified with a more individuated background usually led with notions of student effort, and sometimes followed with comments about community.

Forefronting Individual Effort

To me, "striving" means orienting your life toward progress, change, and improvement. It means setting ambitious goals, accepting major challenges, and working hard to achieve excellence in any chosen undertaking. . . . The corollary to this value is that I find it difficult to tolerate negativity, complaining, laziness, nonchalance, or even inefficiency.

—Norwegian American geography professor

If [students care] about their work, I'll bend over backward to help them learn. If they don't care to work on learning, I don't have to care. They don't need a college degree to be successful in life.

—German Czech American environmental sciences professor

We do not ask for help. We are on time. We work hard. Emotions are to be overcome. Complaining gets you nowhere.

I do not like students' being late. I find it personally insulting on some deep level. Work is work and play is play. Individuals are responsible for their own destiny and must follow the rules. Also, I know from experience that most of the students who are late will not have completed their assignments anyway. Most, but not all, and I really want the students to succeed. I want them to feel good about themselves.

—British American accounting professor

Box 4.1: Our Inner Narratives . . .

Consider the previous narratives from faculty autobiographies.

How might each be helpful to some students' learning?
How might each present a barrier to some students' learning?

Autobiographical Themes Spanning Integrated and Individuated Cultural Constructs

As faculty wrote their cultural autobiographies, they began to notice interactions and relationships with students in light of their own educational experiences. Though faculty insights were distinct by individual, they also coalesced around common themes. These themes tended to be related to insights about current teaching and interactions with students. Faculty made connections between their own experience and their interactions with current students on the topic of these core themes. When faculty got in touch with *judgment, isolation,* and *humility* through their writing, they then applied these themes to reflection about students and their teaching practice. Longer-term outcomes related to faculty-identified themes included greater empathy toward students as well as development of their teaching practice to include a wider interpretation and pragmatic application of values.

Judgment. Faculty remembered many times when they were judged for their academic performance or their personal attributes as students in their younger lives. They noted that an inherent goal of their education was to encourage developing judgment, particularly at the undergraduate and graduate levels in their educational journey. Some, however, began to realize that their faculty mentors did not sufficiently distinguish between judging ideas and judging individuals. A master teacher described his own insight that judgment can be transformed into another type of critical thinking, one more conducive to expanding thoughts and perceptions and greater open-mindedness.

> *Judgment versus curiosity, about myself, about students. Education creates judgment. Go for passionate curiosity about one another.*
> —Irish-Danish American math education professor

> *It occurs to me that I may not know how to judge whether a student cares.*
> — Finnish-German American environmental science professor

The science professor quoted previously made a critical and key insight into his own assumptions about students in regard to their level of effort. Previously he had assumed that if students did not demonstrate effort *as he understood effort*, they did not care to learn. Realizing that judging effort based upon casual observation was at best inaccurate, he began to consider different interpretations of student behaviors, understood more deeply, and transformed his relationship with students through conversations and questioning of his own assumptions.

Isolation. One theme we found among autobiographical remembrances was a sense of isolation in the academy. Faculty across cultural identities wrote about feelings of alienation and loneliness, and for many, those lonely experiences continued into the present as faculty members. For many, their educational experiences included a constant reminder of not belonging. They applied these memories in their efforts to welcome students.

> *Often, I did not ask for help and I have never felt completely safe in the classroom. I have always believed [my] experiences contributed to my feeling uncomfortable with my teachers and uncomfortable in the classroom in general.*
>
> —African American information sciences professor

> *Individuals are influenced by their comfort and sense of belonging (or not belonging) in higher education and an appreciation of the many factors that students respond to in their choice to pursue higher education and careers that do not always come easily. I am sensitive to discomfort in this environment and devote care to welcoming students and offering support.*
>
> —Italian American psychology professor

Humility. Humility was an early core value for many of the faculty, especially those who were first-generation college students. When faculty got in touch with this core value, they tended to notice ways that humility influenced their connection with students. Many of the faculty with whom we worked expressed experiences of feeling humbled by the profession of teaching. The following three quotes are from an engineering professor who defines himself more through his rural identity than through his ethnicity:

> *I feel my core values were shaped by growing up on a farm and ranch with a family that valued hard work, perseverance, humility, and a sense of community.*

* * *

> *This is not a core value that's necessarily valued within academics, and I feel like I'm violating this value by claiming it as a value (look at me, I'm so humble!).*

* * *

> *I find that our students [at this university] are more humble and empathetic than usual. In fact, in some cases I find that they actually need a boost in confidence. I respect and appreciate the fact that most of my students are kind and humble and willing to listen to what I have to say while also respecting the needs of their classmates. I also find that a high degree of empathy is very important when dealing with [our] students. Many of them come from backgrounds that put them at a great disadvantage in the world of higher education. Listening to*

them and trying to understand their situation in life is critical. Likewise, pro-
viding flexibility and alternative routes to success can make a huge difference in
their academic careers. I constantly emphasize the need to keep an open line of
communication with me and their other professors when things get out of hand.

An additional outcome of writing the autobiography was a greater
willingness to suspend judgment—long enough to consider a balance
of cultural interpretations, ways of being, and positive attributes in
students.

Faculty realized that to be effective with all students, they needed to be
in touch with their own vulnerability and humility. The process of writing
the autobiography aided in forming a connection with their own vulnerability. An important outcome that arose out of these three core themes
was a greater sense of empathy toward students. Because faculty had fresh
memories of *isolation*, *humility*, and *judgment*, they were more in touch with
student experiences of the same. An additional outcome of writing the autobiography was a greater willingness to suspend judgment—long enough to
consider a balance of cultural interpretations, ways of being, and positive
attributes in students.

Looking Outward: Learning Culturally About Students

Knowing students more deeply and culturally as faculty is helpful to understanding students and their learning. It is also helpful for gaining a better
sense of how students experience our communications and teaching practices. The following are a variety of introspection techniques to assist with
developing a deeper understanding of students and the cultural influences on
their behavior, interpretations, and learning.

Observe and Ask

To learn about students' cultural influences, it can be helpful to both observe
them and ask them directly about what you observe. Observe some specific
student behavior in classes or as manifested through assignments; then ask
individual students how they go about studying, completing assignments,
and preparing for and taking tests. Probe gently for explanations about
how this is helpful to their learning or where they learned to do things the
way they do. In our studies of students that informed the Cultural Frameworks in Teaching and Learning model, we asked students to describe the
process they use when they really need or want to learn something.

Observing and asking can be especially helpful when applied over time to students from a variety of cultures. The action of observing and inquiring often leads to surprises about what we assume about students. Sometimes we learn that what we thought we knew about students is not the case, but sometimes it is. Usually we learn about the variety of ways students learn.

> To learn about students' cultural influences, it can be helpful to both observe them and ask them directly about what you observe.

Conversations with students can be done before or after class, during a class break, via e-mail, or even during a class session, such as, "I've been noticing this kind of behavior in classes when I do this and I was wondering what that is about. I really want to understand how you learn best, and your assistance would be really appreciated. Would some of you be willing to share?"

Invite a Student for Deeper Conversation

Deeper conversations with students are very powerful tools to understanding. Consider inviting a student from a different culture from your own to take a campus walk, meet with you in your office, or share a beverage at the student union. Ask the student to help you understand how he learns best and what in your teaching is helpful, not helpful, or even a barrier to learning. Or ask him to describe the process he uses when he most wants or needs to learn something. Ask what is helpful about this process. It might be helpful also to ask how teaching in college is similar to and different from teaching at home by families and other early teachers. Over time, we can gain greater insight from conversations with a variety of students.

Use the Cultural Frameworks Model With Students

During a class session or as an online class activity, hand out copies of the Cultural Frameworks in Teaching and Learning model in (Table 1.1). Explain to students that you would like to understand more about their natural or preferred ways of learning. Ask students to go through the model and, in each of the eight continua, place a mark where they believe they are in the ways they learn most naturally.

We recommend that you allow students to choose whether to identify themselves or not. You may have students who wish to talk with you individually about this model or the experience of identifying how they learn. Some may show concern, feel grateful, or even feel intruded upon.

All of these are helpful clues about how students are experiencing learning in formal environments. A follow-up question can assist you in gaining further understanding, such as, "You seem very concerned about this. Would you be willing to share more about that with me?" You could also sit down for longer conversations with individual students or with a small group of students to ask them to share some of the meanings behind and examples of where they are on the cultural frameworks continua. These conversations often lead to deep and helpful understandings about learning and culture.

Explain to students that you would like to understand more about their natural ways of learning.

Even a few minutes of class time spent exploring how students learn will garner a great deal of information that can assist you in teaching more effectively across student similarities and differences in learning and interacting.

You can take the exploration of student learning further immediately or over several class sessions by asking students to chat with a partner or free write on the back of the form using the following prompts:

- Describe how you learn most naturally in relation to integrated and individuated cultural frameworks. What about this is important to your overall learning?
- Write about how your family members or other early teachers taught in relation to the individuated and integrated frameworks. How is this teaching still present in the ways you learn? How is it now different?
- Compare and contrast how your natural ways of learning may or may not be present in your experiences of college or high school classes.
- Develop (in partners or small groups) your ideas for teaching within each of the eight continua, and then we will compile these as a class.
- Reflect on and then let us brainstorm as a class some of the teaching techniques you suggest within each of the eight continua. (This could be done one continuum at a time over a course of eight classes, or you could divide the class into eight teams and ask each team to brainstorm for one of the eight continua.)

- These are several ways I've learned that students take in knowledge. How do you do take in knowledge most naturally?

You could also have students self-select into three groups according to where they see themselves on the model: one for integrated, one for individuated, and one for some of both. Ask each group to brainstorm teaching and learning ideas on newsprint and then share with the class.

Read About a Particular Cultural Population of Students

There is some very helpful literature about teaching among specific cultural populations of students. Remain cautious not to assume that every student from a specific cultural origin has similar characteristics or learns in the same way. Yet it can be very helpful to understand the possibilities and to include pedagogical techniques that are more common to specific cultural norms.

For example, in some cultures, silence for thinking is designed into class time. Alternating some discussion time with some short thinking time before discussion or responses to instructor queries can be helpful to certain learners' processes. Silence can be in the form of taking a moment to gather thoughts, jotting down a note or two, drawing ideas, or other techniques that serve as catalysts for thinking.

There is also a great deal of literature on cultural, ethnic, racial, and other identities among college students. In addition, collections of narrative writings by college students display how their identities influence their college experiences (see books edited by Andrew Garrod).

Consult With Campus Professionals

Many campuses include cultural offices or centers, diversity specialists, centers for teaching development, ethnic studies programs, student success and retention specialists, or education faculty who specialize in studying or providing service to specific populations. Consulting with other professionals formally or informally can be very helpful. Even a brief conversation can inspire ideas in our teaching as we learn more about the needs, ways of being, and life challenges of students.

Conversations with professionals and others who can serve as informal *cultural interpreters and translators* can give us insight into new ways to work with students, things to watch for, and ways to show respect to someone from a culture new to us. Community members can be helpful as well. Reaching out to ask for assistance, brainstorm ideas, or request advice often leads to identifying new resources and expanded pedagogies.

> Conversations with professionals and others who can serve as informal *cultural interpreters and translators* can give us insight into new ways to work with students, things to watch for, and ways to show respect to someone from a culture new to us.

Conclusion

By going inward to our early learning influences and our current teaching practices, and going outward toward a greater understanding of students, we gain the possibility of a deeper understanding of learning—our own and our students'. We included several quotes and themes from teaching autobiographies to give you a sense of the possibilities inherent in this kind of introspection. We also included pragmatic ideas for increasing awareness and knowledge of students and their natural ways of learning.

We encourage faculty over time to become purposefully introspective about intersections of culture and teaching as well as culture and learning.

5

Strengths-Based Teaching
in Cultural Context

It was kind of a humbling awakening to learn that even though I've been awarded honors for my teaching, I was really missing it with some groups of students. It never occurred to me that there might be different cultural modes of knowing or learning. I figured that if I taught like my own best college professors, students would learn. And I should know better. I focus my research in the cultural underpinnings of my own profession yet I hadn't considered culture in relation to teaching or learning. Recently one of my students came to me and shared that she was struggling with learning in my classes because she was taught so differently in her home country. After this, I began to apply my understandings of cultural epistemologies from my research to my teaching, alternating a wider variety of pedagogies, ways of interacting, and kinds of evaluation techniques. This student thanked me profusely, and I felt humbled again that it took me this long to apply something as fundamental as a cultural epistemology to my teaching.

—Cuban American medical professor

ultural strengths underlie teaching and learning in college. Usually without realizing it, we design and facilitate the courses we teach by applying the cultural strengths with which we are familiar or comfortable or that relate to the way we were taught in college. We expect students to come to class with certain competencies and skills, often because we were expected to bring them to our learning when we were in college. The challenge as we continue to diversify in student enrollments is that different competencies and skills are expected and cultivated in different cultures. Students bring varying strengths to learning from expectations developed through cultural upbringing. When we harness a wide variety of cultural norms and strengths to enhance learning, we are more likely to engage *all* students. This takes an ongoing dedication to discovering the many ways students learn and then designing this multiplicity into our teaching practices.

Some cultures, especially integrated cultures, place great value on relational skills and less on skills that accomplish immediate tasks. In many of these cultures, it is believed that through strong interpersonal skills we will build necessary relationships for accomplishing tasks over a span of time. Within this framework of culture, students and professionals are expected to come into an environment already highly skilled at relational competencies such as conflict resolution, empathy for others, collaborative or teamwork abilities, an expectation to focus on the greater good, an ability to draw out the strengths of others, and keen communication skills. Students in these cultures are often used to learning through collaborative pedagogies. In this kind of cultural environment, teachers and supervisors *expect* to teach other skills needed to accomplish specific tasks and goals because the relational skills are assumed.

Alternatively, some cultures place a high value on accomplishing immediate tasks. In many of these cultures, it is believed that by prioritizing skills required to accomplish a specific task, long-term tasks and goals will be met. Because of this cultural focus, students and professionals are expected to come into an environment already highly skilled in specific areas related to the class or job. In this kind of cultural environment, teachers and supervisors *expect* to teach other skills needed to collaborate or learn the academic topic because the task-oriented skills are assumed as basic. Many workplaces in the United States expect to train new employees in interpersonal skills but not in writing or the basic skills needed for a specific job. In countries where the culture(s) are more relationally oriented, workplaces often expect relational skills to be in place and to train new employees in other skills related to the job.

We do this in higher education as well. We expect students to come into college courses with certain aptitudes and skills we consider basic, such as knowing how to write, take tests, listen quietly, take notes, and volunteer answers in class. These can be thought of as *cultural strengths* or *cultural educational capital* (Yosso, 2005) because they are widespread within individuated cultural processes common to U.S. colleges. Students who originate in individuated cultures and educational experiences expect to find these norms and usually have experience with them.

Alternatively, some students are acculturated within a different set of basic educational skills, such as knowing how to help other students learn; how to understand through symbols, reflection, or action; and how to wait respectfully for individual invitations from the teacher to share thoughts (Brendtro & Brokenleg, 1996). With these students, often those from integrated cultures, our commonly held pedagogies and interactive processes are usually less equipped to enhance learning. Students who originate in integrated cultures and educational experiences find few of their own natural modes of learning within the highly individuated educational cultures of most college classes. We, in essence, are not teaching to these students' cultural strengths, and the cultural educational capital they bring is less likely to be normative in the ways we teach. We are also losing out on the cultural gifts and learning they bring to individuated student peers, to the academic subject, and to our own learning. We are not embracing the strengths that structural diversity offers to learning (Milem, 2003). We may interpret these students as less than because they do not bring what we consider the "basic" skills to learning.

> *All through my earlier schooling, I was a strong student. I often worked to assist other students who were struggling; this was encouraged and also helped my learning. All of a sudden in college, I feel like we are all competing against each other, not because there are overtly competitive activities but because we are all in it alone. I wonder sometimes why we even come together because we are not really learning together, just occupying the same space for a while. I don't feel like I'm learning much because we never compare ideas with each other, never hear a variety of interpretations of any one thing, never get to share our insights with anyone but the professor. I feel like I'm a widget in a factory instead of a contributing member of a community of learners.*
> —Guatemalan American management information systems student

By teaching mostly within only one cultural framework, we are not teaching in ways that incorporate a diversity of cultural strengths. Subsequently, we create learning environments that privilege some kinds of learning and underserve or even repress others. This is one of the reasons some cultural groups have greater success and retention rates in college than others. This factor is also contributing to creating differential learning rates between cultural populations. Viernes Turner (1994) describes this experience, especially for domestic and international students of color, as similar to being *guests in someone else's house* whose pictures are not on the wall, whose traditions are not present. Even when all students are welcomed into the college environment, not everyone's ways of learning are present, expected, designed for, rewarded, or understood. Our challenge then is to balance our learning designs to include a wider variety of cultural strengths and frameworks in everything we do and in everything we ask of students. In this way, we continually offer each individual student some of their own natural ways of learning and some ways that are new to them.

Facilitating learning across cultures has to do in great part with developing pedagogies, relational dynamics, and assignments that promote a healthy balance of resonance and dissonance with a diversity of learners, which means teaching with an understanding that students learn in a variety of ways. To do this, we recommend designing courses and learning experiences that balance cultural strengths, blending integrated and individuated frameworks across learning design and facilitation. When we do this, each student in our learning environment will sometimes feel the confidence of working within their own natural basic skills and aptitudes and sometimes the challenge of gaining new ones.

> Facilitating learning across cultures has to do in great part with developing pedagogies, relational dynamics, and assignments that promote a healthy balance of resonance and dissonance with a diversity of learners.

This chapter offers concrete tools for the critical practice of assuming and working from across a diversity of student cultural strengths. We provide two sections on integrating cultural strengths in teaching. The first is about getting started and conceptualizing, with subsections on teaching philosophy, starting where students are developmentally, and balancing cultural capital. The second is about pedagogy across cultural frameworks, with subsections on course syllabi; individual needs; evaluations and assignments; time, timing, and scheduling; ways to facilitate a multiculturally empowering course climate; student engagement; and ways to balance activities across cultural frameworks. Finally we provide sections on several areas for additional consideration, including ongoing access to course materials as a form of oral history helpful to learning, teaching in the moment across cultures to balance content and process, and cocreating knowledge across cultures.

Getting Started: Conceptualizing

We now live and work in a world where vast knowledge is readily accessible to many through a variety of sources. Collegiate learners at this point in history grew up with ready access to knowledge sources and often have more practice in accessing knowledge via technology than the faculty who teach them. This doesn't automatically translate, however, to engaged learning. As we reconceptualize our courses and our teaching, it is helpful to design in a way that does not let content dissemination alone drive our design or facilitation. Instead, conceptualizing from a place of process-based learning is most helpful in engaging learning among students. Many faculty still teach from a *content*-driven framework, yet for most students, learning happens more from a *process*-driven framework.

A process-based learning orientation turns dissemination of knowledge on its head, replacing it with a balance of many ways of learning through teaching designed toward learning goals or outcomes. Learning happens when faculty work interactively and iteratively with students over time to check constantly for understanding. Faculty do this in multiple ways: paying attention to student verbal and nonverbal communication, helping students make sense of and apply what they are learning, challenging students to figure things out for themselves, and developing new pedagogies in the moment when students are struggling to understand through the methods we initially planned.

As discussed in earlier chapters, especially in Chapter 1, a balance of cultural frameworks is necessary if we wish to facilitate engaged learning among all of our students. Students learn most naturally within cultural frameworks with which they were raised and also benefit from the challenge of learning through less familiar pedagogies. Alternatively, when their natural cultural frameworks are mostly or completely absent in learning environments, students struggle to learn because they are both struggling to learn and struggling with how to learn. When only one's own cultural framework is present, he or she will miss out on many kinds of learning and understanding that may be necessary in the future. Balancing across integrated and individuated cultural frameworks of teaching and learning facilitates learning across the many cultures present in a college classroom.

Many faculty still teach from a *content*-driven framework, yet for most students, learning happens more from a *process*-driven framework.

Reimagining Our Teaching: The Influence of Teaching Philosophy on Learning, Student Success, and Retention

A most influential factor in facilitating learning, success, and retention among students is the philosophy that faculty hold about learners. Learning, success, and retention are elevated at colleges and universities where faculty widely believe they hold responsibility for student learning, success, and retention (Kuh et al., 2010; Woodard et al., 2001). This is the case even when controlling for entering factors such as grade point average, ethnicity, income, and test scores. Faculty with this belief actively find and innovate ways to engage and facilitate learning among their students. When students are not learning or succeeding, a culture of belief in students encourages faculty to try alternative pedagogies and interrelational techniques *until* something works. These faculty often believe in engaging the individual strengths of students toward learning and openly communicate their belief with students that they can and will learn (Woodard et al., 2001).

Alternatively, learning, success, and retention are lowest at institutions where faculty believe their job is to weed out the poor or bad student, even when controlling for entering factors such as grade point average, ethnicity, income, and test scores. Faculty with this kind of belief often see it as their responsibility to separate the good students from the bad students by posing a series of increasingly difficult evaluations and tasks. Faculty with this philosophy often believe that learning, success, and retention are firmly in the hands of students and that students must adapt to the way things are in college courses or move on (Woodard et al., 2001). This distinction is important; because colleges and universities in the United States were founded in specific cultural frameworks, students from any other cultural framework will naturally be disadvantaged. National student enrollment, retention, and success rates bear this out.

Because students come from such a variety of backgrounds, we as faculty must reframe how we think about our teaching and about student learning. We must take on responsibility in partnership with students for learning, success, and retention. This requires that we work with students over time to figure out what fosters their learning and what does not, how to balance a variety of learning processes in our pedagogical designs, and how to continually assess understanding among students *during* our teaching so that we can change approaches whenever necessary. In many ways, it also takes a philosophy of starting with students where they are and bringing them along toward learning and understanding. In essence, we must entirely reimagine our teaching and student learning.

We must reimagine our teaching and student learning.

Starting Where Students Are Developmentally

Starting where students are in their learning and levels of engagement takes an understanding of how students learn and develop. We can use many approaches to develop this understanding, including continual observation of and input from students, flexibility in our teaching practice to try new methods when students are not coming along in their learning of particular concepts, and an ability to engage students' natural curiosity, empathy, and pragmatic design to accommodate the realities of students' lives. Starting with students in mind is especially challenging when we are faced with constantly changing students as new generations experience evolving realities of our world.

College students are no longer predominantly 18- to 22-year-olds momentarily liberated from societal responsibilities while they focus on academic studies, fun, and transition into adulthood. Students holding down full-time jobs, raising families, and even taking care of parents are now the majority in most colleges and universities. Starting where students are increasingly means consideration of a diversity of cultures, socioeconomics, nationalities, familial and work responsibilities, and other identity dimensions.

When we as faculty consider these important student factors in the design of our teaching practices and systematically build in flexibility for the responsibilities that students contend with on a daily basis and the naturally diverse modes of their learning, we are more likely to devise teaching that engages and effectively facilitates learning as well as success and retention. When we balance multiple cultural frameworks and learning processes underlying the design of learning contexts, we meet students where they are as learners, incorporating diverse continua of taking in and processing knowledge, varied lenses of interpretation, and experiential as well as abstract ways of sequencing learning. We hold in our hands possibilities of learning for and with students.

Balancing Cultural Capital

Cultural capital is familiarity and comfort with the prevailing or dominant culture and is learned early in families, schools, religious institutions, and communities. It consists of general cultural knowledge, language, language patterns, manners, and skills expected in a particular society (Lamont & Lareau, 1988). Cultural capital enables individuals to negotiate social environments with general sanction, assistance, and support from others. Behaving within general social and cultural rules and norms helps a person negotiate the environment successfully, while not knowing the rules and norms usually leads to disapproval, ostracism, exclusion, isolation, and sometimes to active discrimination or harassment. We often know immediately when we have stepped outside of social norms because we feel disapproval from others around us. Those who have less cultural capital in an academic environment are those whose cultural, familial, and social upbringing have taught them different norms. The reality for these individuals is that they must negotiate unfamiliar cultural norms in social and academic environments.

Educational institutions are not socially neutral institutions but are made up of experiences and norms of those in the dominant cultures of a society (Bourdieu, 1977). Cultural imbalance and learning disparity are often created from unspoken rules and codes for participation enacted in classrooms (Delpit, 2006). A disproportionate influence on learning takes place when some students are already culturally well versed in classroom rules and norms while others are not. These classroom rules echo the dominant society to a great extent, and because they are usually unconscious and unacknowledged, they remain unexamined and unchanged.

A lack of cultural capital is exacerbated by the reality that some students come from families with parents or siblings who attended college and thus have close relations to turn to with questions or concerns, continually increasing their cultural capital. New friends of similar background also serve as translators of college norms and expectations. But some student populations—especially those who are the first in their families to attend college and those not originating in the more common cultural origins currently predominant in higher education—start out with few or no family or friends to serve as translators of college norms. In addition, when students are obviously different because of skin color, phenotype, language, accent, nationality, or other identity characteristics, other students are less likely to reach out to offer assistance, friendship, or support. Finding some cultural norms of their own in our classrooms and teaching can mitigate these inequities in cultural capital and go a long way toward helping these students feel more at home and be more successful in college.

Becoming more aware through inward and outward cultural introspection and actively balancing cultural norms and pedagogies in classrooms are ways to begin creating a more effective and equitable learning context across cultures. The Cultural Frameworks in Teaching and Learning model (Table 1.1) can be applied as a guide and decision matrix for this purpose. Over time, observing, analyzing, and then culturally rebalancing all the components of a course will, to a great extent, provide greater equity in learning, success, and retention for all students.

> We find it helpful to choose some major aspect of a course each semester to culturally analyze and balance across integrated and individuated cultural frameworks.

The following sections focus on many of the specifics of designing and facilitating a college course. It is helpful to systematically transform each course to deepen student learning by analyzing and then balancing cultural frameworks in every aspect of pedagogy. We find it helpful to choose some major aspect of a course each semester to culturally analyze and balance across integrated and individuated cultural frameworks. In this way, transforming our courses occurs over time, and we are less likely to become overwhelmed by the challenge of new modes of teaching or increased workload.

When *Everyone's* Learning Is the Objective: Pedagogy, Facilitation, and Interaction Across Cultural Frameworks

I know in the first session whether a professor cares and wants me to learn and succeed in their class. It is in the syllabus, and the way they talk to us, and whether or not they are interested in us or just in what they are teaching. I'll drop a class and add one that is much tougher to learn with a professor who cares.

—Picuris Pueblo biology student

When learning and student success become the intention, the environment changes in a class. When *everyone's* learning is the objective in a course, learning transforms for everyone. If our objective as teachers is simply to disseminate knowledge and expect students to take it in on their own or even with our assistance, the outcomes are uncertain and less influential to learning. If, however, we embrace a role as caring facilitators of all student learning, understanding, and success, something amazing happens. We begin to see students and their learning as our privilege, challenge, and responsibility. We begin to learn from and with our students, deepening exploration of subject areas. We find that many faculty also begin to experience real joy in the creative challenge of teaching and working with students. This, in turn, facilitates learning across many cultures and other student differences. The following sections offer a guide to designing and facilitating courses with care and a balance of cultural frameworks to enhance learning among students.

> When everyone's learning is the objective of a course, learning transforms for everyone.

Course Syllabi

Syllabi can act as one of the first indicators of care, cultural balance, and learning in a college course. How a syllabus is designed and what it includes helps to set the character and tone of a course. It is one of the important opportunities to initiate a learning partnership between faculty and students. The words we choose, values we communicate, and expectations we delineate let students know if their learning and success matter to us. Each element represented in the syllabus sends a message to students about whether who they are is truly welcome and safe and if they are encouraged to learn and succeed in class. Our syllabus often conveys whether we are dedicated both to the academic subject and to them.

The balance of cultural frameworks in the form of a diversity of elements across a syllabus signals to students whether they will find themselves, their ways of learning, and their ways of communicating in our class. Much of this is felt rather than consciously held, as students review a syllabus for the first time. They quickly sense through words and the framing of expectations and assignments in the document whether they (and the academic subject) genuinely matter to the faculty. Even when we care deeply, we may not purposefully convey this to students with the often-removed, third-person language of academics. When we begin to purposefully reflect on our words and messages from this perspective, we develop syllabi that engage and support students and their learning from the beginning.

Think of the syllabus as one of our first communications with students and a measure of the cultural possibilities in a class. With each aspect of the syllabus we can begin to offer a balance of learning elements across integrated and individuated cultural frameworks. Following are some ideas to create pedagogical balance:

- For expectations we might include some individual expectations of students and some collective, communal, or group expectations.
- Some assignments might focus in the abstract theoretical or philosophical realm while others focus in application to real-world, even local or student-focused, challenges or issues. Each assignment could alternatively merge aspects of both application and theory.
- Exams or quizzes could be made up of some individual and some partnered pieces; they could also vary in time and place by having some take-home and some in-class quizzes and exams. In online classes, some could be timed and some could offer a wider deadline, allowing students the option to come and go.
- We could go beyond offering information on ADA or religious accommodations and services to encourage students to see us about adaptations for familial, tribal, and nondominant spiritual/religious obligations. The following is from a syllabus currently in use by a professor in our culture and learning cohort. The first paragraph offers institutional language offered in many syllabi; the second paragraph goes beyond what is required by the university to openly support and offer flexibility for additional student responsibilities and needs.

Individual Needs

Students with physical or learning disabilities or with other individual needs are encouraged to contact the professor early in the semester if there are services or adaptations that would be helpful in accommodating your individual needs. For information on assistive technology available for student use and additional information on services available through UNM Student Accessibility Services, see http://as2.unm.edu

I am very aware that students have important familial, tribal, community, spiritual, and/or religious obligations. I try to be as flexible as I can in support of your learning, and I can be most helpful when you take a few minutes to let me know your needs or to meet with me so we can work together to develop solutions.

* * *

I wanted students to know that I empathize with their responsibilities for more than academics. I rarely have students who ask for anything special other than a few extra days for an assignment, yet I often hear from students that as soon as they read the individual needs passage in my syllabus they calm down and know things will be okay if something happens in their lives. This seems to reassure them and open them up more deeply to learning.

—Mestiza education professor

Some faculty develop syllabi that provide a synopsis of every aspect of the class, including policies, expectations, course description, learning objectives, assignments, evaluations, and a calendar for the semester or quarter. Others may provide some of these items and wait until relevant times to provide more detail, especially on course assignments or the course calendar. Different students benefit from more or less information up front. Providing as much as possible at the beginning of a semester or quarter can assist those who need to plan around busy family, community, and work schedules. Encouraging students to look as far ahead as would be helpful reassures them that it is okay to take in the syllabus at their own pace.

Working systematically and systemically to review and culturally balance everything in our syllabi and supporting materials will take us a long way toward enhancing learning for all of our students. Doing so a little bit at a time helps us to mitigate the effects of the changes on our own demanding lives.

Now you try it (see Box 5.1).

Box 5.1: Reimagining . . .

Take a few moments to reimagine some basic part of one of your syllabi—perhaps how you address students, how you welcome them in writing, or what you include in an individual needs section.

Evaluations and Assignments

Culturally, balancing exams, quizzes, assignments, projects, and presentations is something to think about and transform over time. It is helpful to balance these components in terms of individual and group orientation, timing, sequencing, and ways of knowing (see Table 1.1 in Chapter 1).

Exams and quizzes. Exams and quizzes can be modified without much change in time required for grading by developing techniques to alternate the way students experience them. Some of the faculty we worked with thoughtfully developed ways to evaluate with a focus on "the context of learning instead of the context of testing" (Tsuchiya, 2014, p. 45).

> *Before I was always testing to hold students accountable. I hadn't really thought of it in terms of learning. Go figure! When I really began to think about things from a learning perspective, things really changed. Suddenly I was thinking of ways to use quizzes and exams in partnership with other activities to CHECK for student learning . . . not so much to hold them accountable but rather to hold ME accountable for their learning. If it was clear they had not learned something, it became my role to keep trying pedagogical methods and activities until they could really demonstrate their learning. Tests and exams turned into opportunities to check in with students about their learning instead of a penalty for not learning or a reward for learning.*
>
> — Austrian French music professor

Some professors developed quizzes that combined the learning assistance of figuring things out together with individual accountability. They facilitated students collectively discussing and solving the quiz problems, then submitting quizzes individually either in class or later online. We observed faculty doing this both in class sessions and through online discussions and submissions.

In a large geology course (60-plus students) taught in a shared learning laboratory where students sit at large, round tables together, the professor presents a local geological situation on the overhead screens while handing out a worksheet to students. He has students work in groups on the case study for much of the class period, wandering through the room while answering questions, encouraging, and challenging students. Toward the end of class he reminds students they will need to turn in their final solutions to the case study individually online by a specified date. Later, in an interview he explains,

> I find that this new technique of collaborative solution development combined with individual write-up of the solution creates a dynamic balance of learning and accountability that enhances student learning over the long run.
>
> —German American geology professor

Quizzes themselves can take on a wider meaning and process by combining multiple ways of taking in and processing knowledge. Some examples include using memory questions with simulations, enactments, oral storytelling, Socratic questioning (within the larger class or individually as professors walk around the room asking questions of individual students), gaming, media, and other innovative designs. It can be helpful to include collaborative, individual, and competitive quizzes and quiz-like activities. Students are often comfortable with some aspects of the process initially and not so comfortable with others, which sets up a dynamic tension of opposites and balance of cultural frameworks helpful to student learning.

Varying the rhythm or feel of quizzes can also increase the sense of class community or make a tough topic more relaxing by changing the pace to fit the affective needs or engagement of the class.

One professor developed a team competitive game to assist students in understanding and applying organic chemistry principles, combining the excitement and pressure of gaming with the help and reassurance of peers to develop shared solutions.

Another professor noticed that a specific theory often caused fear and tension in her class, so she made the quiz an ungraded one in which students worked with partners to figure out the accounting problem, then brought their answer to show her privately at the front of class. Those who finished first were then expected to circulate and help other students until all were able to figure out the problem. She shared with us later that she had read that learning really "sets in" when you have to teach someone else.

Another professor discussed working with a peer mentoring program for one of her courses in which students who had successfully completed the course provided in-class mentoring to other students as well as worked with the professor to redesign and facilitate the course in ways that worked better from student perspectives. Peer mentors circulate through the class during quizzes and learning activities, answering questions, providing tips, and offering encouragement and reassurance. This innovative, instruction-based peer mentoring program was later studied by a doctoral student for her dissertation (Gomez-Chavez, 2014).

Because some cultures are very time- and task-oriented and others are less so, it can be helpful to alternate how exams are administered. In this way, they are framed in a wider cultural set of natural inclinations. To do so a professor might alternate in-class and time-limited exams with take-home, open-ended exams, and with a choice of online or paper submission. Alternatively, some exams could be completed orally or at the board, while others might consist of researching a theory in teams online during class or between classes and later explaining the theory for the benefit of the whole class.

Larger exams can also combine collective and individual work, perhaps with a discussion to place the exam in the context of how professional pressures and expectations require both at different times. It is helpful with exams to also offer some that focus on abstract theory while others require application of theory to an actual situation or case study, either posed by the professor or identified by the student or students.

When learning (rather than evaluating) is at the core of exams and quizzes, thinking of them as opportunities to check in with student learning encourages much greater flexibility in design. Informal check-ins are helpful to this process. For example, having students start class regularly by writing one important insight they learned from the assigned readings and then processing the insights collectively is a way to see what students think is important in readings. It also provides an informal check-in to student learning. This technique could be used to have students share one thing they found confusing or about which they have disagreements or questions. This quick technique can also provide the professor with a better sense of what students are having difficulty understanding or what they identify as important.

Some techniques generate a fun yet elevated pressure to come prepared and to assist in others' learning. Some faculty facilitate discussion between pairs of students in the class and then ask for different students over time to explain to the entire class what they discussed. One professor designed a bingo-type game and each class period would randomly choose student names from it to call on throughout class. Encouraging and teasing students helped make this a fun activity that also provided constant check-ins for student learning. Over time, even the shyest and least confident of students became adept at responding. Another professor constantly questioned the class to garner student interpretations and applications of theory, writing student ideas on the chalkboard. Students later wrote in evaluations that this technique served as a validation of their thoughts and ideas and that they really felt that this professor listened to and cared about them.

Use of cultural frameworks in assignments, projects, and other work. More engaged learning can also mean moving beyond asking students to demonstrate their learning through exams and quizzes to including a wider mix of projects, presentations, teamwork, writing assignments, simulations, and poster presentations. These options often include both online and other modes of work, as faculty find and are encouraged by their students to use newly helpful software, online tools, and sites. Helping students take a larger role in offering feedback, finding and sharing academic insights, helping each other, and even tutoring or evaluating can all be helpful to the learning process as well as to the professor. Facilitating students' learning deeply from each other personally and from each other's intellectual and creative works can enhance learning. In our work, we have observed and discussed a wide variety of innovative assignments and projects assigned by faculty as learning experiences for students.

A key to deepening learning through the application of cultural strengths in coursework is often rooted in offering variety, sometimes within an assignment and sometimes by requiring a collection of assignments over the course of an academic term that include strengths from both individuated and integrated cultural frameworks. We find the following cultural continua from Chapter 1 (Table 1.1) especially helpful to deepening learning: purpose of learning, sequencing, interconnectedness of what is being learned, ways of taking in and processing knowledge, responsibility for learning, and student interactions. We discuss some pedagogical applications of these continua later.

Balancing the purpose of learning, sequencing, and interconnectedness of what is learned works by asking students over time to delve into learning through specific academic, professional, and individual-related goals as well as by applying some learning to the betterment of known communities. Some students learn best without the pressure of connection to real-world responsibilities and realities while other students benefit most when learning is placed in a familiar context or applied to family, tribe, or community.

Likewise, some learn best addressing separate components one at a time, while others learn best within the context of component connections. Including assignments that require students to study for both purposes during the term deepens learning for everyone.

> One geography assignment we observed asks students to delve deeply into the meanings of social, economic, geographic, language, and cultural concepts within their own home communities, analyzing how these factors influence people of the area. Another assignment asks students to study specific components of these same concepts one at a time in another country to gain an overall sense of its geography.

To sequence, it is helpful to alternate between starting with broad abstract concepts and starting with broad concepts in context with their practical applications. Alternating between individuated and integrated cultural frameworks of these elements helps students to start at times with their own strongest, most natural processes and at times with those that are less comfortable. Over the course of an academic term, students develop greater proficiency in each. Try practicing developing this balance using the exercise in Box 5.2.

Box 5.2: Culturally Balancing Graded Elements . . .

Choose an assignment in one of your courses—or alternatively, a quiz or exam. Reimagine how this assignment or evaluation might be redesigned to balance across integrated and individuated cultural frameworks in one or more of the teaching and learning continua.

> How might you relate it or have students relate it to a local situation or need?
>
> How might it be completed through a combination of collaborative in-class processing and individual synthesis and submission?

Multiple ways of taking in and processing knowledge are also helpful to balancing cultural strengths across integrated and individuated frameworks among students.

An assignment in a geography course asks students to choose and report on a creative work from among a list of movies and novels about one of the countries or regions studied. This assignment is designed for students to gain an overall sense and feel for a specific country or region of the world. The use of story and characters in movies and novels enables students to imagine and relate to life in that country or region.

The professor discussed the use of movies and novels with us in our project as an important way for students to learn—accessing emotions, gaining a contextual sense of place, and learning through story as well as learning to be savvy consumers of information in all forms. Going further with this kind of assignment and having students share their insights and critique in some way with each other would also be helpful to all learners. This could be done online or in class discussions, or perhaps through having students share one insight on the board or online.

Some faculty design assignments to purposefully include a variety of learning processes or multiple intelligences (see Gardner, 2006) into assignments, believing that studying something from a variety of lenses deepens learning and understanding.

- One professor requires students to incorporate at least three intelligences into each paper or project.
- Another provides at least one assignment that allows students to choose from among several different assignment options designed to study something in different ways, encouraging students to choose either the assignment that most excites or feels most natural to them or instead choosing one that will take them outside their comfort zone. Each iteration of the assignment has the same learning components, yet students can choose different ways to accomplish them.
- Another professor offers students the option of several formats to complete the same assignment, including a paper, electronic poster, PowerPoint, website, or some other medium. The assignment is then easily shared via a course website so that students can access and learn from peers in advance of a class session or in preparation for an online written or spoken conversation during which assignments are discussed.

Another way connectedness matters in coursework is in how individuals from different cultural upbringings present information. Individuals from integrated cultures are likely to interweave ideas, showing connections and depth across a strand of thought. Overlapping circular images of connections are common, and in some cultures circling back to previously presented ideas through story and larger connections is likely. Starting with symbols or imagery is often helpful for organizing thoughts.

Individuals from integrated cultures are likely to interweave ideas, showing connections and depth across a strand of thought.

Individuals from individuated cultures are more likely to present things as discrete components in a step-by-step manner.

Designing in options for both is helpful to learning across cultural frameworks.

Individuals from individuated cultures are more likely to present things as discrete components in a step-by-step manner. Starting with an outline is common among individuated individuals and often helpful to organize thoughts.

Because of these different orientations, requiring a specific organizational set of rules rather than specific elements or outcomes can serve as a barrier for either kind of learner. For example, if we require that students start with an outline, this approach is unlikely to assist and may detract from an integrated learner's process. If, instead, we ask the students to formulate and share their ideas in some way, and perhaps offer examples—"You could draw or outline your ideas first"—we are providing a more flexible process to allow students to engage their own natural starting points or *ways in* to projects and assignments. One Arabic American professor shared,

When I did my dissertation proposal, my adviser required me to approve each chapter with her before moving on to the next one. This linear, separated process was so impossible for me that I finally wrote all three chapters and then handed them in one at a time for her approval. I needed to weave the whole together so I could understand the parts. Even when I tried to explain this to my dissertation chair, she refused to believe me, perhaps thinking that I was trying to get away with something. So I had to hide from her who I am and the way I think to do what needed to be done. I shudder to think how many students drop out of college because a professor or more than one over time remains unopen to or unknowing of the varied ways students think, process, and learn. As a result I strive to make sure I'm offering many options and ways for them to do their own learning. I also work to remain open to and ask them about what works for their learning so that I can continually develop new avenues for them toward learning the same things through a variety of means.

It is helpful to facilitate in class to provide learners with a balance of integrated and individuated processing to organize and collect their thoughts. Offering a choice of where to start provides each learner with a chance to begin in their most natural mode of processing. One professor shared,

> *For larger classes I ask students to take out a piece of paper and take a few moments to outline, draw, or otherwise collect their thoughts about an upcoming assignment. In smaller classes, I'm known for my bag of crayons, and students add color to their process. I find that students in the larger classes often begin to bring colored markers or pencils with them to class, knowing that it is something we'll do during our time together, not only for assignments but for everything. As I move around class while they are gathering their thoughts I notice a wide variety of what is on their desks . . . flowcharts, drawings, words in different colors, models, symbols, timelines, and more. Nowadays, this also takes form in visual and other elements on their laptops. Observing what students are doing often gives me new ideas for how I might work with students in future.*

—Mestiza education professor

A variety of approaches are available to balance *individual and collective responsibility for learning* within coursework, which also has the added benefit of expanding knowledge and lenses into that knowledge by engaging students both as learners and contributors to others' learning. We find that when students know their work will be read, seen, or heard by other students, their work tends to improve and they often move beyond thinking about something from only their own perspectives toward considering multiple perspectives. Designing courses that include both individual and collective assignments can mean many things.

One professor includes at least one assignment in which students' individual work becomes the reading for the following class sessions. Students are required to post their work on an online course site and then discuss insights from at least three peer works in the next discussion.

Another professor offers extra credit when students choose to work with a partner on one assignment. She explains the extra credit is for the extra effort it takes to work in collaboration with and learn from each other and lauds benefits from often complex understandings and results as students make sense of dual interpretations of what is studied.

Including individual assignments is also important to encourage students to delve deeply into their own insights, intelligences, and interpretations, which allows students to feel responsible only for their own learning. Balancing individual and collective responsibility for learning in a course engages students in a variety of ways, deepening learning for everyone and expanding knowledge and possibility. We have learned extensively from the insights, knowledge, interpretations, and innovative creativity of our students who always seem to bring new wisdom as well as new content to our courses. One professor shared,

> *One of the added benefits of having students develop their own theories and knowledge as well as share what they find in the literature, on the Internet, and from their own lives is that I am constantly made aware of new knowledge and insights that I would not have found on my own.*
> —Scottish American psychology professor

In her update of culturally relevant pedagogy, Ladson-Billings shared an insight about the power of students as teachers in her course. In a class session designed for multimedia presentations from students and teachers, one teacher expressed apprehension about presenting immediately after a characteristically powerful student presentation when she exclaimed, "You expect me to go on after *that*?" (Ladson-Billings, 2014, p. 79). Students communicate powerfully and teach effectively to one another in ways that professors seldom emulate. Students interpret the world from a variety of perspectives and offer those to each other when given the opportunity. By continually creating positive opportunities for students to create and share, we gain new insights and knowledge in our academic discipline as well as new ideas for our teaching practice.

Student interactions through coursework hold great possibility for contributing to learning. When group papers, presentations, and projects are assigned, students gain opportunities to draw from the diverse abilities, perspectives, and knowledge of others. Assignments are most effective when they are carefully crafted, facilitated, developed, and monitored over time.

One professor facilitates in-class time for teams to spend working together on ungraded activities before a team assignment. She finds this very helpful to develop key relationships within a team before members move into the more stressful graded part of the assignment.

Continuing some in-class time for teams to meet and work together in the presence of the professor can also help students work through conflict, take on different roles based on their own strengths, ask for insights from the professor, schedule outside meetings, and share key information during times they can count on regularly. Students who are less likely to enjoy group work are sometimes reassured when they are given the opportunity to evaluate each others' individual efforts. Group work is often most successful and satisfying when professors provide some structure and avenues for working through conflict situations.

> One professor had the class brainstorm "rules of engagement" about working together as a team, discussing areas likely to cause conflict and resolution of these conflicts as well as ways to maximize learning and outcomes for everyone on each team.

Over time and with student input, it becomes easier to anticipate issues and challenges and to design for these eventualities. Having a balance of individual and team assignments can also reduce grading time for professors and open up time for other work. One professor discussed making herself grade presentations and offer quick feedback during the presentations, stating,

> That way, students are happy because I give them their grade and feedback immediately, and I'm done with grading for that assignment by the end of class!

Time, Timing, and Scheduling

Over time, faculty develop a sense of what works best for learners at various points in an academic term or program. For instance, assignments that build on each other over the course of an academic term deepen learning by building complexity of thought over layers of coursework. Faculty also develop insights about how students are processing new knowledge, in what order they learn concepts most easily, and how long it takes for a complex concept to be generally understood. One professor shared,

> *It took me years to realize that our MBA students were always stressing out in the seventh week of our program. I began to talk with them and observe their reactions and behavior. I finally realized that the seventh week marked a point when all the requirements as well as the reality of having so many of their worldviews challenged in our very diverse program proved overwhelming.*

Understanding this helped me design in discussions, assignment ordering, and even a fun, stress-relieving activity during the seventh week to help students get through this tough time and continue learning.
                        —Irish-British American management professor

Not everything in a course or program is this drastic, yet how we order assignments, activities, deadlines, and new topics affects students in many ways. This order also affects our lives and work.

> One faculty participant realized that by accommodating late papers without penalty, her own grading work was better sequenced.
>
> One professor routinely asks students in a cohort program for the syllabi of congruent courses, or speaks with those course professors, and subsequently schedules key assignment deadlines during weeks that do not share deadlines with congruent courses. The professor also shifts deadlines mid-semester when it becomes clear that the cohort's overall schedule is becoming overwhelming and a detriment to learning.

Planning activities that facilitate students' getting to know each other and us during the very first class session has profound effects on their learning throughout the term (see later in this chapter the section on engaging students from the first class). Finally, by noticing when students are stressed or relaxed in general, we can plan course schedules to ease their stress and maximize learning.

Time is also highly related to how individuals are taught to think within their own cultural upbringing. In some cultures, individuals are encouraged to take the time needed to think deeply, including time for clearing the mind, for sleep and dreaming, or for meditation. (See Box 5.3 for some reflection in this area.) Timed, in-class exams do not usually allow for this kind of reflective processing, so students not used to accessing time in this way are underserved when timed, in-class exams are expected and the only form of evaluating learning. It is helpful to alternate take-home and in-class exams to balance a variety of culturally based ways of processing. In this way, sometimes exams are natural to those who are used to processing quickly and in a specific location while they are natural at other times to those who most often take time, different kinds of reflection, and varying locations to process.

One professor shared,

Once I started to think outside my academic "time" box, I began to see how many different kinds of evaluations, assignments, and in-class activities would be helpful to student learning as well as to my own engagement with my academic discipline.

—German math professor

Box 5.3: The Influence of Time . . .

Consider some timing aspect in the way you teach. How might you balance time within this element across individuated and integrated cultural frameworks?

Climate, Facilitation, and Interaction

How we work with students is just as important as what we have them do. Creating a safe and engaging environment with a balance of challenge and support is critical to student learning.

Facilitating a Multiculturally Empowering Climate Beginning With the First Class Session

A variety of research studies suggest that certain contextual elements help professors create multiculturally empowering learning communities through attention to climate, tone, and context. Attending to climate provides a learning atmosphere in which individuals are able to work together toward learning as well as toward constructing new or alternative knowledge and questioning established norms. In the words of bell hooks[1] (1994, p. 147), these learning communities are involved in "education as the practice of freedom" across identity and background differences. The following elemental dynamics are especially critical to empowering or liberating multicultural learning communities in higher education: (a) climate of safety, (b) spirit of risk taking, (c) congruence, (d) proactivity, (e) multiplicity, and (f) reciprocity (Chávez, 2007).

In a multiculturally empowering learning community, professors work with all students to create collective, empowering learning experiences that utilize and honor multicultural realities within a shared and rigorous academic experience. This kind of learning environment has an underlying culture of belief in which faculty believe that students are fully capable of learning in their own ways and stretching into other ways as well (Leaver, 1997). In this kind of learning context, students feel safe enough to be more fully themselves and draw on their own cultural strengths and abilities for the benefit of learning.

Climate of safety. Support, trust, individual dignity, respectful communication and confrontation, absence of judgment, power with each other rather than over each other, and minimization of the effects of hierarchy are all essential to creating a climate of safety. One indicator of a safe environment is the willingness of students to respectfully challenge the professor, ideas presented in the readings or in class, and each other. One professor described this indicator with some humor:

> *I encourage my students to question everything—theory, knowledge, sources, and of course the first thing they question is me! I love this even though it can be a bit uncomfortable at times because it means they are learning and growing in more complex, more confident ways. I was not raised this way in China, where educational systems are mostly about learning from and not questioning the teacher or professor; yet, I believe that everyone's knowledge is enhanced through student questions. From my personal experiences being discouraged to question anything publicly during my early education, I know just how much a feeling of safety is enhanced when encouragement to question things is the norm in classrooms. Even here in the United States, students in my classes have to be encouraged and coached before most of them will question anything.*
>
> —Chinese education professor

An education professor shares that at times she has to remind herself that some students, often from individuated cultures, learn through what Belenky and colleagues (1986) call *separate knowing*. Separate knowers learn new material most naturally by separating themselves from the new material, creating distance through critique, in order to analyze the new knowledge and choose how and whether to incorporate it into their own understanding. *Connected knowers* (Belenky et al., 1986), however, learn more through experiencing new knowledge from the perspective of the one offering the knowledge before incorporating it into their own understanding. Remembering that some students are naturally separate knowers helps this professor not to personalize but to welcome challenges and disagreements from students because they enhance some students' learning.

In a safe learning context, teachers encourage, welcome, and incorporate respectful challenge. This climate encourages students to stop following the rules and begin to assist in creating them, an indicator of critical thinking. One helpful role of a professor is to facilitate the development of safety guidelines—what one professor called the "rules of engagement"—by the collective, to ensure accountability for those guidelines, and to nurture the healing process when guidelines are breached.

In a multicultural learning climate of safety, individuals are encouraged to take increasing responsibility for their own safety and the safety of others. In this way, students learn to be full participants in the learning community. In this kind of learning environment, professors may find the following behaviors as well as others helpful:

1. Speaking from personal experience and insight
2. Allowing for reflection and some choice in what to share
3. Listening intently to others
4. Showing with positive nonverbals, such as nodding and comments, that many experiences and viewpoints of a subject are welcome points of exploration and critique
5. Making it clear that putting down others is not acceptable, yet all ideas are welcome
6. Acknowledging and supporting that each person is in a different place with the subject and still learning
7. Encouraging students to challenge ideas and assumptions
8. Stepping in to facilitate when necessary to redirect or stop disrespectful or hurtful discussion or behavior.

Respectful conflict, mistakes, and even discomfort combined with safe spaces and encouragement are necessary for complex learning. In the words of Maslow (1968, p. 204), "Growth forward . . . requires courage, will, choice, and strength in the individual as well as protection, permission, and encouragement in the environment."

In a multiculturally safe learning environment, professors don't hesitate to intervene during times of discomfort or disrespectful student behavior in ways that reengage students in discussions after difficult situations have arisen. A safe learning space is a place where professors are willing to admit, learn, and apologize when mistakes are made. Students listen to the ways we acknowledge our own mistakes and the ways we respond to those of students. Compassionate responses are essential to safe learning environments. A multicultural learning community is not one that is mistake free but rather one in which individuals constantly commit themselves to stay engaged and work through difficulties. It is also a place that can include students doing poorly on evaluations or assignments and still feeling welcomed and encouraged to keep learning. Finding ways to reengage students after they have performed poorly on an assignment or said something awkward in class is one of the important ways that we build and maintain a safe learning climate.

As groups become empowered, students may begin to call each other on destructive behaviors as well as encourage and applaud positive ones, especially if encouraged to do so by the professor. One helpful technique is to ask students who are doing well to mentor or offer assistance to those who are struggling. Learning is enhanced by the act of teaching others, so this approach is often helpful to both students. Peer support can also help students develop a sense of care and empathy for each other. We encourage faculty to facilitate during uncomfortable classroom situations and to always be ready to confront hurtful comments and behavior. Gently interrupting microaggressions may feel awkward, and we may not do it perfectly, but the risk of interrupting hurtful comments is far less than the risk of allowing harm within the learning environment to go unchallenged.

Engaged learning can affect people in ways that are deeply unsettling, and issues may not be resolved within a session or even within the period of the course (hooks, 1994). Sometimes it is necessary to return to discuss an issue later if we miss the opportunity or need to reengage students more than once to get learning back on track. Our own startled response to something unsettling during a class session can sometimes mean we hesitate for what feels like too long to confront and resolve a situation. We encourage faculty to return to issues in the subsequent class if necessary rather than letting tensions continue to build or behavior go unchallenged. There is not a time limit on addressing issues. What we *don't* say or do often has more of a negative impact on safety and risk taking than anything we do say or do.

> *I learned there is no statute of limitations on apologizing for my own mistakes or on addressing difficult moments from prior class sessions in subsequent class sessions. After a tough conversation with students about their failure to read course material, I reflected that I had not been clear enough with the use of readings in the course. I began the next session by apologizing for my assumptions and impatience, and then facilitated a discussion about how to use the readings in ways that would work best for student learning. The students came forward right away with effective responses to how readings could be used and the class moved forward with ease. It was almost as though the whole class breathed a sigh of relief and were able to continue learning together with greater confidence because we made it through a tough situation together.*
> —Northern European American education professor

Spirit of risk taking. Risk taking is essential to learning and teaching across cultures. It is necessary to take risks outside our comfort zones as teachers and learners in order to contend with complexity, new ideas, and learning processes that are unlike our experiences and cultural frameworks. There are many kinds of risk taking among students—for example, speaking up first or sometimes at all, deepening ideas, stretching thoughts to new places, offering critique, and questioning worldviews.

> As Professor Nair encouraged us to question everything, we sometimes offended or hurt others. Unlike most classes I've been in where either the "prof" didn't brook any questioning or where they did but conversations quickly deteriorated into arguments and then silence, this professor just gets us through that risky stage. How? Well, he stays calm and nods at every idea yet gets us to expand on what we say. He also helps us to process emotions. I can tell you, I've almost never seen that in a class. It's like we start off in our respective corners all defensive and once everyone knows their ideas won't be dismissed or overlooked, everyone calms down and starts to listen and at least consider other perspectives.
> —William, African American bilingual education student
> (Chávez, 2007, p. 280)

Trying new, sometimes less comfortable kinds of assignments is often easier for students when they are offered a choice; an individuated learner may choose to add a drawing or poem, and an integrated learner may work in linear, sequential steps. Each student experiences areas that feel risky, which may be ones that other students find comfortable.

Some discomfort at appropriate levels is a sign that risk taking and safety are balanced well. It is helpful for faculty to acknowledge that each individual, including us as instructors, will sometimes feel comfortable and sometimes uncomfortable during our learning process together.

> *I often start classes by letting students know that we will go through a range of emotions in this class, that we will find joy and experience discomfort together, all to learn deeply. I tell them that I will be with them along the way to support, encourage, feel with them, think with them, and learn with them.*
> —Russian American psychology professor

Instructors need to acknowledge the discomfort of risk taking as a natural part of learning and working together. We might offer a learning road map to students, letting them know that discomfort is likely because of the variety of learning needs, personalities, cultural frameworks, and perspectives within any group and with many new kinds of content. We can then help them understand that discomfort is a natural and often necessary part of learning.

Just as critically, we need to take a deep breath when we strongly disagree with something said and find a way to encourage a variety of perspectives even as we clarify, correct, or expand. Some faculty we observed encourage risk taking by finding something right with and responding positively to student comments. Because each student is watching our response to every student, responding positively to the first comment elicits more risk taking from other students. Some use a combination of humor, teasing, and personal vulnerability to encourage and model risk taking. We also find it helpful to acknowledge positive feelings that can come from taking risks and making it through these experiences, whether successfully or not.

Congruence. Congruence between behavior and dialogue, or *walking the talk,* is critical to effectively facilitate learning across cultural strengths. Individuals from marginalized groups are often adept at identifying incongruent behavior; this skill is developed from the vulnerabilities of negotiating cultures not their own (Thomas, 1991), and these individuals may always be on the lookout for behaviors that belie more welcoming dialogue. Because of this actuality, "Teachers must work to maintain congruency in their behavior to be trusted and effective across cultures" (Chávez, 2007, p. 282). Incongruent behavior confuses students and undermines learning as individuals struggle to make sense of the incongruence, their feelings about it, their assessment of safety, and their decision whether to abide by the teacher's words or instead by their actions. The integrative nature of many marginalized student populations makes congruence even more important since word of mouth quickly spreads about professors who can be trusted and those who cannot.

> I've had way too many teachers who encourage us to share our ideas but then scoff at or dismiss what we say. Sometimes it's their nonverbal [affect]—an impatient sigh, a negative shake of their head, or a disappointed look. It's enough to freeze any additional sharing by students.
> —Navajo special education student (Chávez, 2007, p. 282)

Incongruence can also arise when a professor teaches ideas that go against core beliefs within a student's upbringing. At times this is inevitable as we introduce students to a wider world, yet how we show respect for multiple beliefs about the world is important to developing trust among students over time. A biology professor discusses this in relation to theories of evolution and creation:

> *Because I teach about evolution, I often see students begin to shift in their seats or get looks of discomfort on their faces at certain points. By having a teaching observation and some discussions with a colleague, we came up with some ideas, and now I first make it clear that scientific theories including those in biology are just that—theories—and that historically, theories are often replaced by*

new understandings. Then I offer multiple conceptions of evolution and crea-
tion from a variety of cultural, spiritual, and religious sources, using quotes
and images to bring these alive for students. I then ask students to discuss their
own conceptions of evolution and/or creation with a partner and ask for a few
to share their own sense of things with the class. We then have a positive, lively
discussion that helps us learn from many theories of evolution and creation, to
compare and contrast, and to place evolutionary theories and creation beliefs
within a larger and continuously developing context.

—Japanese American biology professor

At times our teaching challenge is in systematically developing internal congruence of teaching techniques, cultural beliefs, and overall learning
objectives. The following faculty narrative offers an example within a cultural
context.

I was at a local coffee shop and came across a former student. We struck up a
conversation, and I learned that this student who was enrolled in medical school
had dropped out. He explained that he is unable to take an anatomy course
because of required work with human remains. His cultural and spiritual beliefs
restrict him from this practice. After some thought, I asked him if he would feel
comfortable if I contacted one of the medical professors known for integrative
medicine to see if we could develop another option for learning anatomy.

I called the professor, and we met with the student to see what might work.
The professor became very excited because the medical school had two ongoing
concerns about the anatomy course: first, that it seemed to encourage disrespect
for human remains and the human body, and second, that a doctor's work after
medical school is with living bodies, so learning anatomy just from human
remains is not enough. Together the three of us came up with the idea of having
a small group of students, including this student, do a series of internships with
surgeons so that greater respect for humans and the body could be cultivated
and students could learn about living systems. This resolved a number of cul-
tural, spiritual, teaching, and learning dilemmas for the student, the medical
faculty, and the program.

—Mestiza education professor

This professor's narrative illuminates an ongoing challenge faculty face
as we develop curriculum and teaching practices that may or may not be
congruent with the actual learning we wish to facilitate. We find, as did many
of the faculty with whom we have worked, that striving to teach across cultural continua and frameworks can promote greater congruency between our
learning objectives and learning among students. A wider look at pedagogical
options and gaining skill in teaching across cultural frameworks facilitates
congruence over time.

Proactivity. Teaching professors must progress proactively beyond gaining knowledge about culturally balancing teaching into its purposeful and studied practice. We hold the responsibility for establishing a community of learners that is inclusive of and permeating with individuated and integrated cultural elements. *Awareness, knowledge, education, skills,* and *action* are five levels of proactivity needed in a cross-cultural learning community (Pope, Reynolds, & Mueller, 2004). Professors can be multiculturally proactive in developing awareness by getting to know themselves culturally, gaining knowledge and understanding of individual students' learning processes, and educating themselves about the role of culture underlying teaching and learning.

We can then take action by analyzing and balancing cultural frameworks. Over time we can explore our cultured selves to develop greater understanding of our teaching. We can take risks to incorporate pedagogical techniques from outside our own cultural frameworks as well as facilitate respectful comparison and contrast of multiple perspectives and interpretations for any one concept we are learning. Finally we can ask students for their ideas about teaching and maintain a continual openness to learning. Proactivity means taking a diversity of ideas and turning them into practice. One professor stated,

> Ideas that emanate from students must be appreciated and put into practice so they feel a sense of empowerment. They can and do make a difference in terms of the structure of the classroom. In fact their ideas often make more of a difference than my own. (Chávez, 2007, p. 283)

One of the reasons student ideas make such a difference is because it can be highly challenging to even imagine teaching techniques centered in a cultural framework different from our own. Students, especially those from cultures different from our own, often provide cultural insights as well as techniques they think of or have experienced in their own communities.

We urge you to go beyond the intellectually stimulating activity of reading this book to find your own proactive means to begin and sustain a practice of transforming your teaching to balance integrated and individuated cultural frameworks. We offer several concrete suggestions for practice: form or join a faculty learning community, apply for a course release to create time for redesigning teaching practices, ask to be observed by a professor who teaches very differently than you and is perhaps from a different cultural origin from you, seek out faculty mentors, converse with students about how they learn best, and find like-minded colleagues who also care about learning among students of all cultures.

Multiplicity.

> It's funny. I've noticed that when some of my own ways of learning and interacting are present in a college classroom, I'm also more able to learn in ways that are not my own. But when my ways of learning are completely absent, like in most of my classes, I feel off balance, like I'm hanging upside down trying to make sense of my surroundings.
> —Hopi sociocultural studies student (Chávez, 2007, p. 283)

Challenging one-dimensional perceptions and introducing contrasting ideas, knowledge, and experiences is critical to teaching effectively across cultures. Using a multiplicity of knowledge, methods, styles, and relationships in various processes is essential. bell hooks (1994) urges that learning needs to be multifaceted to be effective and that "there can never be an absolute set agenda governing teaching practices" (p. 7). hooks uses lecture in small amounts and problem solving, discussion, media, drawing, case study, and multiple modes of processing to create multiplicity in her teaching. Designing and facilitating purposefully across individuated and integrated cultural frameworks, as discussed in Chapter 1 (Table 1.1), is useful for developing diverse and balanced forms of pedagogies and interactions.

> Flexible agendas, multiple realities in knowledge, sharing of personal experience and spontaneous shifts in direction are common [in teaching across cultures]. . . . Multiplicity means in part that the full mind, heart, body, and spirit of the students must be brought out in relation to the academic course subject. To realize the full benefit of a multicultural learning community, students and teachers must engage in a multiplicity of ways of knowing, knowledge sources, realities, relationships, and experiences. (Chávez, 2007, p. 282)

Flexibility is especially important to promote learning across a diverse group of learners. Negotiability in grading methods, priorities, reading materials, assignments, relationships, and roles are essential. As one professor described,

> I don't force my students into anything; I try to work with the class to create the learning process. Some students are more "ready" for a particular learning phase than others, so I usually offer assignment and activity choices. (Chávez, 2007, p. 282)

When we create systematic means for students to make choices beneficial to their specific learning processes and phases, we can also minimize grading time, a very real consideration in our lives as faculty. Students are likely to choose a variety of formats, and many of these formats will enable faster grading.

If we are to facilitate learning among students across cultural strengths, we must learn to provide a variety of means to achieve the same learning outcomes. Ten different students may need 10 different learning processes to get to the same learning outcome. Blending a variety of techniques over the course of a term usually ensures that everyone can find their own natural ways of learning as well as new ones to enhance understanding. When we try too hard to control the process instead of modifying our pedagogy on the basis of need and context, we miss opportunities to harness the full learning potential of each student.

Reciprocal relationships and roles.

> When I first began to teach, I felt oddly uncomfortable about having set up a typical syllabus where students did large papers and projects, where other than brief presentations, no one was learning from these assignments except me and each individual student. I pondered this for a while and then decided to try several techniques that assigned students to read each other's papers, review and critique student research, and apply theory or research developed by students to professional scenarios. I am much more comfortable with these pedagogically collaborative techniques, especially because now everyone in the classroom is learning from a wider variety of teachers—each from a different identity and experiential background, each with different priorities and values, each bringing their own wisdom into our learning community.
> —African American education professor (Chávez, 2007, p. 284)

Varied outlooks on acceptable knowledge and perspectives have produced a contested canon in academe throughout its history, which gets to the heart of the question: Whose knowledge do we study? In a multicultural and academic context it is important to purposefully bring a variety of perspectives, insights, and worldviews to the table to enhance academic integrity and deepen learning. One way to do this is to facilitate learners in bringing what they believe is important to the table to enhance everyone's learning. In this way, we all benefit from many lenses, many voices, and many ways of looking at the world.

To offer varied perspectives in a cross-cultural context, reciprocal relationships and roles are necessary to broaden the font of knowledge naturally, which means designing and facilitating courses in which the whole group shares their thoughts, resources, and critiques in relation to the subject. "Reciprocity or parity among groups of people in relationships involves power and idea sharing as well as reciprocal validation of each other's ideas" (Chávez, 2007, p. 285). Reciprocity assists in the creation of a balanced, cross-cultural learning environment and encourages equal but different participatory roles for each person in a course.

A professor's role is to create an environment in which diverse student strengths, knowledge, and perspectives are integrated and valued. Then we must design ways for students to naturally contribute to their own and others' learning. Having students teach each other, provide regular feedback, and learn from each other's assignments can have a profound effect on learning. Much of our motivation to engage in learning comes from our capacity to find interest in one another and to hear each other. To do so, the professor models validating others.

> The teacher must genuinely value, seek out, and reinforce the contributions of every member in the classroom; often this means those who make us most uncomfortable because they are unlike us in key ways. We must continuously resist the traditional notion that the professor is the only one responsible for classroom dynamics, knowledge, and insight. (Chávez, 2007, p. 285)

Our natural tendencies toward cross-cultural judgments, misunderstandings, and differences in what we believe important can disrupt reciprocal learning. Some kinds of knowledge and skill can mediate these disruptions: greater cultural self-awareness, self-observation in the learning environment, careful course design to include student knowledge creation and sharing, development of effective facilitation techniques, and a constant positive narrative toward student insights and perspectives go a long way toward facilitating reciprocal learning among students.

Initiating and Sustaining Student Engagement Across Cultures

All students benefit from engagement in learning. Engaging their curiosity, connecting subjects to their current and future lives, and creating an environment where they feel empowered enough to learn are all critical aspects of teaching. What is less understood is the criticality of engaging students right from the beginning of a course. We previously discussed the role of the syllabus in early development of connections. In this section, we offer some suggestions for engaging students interpersonally in the first days of a course. Engaging students in the academic subject, with us as teachers and with their peers in the class, is an important part of learning. Meaningful interaction and dialogue with peers, especially across cultures, develops students' openness and furthers their critical thinking (Longerbeam, 2010). Peer and professor engagement and openness are critical because learning is a reflective and often interpersonal act that benefits from purposeful relationship building.

Not everyone is comfortable with the thought of building relationships with students, yet there are many ways to do this from the more academic to the more personal. Some professors take a very academic approach to relationship and trust building as well as to engaging student interest in the subject. Many activities can be devised and facilitated to get students curious and talking about the academic subject.

One chemistry professor who teaches a course with 500 students engages students immediately in the first class by discussing and visually offering students a few examples of chemistry in their lives, using food, soil in and around their homes, and the toothpaste they use every day. He then asks students to brainstorm in trios a list of items with chemical properties in their own lives as well as their thoughts on how they are affected by the chemical nature of these items. After they have brainstormed for a while, he asks the groups to write their most unique item and the way it affects their lives on the board. He discusses some of the more unusual items and then begins to connect the discussion to what they will be doing in the course during the term.

* * *

Other professors use their own stories and experiences with their academic subject to connect with students and begin engaging them with the subject.

* * *

Some professors use trust-building exercises to get students to know each other around nonacademic subjects before moving into the subject itself.

* * *

Still others have students freewrite their feelings or thoughts about the subject and then facilitate discussions about their fears, hopes, or concerns—alleviating concerns with reassurance and ways they will assist with learning as well as connecting their hopes to what they will learn.

* * *

One professor uses technology to have students upload anonymous freewritten paragraphs on the first day to a shared course site so that students can see their common worries, hopes, and insights. She then processes some of the common themes in the next class, offering reassurance and connecting to what they will be doing throughout the term.

One of the keys to connection is drawing from our own natural strengths, interests, and ways of interacting as well as adding a few activities that may be outside our personal or cultural comfort zone.

> A highly extraverted professor, comfortable with group discussion, starts with discussions between pairs, trios, or groups of students followed immediately by individual reflective drawing or freewriting about the subject.

In this way, a culturally balanced engagement is achieved by including both discussion and reflection. This professor started with an activity that he as an extravert was more comfortable with (discussion) before moving to one with which he was less comfortable (reflection), knowing that there would be introverts as well as extraverts in his class. By continuing to purposefully design and facilitate both within and outside our own cultural and personality comfort zones and trying new techniques when we feel ready, over time we build a strong repertoire of pedagogical techniques to sustain student engagement through the semester.

Balancing Activities Across Cultural Norms, Learning Processes, and Personalities

A key to developing a balance of integrated and individuated cultural frameworks is alternating between and blending both in designing and facilitating activities. For example, in an online format, it is helpful one week to have students interact in either an asynchronous or a synchronous activity. This could be in written or spoken discussion. The next week you could then ask students to journal privately with you or in reflective preparation for other activities. In this way, students gain from elements in integrated and individuated modes of learning.

Some key areas to balance within class activities include the following:

- Offering indivual and collective activities
- Starting with theory first and later starting with an example or story first
- Problem solving and creative activities
- Allowing time for silent reflection and interactive discussion
- Using one part of ourselves, such as the mind, and using many senses and processes, such as some combination of mind, emotions, observation, touch, sound, taste, and intuition

- Mixing modes of taking in information such as lecture, symbols, metaphor, story, case study, imagery, or application

The more we guide students through complex activities as well as build on previous learning and connect a variety of kinds of knowledge, the more robust their learning.

Additional Considerations

Provide Ongoing Access to Course Materials as a Form of Oral History Helpful to Learning

Many students find it helpful to have ongoing access to course content. This is true especially for those who learn most naturally through visual means or through oral history. In a study of Native, Hispano, and Mestizo American students, Native American students commonly discussed the importance of continued access throughout an academic term to lecture and other class materials and information. These students likened this access to oral history, enabling them to return to review and recapture knowledge beyond a specific learning module or class session, similar to recurring teaching stories from Elders in their tribes.

Over time, faculty can build course websites or use other available technology to provide ongoing access to materials and links, as well as course information and updates. PowerPoints, e-posters, video or audio recordings of class lectures, lecture notes, and other materials and links can be provided after or even before class sessions so that students can review or preview information. Many colleges and universities have staff to assist with these technologies. In addition, students and colleagues can often point us to do-it-yourself, often free software (freeware) available online. Campus libraries may have e-reserves available for faculty to use in providing materials to students.

Teach in the Moment Across Cultures to Balance Content and Process

One of the memorable things we observed and discussed with faculty in our project was what we came to think of and refer to as the *tyranny of course content*. Most faculty felt a constant and strong pressure to get through a certain amount of course content during each class session or learning module. Some felt additional pressure because of curricular requirements determined for a specific course.

The difficulty with this common sort of pressure is that it contradicts how learning actually takes place. Learning is a process that must flow and change as we facilitate it among a diversity of students; students need to be able to access, connect, and apply new information to learn it. Learning is more about the process of *using* content than about the content itself (Zull, 2002). Even when working with one student, learning is not a static phenomenon. Paulo Freire (1993) urged teachers to move beyond a conception of *pouring knowledge into a learner's head* toward a process-oriented approach. Many learning theorists encourage checking in with students over time and guiding students through learning processes in ways that allow for modification midstream when understanding is not occurring. This process takes paying close attention to student nonverbals in a class session, as well as to other communication indicators, such as silence or an overabundance of confused looks or questions. Other indicators can also serve as clues that learning is not taking place, such as widespread low scores on assignments, exams, or quizzes.

The key even when we start with a design in advance is to have a variety of strategies at the ready for a specific session. Then we can choose the ones that are most helpful to where students are in their learning. One professor described it this way:

> *I'm the kind of person who loves to organize and plan my class sessions down to a T, so when I began to realize that not everyone was getting it in my classes, I had to really think about how to balance my own need for planning with the reality of student learning processes. These days, I plan extra activities into my overall session plan so that I have both a plan for when students take longer to understand and a plan for when students are further ahead than I anticipated. I've also challenged myself to develop my ability to create a new activity on the spur of the moment when needed, though this is less comfortable for me.*
>
> —Filipino architecture professor

We must become adept over time at designing pedagogy on a moment-to-moment basis. It is helpful to regularly make use of strategies to check in with students, sometimes by paying attention to nonverbal cues and other indicators of learning. Students leaning forward, heads nodding, plenty of eye contact, and other positive learning behaviors can indicate that students are engaged. Multiple members of a class offering answers to questions out loud during lectures or activities can also indicate positive learning, though notice if this only includes the students who are already doing well in the course and are comfortable speaking up.

When students frown or show other nonverbal signs of confusion, it may well be time to try a different strategy. We encourage you to ask students outright what their concerns are, or even "test" student knowledge by having a number of students come up to the board and show you or explain to the class. When interaction around learning moves back and forth between professor and students as well as among student peers, learning is happening. Some professors are reluctant to put students on the spot, yet we find that when professors combine care, overt reassurances, and a constant positive narrative that includes encouragement that it is okay and even helpful to make mistakes, students engage in and benefit from this kind of on-the-spot problem solving, trying, and even testing. We observed even very shy and reticent students benefitting from this approach.

Keep in mind, though, that silence is not necessarily an indicator that students are confused or not learning. Some learners need time to think and internally process. One study found that Navajo students tend to wait six to 10 seconds to offer a response when asked, while non-Native learners typically respond within three to five seconds (McCarthy & Benally, 2003). Another study reported that Navajo and Apache students prefer 15 to 30 seconds to think reflectively before responding (Plank, 1994). Students who are naturally introverted also find it helpful or even necessary to process internally before sharing, and many benefit from quiet time during this thinking process. For these students, silence is necessary to learning and, when provided in class, offers a time to collect or process thoughts before sharing.

> One professor we observed asked students each class session to pick up index cards from the front and send them out to the aisles for him to pick up whenever they had a question or needed something reviewed. This professor would circulate while he was talking or while students were working in small groups to pick up cards and address concerns and questions as the class session progressed.
>
> * * *
>
> An innovative peer mentoring program we observed placed student peer mentors move around quietly in class in an active fashion. They answering questions and assisting students while other activities are in progress (Gomez-Chavez, 2014).

Teaching pedagogies across cultural frameworks are infinite in their possibilities. We hope that you engage your creative energies, learn with and from students and colleagues, share your ideas, and risk transformation by garnering strengths from across cultural frameworks for the benefit of all students.

Note

1. bell hooks chooses not to capitalize her name in an effort to show equity among and solidarity with others. We honor her choice in our writing.

6

Top 10 Things Faculty Can Do
to Teach Across Cultures

This chapter addresses the common pressure that faculty feel to gradually transform their teaching within busy professional lives. The many responsibilities pulling at faculty time and a common preference for deliberate, purposeful development of teaching practice make it more likely that faculty will progressively incorporate new or modified pedagogical techniques gradually. Faculty can take on one or two strategies at a time, trying out different practices, observing student responses and student learning, and transforming practice in a sustained manner over the life of their teaching.

In our Culture and Teaching Faculty Development Project, faculty typically engaged in one fundamental or profound transformation in their teaching. For example, they may have purposefully questioned assumptions they made about students, knowledge, or learning on the basis of their own cultural values related to teaching and learning; chosen one cultural construct and added or modified a technique from the other side of the continuum from their own; or made time to talk with three students from cultures other than their own about how they learn best. Since then, many have continued to develop their teaching incrementally, sharing with us some of their revelations and techniques. The following sections discuss each of these top 10 things (see Figure 6.1) faculty can do in more detail, providing examples and tips to assist in transforming practice over time.

Self-Reflect Culturally

Deep reflection on our earliest cultural influences is critically important to uncover our natural ways of teaching, integrate our cultural strengths,

Special thanks to Dr. Gary Weissman, professor of Earth and planetary sciences at the University of New Mexico, for suggesting the concept for this chapter.

Figure 6.1 Top 10 Things Faculty Can Do to Teach Across Cultures

Top 10 Things . . .

1. Self-Reflect Culturally

2. Modify One Cultural Continuum

3. Talk With Three Students

4. Explore One Negative Attribution

5. Share With Students the Value of Balancing Cultural Frameworks

6. Connect to Student Lives

7. Partner With Students

8. Make a Personal Connection

9. Assess Creatively

10. Consider the Rewards

and challenge ourselves to adopt practices reflective of the range of cultural frameworks. Our work with faculty in writing a culture and teaching autobiography (see Appendix A for a guide to creating your own culture and teaching autobiography) affirmed our belief that reflection on our early familial, community, and educational experiences gives insight into how our natural ways of teaching and learning—our own cultural strengths—became a part of our college teaching. As a Norwegian American faculty member in physics reflected after she had written her cultural autobiography,

> *I wasn't turning the lens back on myself. Self-reflection was an eye opener and made me more patient. I used to think they can't be late, can't miss deadlines.*

This professor now understood her early cultural influences and eased up on herself and her students with respect to the cultural construct of time. She began to decouple timelines from learning and was able in many cases to offer students and herself the time needed to move toward understanding. She learned that learning is influenced by many factors, and maintaining flexibility with time can be very helpful to learning. Once she was able to reflect on her own feelings about time, she was able to refocus her attention on what worked to develop understanding among a variety of students and the influence of time and time constraints on this process. Faculty might also reflect on other possibilities of time orientations and begin to ponder how time influences learning among students and then transform pedagogical design to balance various conceptions of time (see cultural construct on time, in Chapter 1, Table 1.1). Cultural self-analysis and reflection is helpful even for those who are less conscious or even unaware of their cultural origins. Identifying personal values and beliefs and reflecting on their origins in our lives is helpful to understanding ourselves and to consideration of differing values and beliefs among students in our courses.

We learned that writing the culture and teaching autobiography was universally *challenging* for faculty, yet helpful in developing teaching practice across cultures. The challenge of cultural self-reflection was experienced by every one of the 37 faculty with whom we worked over the yearlong faculty development cohorts. One faculty member noted, "It was a 'where the rubber meets the road' kind of an assignment," and another said she is now more systematic and intentional about how she is teaching as a result of writing the culture and teaching autobiography. When faculty were able to self-reflect, recall, and reframe the cultural origins of their teaching methods, especially their underlying assumptions, they were then well on their way to transforming their teaching.

Modify One Cultural Continuum

Choose one continuum and add or modify a technique from the side of the cultural continuum not your own; develop and implement one or two new teaching practices each semester from this alternate side of the cultural continuum. We encourage generally alternating between activities that are on one side of the cultural continuum with those on the other side. This can be uncomfortable at first for faculty and students, but with time and practice, students learn more deeply and faculty see expanded engagement and understanding. The following discussion comprises several examples to illustrate modifications made by faculty during our Culture and Teaching Faculty Development Project. This Scandinavian-German American educational psychology professor explains,

> *I was raised in an individuated culture, and I teach theory courses. Although I love to begin and end with abstract theory, I know that love is not shared by many students. I decided to try one new pedagogical technique on the integrated end of the cultural frameworks' sequencing continuum. Rather than sequencing from theory to application, I started to use autobiographical stories to illustrate human developmental theory. The stories illustrate adult challenges, growth periods, and life successes. This simple shift is remarkably rewarding. Now I always use autobiographical stories to illustrate theory, though I vary the*

sequencing; sometimes I still begin with theory in the abstract, sometimes I use theory and story concurrently, and other times I assign autobiography and ask students to select and apply relevant theories after reflection. I am enjoying the increased student engagement—students are learning by doing, enjoying working with theoretical concepts, and applying new knowledge to their natural ways of learning.

A Mexican American radiology professor shared,

For the longest time I was content in using all group activities and assignments in my radiology courses. I think of medicine as a very collective profession and feel that this kind of group skill building and group problem solving is critical to facilitating healing. At some point, though, I began to learn more about individual learners, reflection, and more linear thinking processes and attained a greater understanding of many of my students and colleagues. I realized that I was connecting more often with individuals from collective cultures like mine and began to make a concerted effort to balance individual and linear activities and assignments with my more naturally comfortable group and circular ones. It made all the difference in my ability to engage all my students in learning.

To create a balance across individual and collective learner orientations, some faculty have students work on quizzes in pairs or trios before having them submit results individually. This places the focus firmly on enhancing learning rather than on evaluation alone. Another faculty member encourages teamwork on assignments by offering extra credit to those who choose to pair up, clearly explaining that the extra time and relational negotiations necessary in collaborative work enhance outcomes yet take additional energy and patience—skills needed in their profession. Many of these faculty grappled with the challenge of structuring assignments and quizzes so that responsibility for learning and student interactions is balanced. Some felt a bit uncomfortable challenging their own beliefs about independence and individual responsibility enough to consider designing activities, assignments, and tests more collectively. Most from collective cultures usually already had experience with both orientations, yet some still struggled because of ingrained academic norms and pressures valuing more individual orientations.

Talk With Three Students

One relatively simple way to find out more about the learning needs of students from cultures other than our own is to talk to three students from other cultures about how they learn best. This exercise may demonstrate the cultural frameworks, making them concrete. For instance, some students learn best by talking with others, some by reading or reflection. They may mention YouTube videos, or perhaps listening, doing, or watching. One

German-Hungarian-Russian geology professor distributed copies of the Cultural Frameworks in Teaching and Learning model in his first class session of the semester and asked students to identify where they thought they were along each continuum. He then facilitated a discussion of ways the students learned best and asked for their ideas as he designed class activities. He even offered to modify the syllabus somewhat to offer a wider variety of assignments, projects, and evaluations across the semester. This faculty member experienced some real surprises and gained many innovations from this simple exercise and discussion. One that startled him the most was that a Navajo student in the class who had never spoken or approached him in previous courses came up and started a conversation and came in several times in subsequent weeks to his office hours to share more about who she is and to discuss geology in relation to some of her hopes. He shared,

> *I think that I opened a door somehow with this student by acknowledging the relevance of culture with that worksheet activity.*

Another strategy is to choose a new student group to learn about each month or semester. One way to choose is to think about students who tend to trigger or annoy you. Annoyance can be an indicator that there are differences in cultural values or nonverbal communication norms. For example, some of us are annoyed by those who stay silent, others by those who talk a great deal. By reflecting deep down on what annoys us and why, we can move through our feelings and learn to work more effectively with these students. We can also talk with them to find out what their silence or talking means and how it relates to their learning. Another possibility is to consider choosing students who are not doing well, to whom you may assign negative attributions. One faculty member in our project decided to make a list of topics and student groups she prefers to avoid and to choose a new group or topic from that list each month to engage with and learn from.

One relatively nonthreatening way in which you might talk with students is to offer them an invitation to conversation through notes on their papers. You might ask a question about something they wrote that you find intriguing or do not understand and ask them to talk with you after class. Through a brief conversation, you might then extend the invitation to walking back to your office together or to the student union for a larger discussion over a cup of coffee. Inviting students in this way may be more effective than simply asking them to attend your office hours. It can be especially helpful to let them know that you would appreciate their insights and that their ideas and experiences will help you improve learning experiences for future students. We find that students are often honored to be asked for their input.

Meeting with even one student a semester takes only a small amount of time and is helpful to improving our teaching and understanding of students.

Early in her teaching career, one faculty member in our cohorts who is Mestiza, a mix of highly integrated Native and Spanish American cultures, kept receiving feedback from students that she needed to be more organized. This was critical for her because most of her students at the time were from individuated cultures with preferences for more linear, step-by-step learning processes. She was struggling to balance her more process-oriented teaching style with their preferred learning style. No matter how much organization she added to her course through activities, handouts, and syllabi, she kept getting the same feedback. She decided to approach several students who seemed very organized and asked them how they learn best and if they had any suggestions for her teaching. One of them described his need for more obvious visual organization so that he could follow along in a more step-by-step manner. He explained that he would find it helpful if she added PowerPoints or some other noticeably visible organizational aspects to her teaching. The faculty member developed a PowerPoint for the next class session and did so in her own way—using color, only a few words to help focus attention, and many visuals such as models and photographs. After this, she stopped getting feedback about needing to be more organized, perhaps because she was reaching more students by more visibly balancing both ends of the cultural frameworks.

Explore One Negative Attribution

Choose one way in which you tend to judge students negatively. Explore this attribution by asking students why they do what they do or considering how they might be engaging in learning from the opposite side of the continuum from your dominant side. Be sure to let the students know that you are interested so that you can understand their learning and so that they don't feel intimidated or become defensive. Compare the meaning made by students with this behavior to your own interpretations. Consider how this difference in meaning affects your facilitation of learning and what you could modify to accommodate both sides of the continuum. One Danish American engineering professor explains the importance of this purposeful reflection, self-analysis, and awareness of students:

> *Master teachers chip away at their blind spots—they figure out one population they weren't reaching, learn more, and then move on to the next one. It is important to chip away, because if we do not, we project our judgments of students, and students comprehend that. I cannot walk into a class with preconceptions, because then they will react to that.*

We strive to think about students who trigger us and make an effort to learn about their life struggles. We share some common attributions we have listened for, with the intent that you may choose to listen for them in yourself and in the faculty culture around you. One common example of negative attribution during class time is related to silence. As faculty we may attribute silence to intent listening or alternatively to apathy or disinterest; this dynamic occurs most noticeably in discussion. When students do not contribute or do not engage in discussion, we might attribute their reasons to wanting to learn from others by listening or alternatively as distance or coldness. Some other widespread attributions are as follows:

On creating flexibility in assignments and assessment, faculty sometimes refer to "lowering expectations" or "coddling and bribing" students. Another way to frame this might be to consider having very high expectations for learning outcomes combined with high flexibility for student needs and processes and offers of compassion and incentives for student learning. Combining high challenge with high support is a core theorem (Sanford, 1967) of student learning in college.

* * *

On working with students of the current era, some may talk about the "student population we are dealing with," students who come to college "underprepared," or "this generation of less motivated, entitled students." Reframing these phrases as a challenge to continually learn about new generations and populations entering our learning environments can shift our innovative attentions toward developing a wider diversity of pedagogies to address multiple learning processes and needs. Each generation of students brings new strengths and areas of struggle, and as faculty we are called to continuously evolve as well.

* * *

Some may ask whether when we change or adjust assignments to meet student learning needs, students are "taking advantage" or are even lazy. Perhaps the best thing we can do is ask ourselves: How am I with students who are not doing well, and what can I do differently that would engage and enhance these students' learning? A Danish American engineering faculty member works with his own vulnerability around classroom disruptions by becoming more playful with challenging students—"those in the back corner always festering about something." He is successful in reaching challenging students with playfulness after he has reframed his beliefs about them from disruptive to engaged in their own way.

* * *

We found that many faculty we worked with had also moved from evaluating student learning, which in many ways felt like judging students, to working with students until they learned. One Mestiza education professor shared that she now assigns a grade to each project or paper with plenty of specific feedback and then offers students an optional week to revise and resubmit for their own learning and an improved grade, a writing process similar to faculty publishing. She says, "It was remarkable. This shifted me more toward a focus on learning, but I am still amazed with how many students work incredibly hard to revise their assignments and they are always grateful for the opportunity."

Share With Students the Value of Balancing Cultural Frameworks

Learning is enhanced when faculty share their metathinking, or road maps, about teaching and learning processes with students. Purposefully communicating the value of balancing integrated and individuated learning processes lets students know its importance to each of them as learners and welcomes them into our own thinking and learning. Sharing our learning journey of facilitating this balance in our teaching entails the expression of humility. It communicates to students that we are learning along with them. It can be extraordinarily helpful to acknowledge our vulnerability in the learning process. These acknowledgments may allow students to take risks essential to learning and thinking in new ways. There is vulnerability for both teacher and student in this whole enterprise. One business professor says he struggles with and in front of students, and tells them, "I'm going to learn in front of you and with you," and that the class and professor "sit with a certain kind of humility to the question," because, as he shares, "my work is deeply engaged in affecting their lives."

It is common to compartmentalize learning in the academy; in fact it is how the entire enterprise is structured (Ibarra, 2001; Rendón, 2009). The interconnectedness of what is learned is rarely addressed in the curriculum, and yet cognitive neuroscience teaches us that humans learn through making connections (Zull, 2002). Many of the deepest insights are gained through leaps of mind and reaches of intuition. When we share with students the value of teaching to heart, mind, body, emotions, and what we know about learning and neuroscience (Medina, 2011), they understand intuitively. When faculty nurture the intuitive response in students, we also nurture thinking at high levels, the kind of complex thinking needed to solve complex problems (Fried, 2012; Weimer, 2002).

One concrete way to highlight the interconnectedness of learning is to tie together themes within and across courses. When assignments connect across a single course and across multiple courses, they support cognitive complexity and engaged learning. Though the academy is already more likely to accommodate those who learn best through compartmentalizing facts, students who naturally learn in individuated processes and prefer checklists and bullet points can still be accommodated through the continued inclusion of individuated pedagogies in balance with integrated pedagogies. The important point is to teach with and across the full range of cultural frameworks.

Connect to Student Lives

Connecting subject matter to student lives in a variety of ways is helpful to learning across cultures. For some, more personal, familial, tribal, or community connections matter, while for others, connections to professional practice provide the pragmatism helpful to learning. Relating abstract theory and facts in some way to student lives is necessary for most students to engage learning and long-term retention of knowledge and proficiencies.

Learning Theory

The human brain learns by building upon preexisting cognitive structures (Zull, 2002). The brain's process to learn new information generally proceeds as (a) accessing material through our senses; (b) connecting new knowledge to what we already know—preexisting structures; and (c) applying the knowledge creatively in our own way, to make it our own. Exercising these sensory, associative, and motor functions is how we learn (Zull, 2002). If our goal is retention and recall of knowledge, these are the steps that will help students learn and remember what they learn.

A geography professor begins class by asking students, "What do you already know about a region?" Facilitating student contributions, the professor draws borders and then identifies geographical markers on a projected map—and then refers to the projected map all semester long. This pedagogy is a good example of sequencing for students who respond to real-life application of knowledge. It is also a good example because the professor uses maps as visual markers, and vision is the strongest sensory tool in learning and retention of knowledge (Mayer, 2001; Medina, 2011).

When we build upon what students already know, students add new knowledge to old, thereby creating patterns. These patterns facilitate retaining and recalling the new knowledge (Mayer, 2001). Some students come from cultures in which this learning process feels natural, and interconnections are valued; others struggle to understand why some contextualized content is relevant to the course. For more individuated students, periodically orienting them with a road map—for example, learning objectives and learning outcomes as well as some of the ways we will learn toward these objectives and outcomes—may reassure them that discrete knowledge parts can still be separated as well as connected.

Content that has an emotional connection for students is particularly helpful to learning; this is where current events are useful because they often resonate with timely emotional responses. Frequent associations to current events give dynamism to class. An accounting professor draws on the excitement of hot-button news items by regularly using Twitter to send web links to current ethical dilemmas in business news. For instance, the professor incorporated news items about the high-risk mortgages that contributed to the debt crisis and recession that began in 2008.

Local Issues and Realities

Some students gain understanding, learn, and respond most when they can relate something to the needs and realities of their home communities, tribes, personal selves, or families. We work with many students in the Southwest who grow up in rural or urban areas among large extended families and Indigenous tribes. For these students and for many others, learning becomes most real when they can situate it early on in their own relational lives because this is often how learning occurred in their younger lives. Elders and others who facilitate learning in many integrated cultures use the world around them to teach, connecting more abstract lessons to nature and to self, especially by reflection on family and community or tribal needs. Students from this kind of upbringing often learn most effectively first through examples, case studies, stories, and application of concepts and theories to the experiences of their own communities, families, and selves. Some professors have students regularly identify local issues, needs, and realities when discussing specific theory or go inward to reflect on their own experiences with a specific concept. A psychology professor asks students in every online discussion to share or imagine specific mental health conditions in their own families; every time a math professor introduces a new type of equation she shares a problem or scenario in which it might be used and later in the term asks students to brainstorm applications on their own; and a chemistry professor guides students to analyze and then consider the impact of mining residue in water, air, and soil on the health of local tribal communities.

Professional Preparation

Some students respond well when faculty include pragmatic reasons for activities and assignments; establishing connections to future practice is an ideal way to make these reasons relevant. A business professor helps students understand their future profession using conversations that encourage them to embrace complexity and understand ethical issues. A science professor relates assignments to various skills that will be required in a variety of related professions. Professional preparation conversations make those connections. When an accounting professor for whom starting class on time is important wants to emphasize the value of time, she reminds students that clients will expect them to be on time for business consultations and that they may lose a client if they are late. She also encourages students to understand their profession well enough and be competent enough that they can explain accounting core tenets to clients and others using "elevator knowledge"—knowledge that can be shared in two to three minutes.

Sharing related stories from your own life and your profession has the additional benefit of sometimes delighting students. They form impressions of us as we do of them, and they enjoy it when we counter their impressions. Students want to see our humanity and know our own journeys and discoveries through our disciplines and our professional lives in order to get a better sense of who we are. A geography professor shares with students her unfinished writing, such as manuscripts, reviewer comments, and editor notes. Students see and appreciate her writing process and the struggles she faces, and are reminded that they also will be required to respond to others' feedback on their writing throughout their careers.

For students who are motivated by thinking about their futures, drawing from learning to practice and from practice to jobs and professional life will help. A pedagogical strategy that supports the connection to professional life is to use practice dilemmas and case studies. By encouraging students to work with cases, faculty build complexity in approaching problems over time. One education faculty member asks students to write papers from the perspective of a student or a family member to encourage students to think with breadth and complexity. Case studies are also ideal for mixing individual and small-group work. When learning is shared between students, active participation is more likely the norm. And active learning, using experiential scenarios, better prepares students for the future, when they will create in teams and make collaborative contributions to their profession (Weimer, 2002).

Partner With Students

Design and Facilitate Ways for Students to Share Their Insights, Knowledge, and Work With the Entire Class

Partnering with students is a key way to develop pedagogies that work more effectively to promote learning across cultures. There are many ways that faculty in our cohorts did this, including giving students ownership of the class to lead class discussion. For example, have the class choose a topic one student is passionate about, or a topic that interests everyone, and do a group project on that topic. Assign students to read other students' papers as course readings and have students review a student project or appraise a paper summary or abstract and comment. A Spanish American astronomy student in a class where projects became course readings shared,

> *There were quite a few concepts that I didn't understand until I reviewed other student's projects. I don't know, there was something about the many ways others came at things, explained things, illustrated things that helped me to get it a little at a time as I reviewed their work.*

A Mestiza education professor shared a perspective she said came from her collectively oriented cultural origins:

> *At a certain point, I began to feel selfish, even unethical. The only ones learning from a student's paper or project were me and the individual student. This gave me the urge to change and I began to have at least one written assignment that students knew would become a reading for the whole class. This had the added benefit of offering a kind of positive peer pressure that improved student work, and students began to really appreciate and sometimes be amazed by what they were learning from each other in deeper ways than just discussion in class or online. I do this in all my classes now, and it is a very powerful way to partner with students in the learning process.*

One teaching strategy for disseminating student thinking and eliciting active participation is to ask students to list five key points from the week's readings on the board when they first come into class. As one architecture faculty member noted, in this way they "take ownership" of their ideas and make them public. This teaching practice also creates a base of student ideas to discuss as a class. In discussion, ask students to comment on or ask questions about another student's reading. Faculty can also write student insights on the board as they process a problem or case. This provides a collective visual map of ideas and processing for class learning. Another strategy to encourage students to share responsibility for learning is to assign class sessions they lead and even design. Teaching others and having to figure out how to do so are highly effective learning activities.

When we observed teaching sessions, we noticed faculty who gave continual encouragement, something we came to think of as a constant positive narrative. Faculty who partnered with students naturally continued encouraging, cheering, thanking, and reinforcing them. The constant narrative also included testing, pushing, checking in, praising, teasing, and challenging. Common refrains included, "You are on the right track"; "The first part of your comment is right on; let me help you with the second part"; and "Tell us more." Faculty did not take silence for an answer, waiting instead. When waiting did not work, they tried new tactics: working to ensure students understood their message, taking it upon themselves to ensure understanding. The constant back-and-forth between faculty and students, and students and students, was a kind of teaching-and-learning dance. We observed this in classes both large and small.

Invite Students to Speak or Share in Some Way

Part of partnering with students is valuing their thinking. Sometimes inclusion happens best when faculty call upon or invite students to speak in class. When we consider what the class can learn from *every* student, we are motivated to include their voices in class conversations. (As you would expect, this invitation does not mean asking students to speak for their culture or only asking them to speak on topics related to their identities.) Students often benefit from speaking, sharing, or responding to develop as intellectuals and professionals. We can shift our thinking to facilitating everyone's learning through invitation to active engagement rather than merely opening opportunities and expecting students to jump in. Waiting for students, or drawing out student input, often implies letting go of content for that particular class and necessitates a shift from focusing on imparting discrete knowledge to developing larger understanding and learning through engagement with knowledge (Freire, 1993). Learning is often enhanced, as noted earlier, via connections to student lives and pragmatic application to problems, issues, and opportunities. It is often helpful to encourage students to share the beginnings of their thinking or partial thoughts. One professor encourages this by calling out, "Half-formed thoughts are good!" This often leads to other students adding to these initial ideas or offering contrasting perspectives.

Ask Students to Suggest What the Class Will Process

Most faculty develop all of the activities, examples, and cases for their students to process in class. An additional way to engage students and diversify learning and focus is to facilitate activities and assignments that instead ask students to identify a case, situation, example, or issue to which they can apply theory or skill. For example, assign a different theory from readings to each of several groups of students in a course, asking them to explain the theory to everyone during the next class session and include a real-life example to assist in everyone's understanding. Students can be encouraged to draw from their own lives or issues in their families or communities or to look in the news or online for examples. In doing so, students must develop a sense of subject relevance beyond the classroom, they must face the challenge of struggling to understand a specific theory first on their own, and they have each other in the group to rely on for different perspectives and areas of understanding. In addition, the professor is not the sole source of ideas for focus in the classroom. This builds a sense of ownership among students as well as connections from the academic subject to life outside the course. Faculty are often amazed that students can figure out even a highly complex theorem on their own and explain it in terms that classmates understand. Study groups among students often form naturally through this kind of process.

This technique is especially useful when students share their insights and perspectives with peers. Informal sharing or formal presentations are a good way to structure this sharing. Posting and then processing student-developed papers, e-posters, PowerPoints, videos, and other assignment outcomes are especially powerful activities for enriching learning for the whole class.

In a research course, the professor was struggling to explain the difference between qualitative and quantitative research modalities to her students. She came up with the idea to ask them individually to read about both and bring in two different metaphorical examples, one representing quantitative research and the other representing qualitative research. Students used their own interest areas to highlight these differences . . . one brought a guitar to class and played a short part of a Bach concerto and a short part of a Mozart concerto; another showed a photo of an Impressionist painting and a photograph to demonstrate the difference, and still another student used a chart with numbers and a grouping of narrative quotes to show the difference. As each student in the class explained and showed the visual or other example, students developed a deeper understanding of each research modality, and most discussed how challenging yet helpful it was to have to struggle to build an understanding that was strong enough to explain to others.

Make a Personal Connection

A geography professor in our study learned faces and names of the 80 students in her class by returning papers while saying the students' names. Personal connections are very important to those for whom the teacher's role is to facilitate learning interactions among students and teachers. There are many ways to personalize learning; the general concept involves sharing of ourselves as faculty and attempting to understand what it is like to be the student in their particular time and place in the academy. One simple idea for understanding what it is like to be a student is to ask students how they are doing and follow up with concrete questions about what they are involved with in their on-campus and off-campus lives. This can often be done in an ongoing process of approaching a few students before, during, and after each class session. Some students are more likely than others to share their personal hopes and challenges, often trying to make a connection with professors. This behavior is common especially among students from integrated, collective cultural origins for whom providing contextual information is expected and problem solving through relationships is common. When we remain open to students' sharing and refer them to appropriate resources on campus for assistance with non-academic needs, their willingness to share becomes a helpful way to support students academically as well as personally—without feeling like we are being taken advantage of or asked for assistance outside our expertise.

One way to get to know students and relate to student lives is by explaining concepts using social media, current events, and pop culture. Sometimes students are able to share what they are watching, and we can then watch the same media to increase connections for them. Many faculty we worked with made these kinds of connections, usually directly from their own personal interest areas such as performance, sports, outdoor recreation, families, current events, children, or pets. This offers the benefit of allowing students to get to know us by sharing within our own comfort zones. Humor, teasing, connecting, and metaphor or imagery are useful for those who learn best by sequencing from the concrete to the abstract. Another helpful way to make connections is through sharing stories of travels and professional experiences to explain course concepts.

Assess Creatively

Use Multiple Means of Assessment

Assessing student work is an area of teaching practice that offers multiple ways to incorporate the cultural frameworks of teaching and learning. Just as there are many ways to learn, there are many ways to assess learning.

Drawing upon more assessment methods will likely draw upon the strengths of all students. One Norwegian American education professor noted that her primary goal in assessment, and what she would exclaim to students, is, "You need to show me, somehow, someway, what you've learned this semester." A primary focus for a German American geology professor is formative assessment, which he conducts through online quizzes, after the in-class learning sessions. Class time is used for active group problem solving more than lectures and exams. The online quiz after class indicates to him the degree of learning on the week's topic. The professor then adjusts the pacing and content of the course on the basis of the formative assessment because he wants to know how students are learning throughout the course and whether he is intervening effectively at critical moments. This professor uses his own natural analytical interests and abilities to assess from a variety of student data points to track how students are doing and to connect with individuals when he has concerns or wishes to provide affirmation.

In reflection on the benefits of using multiple assessments, the professor observes that using multiple forms of assessment helps him to understand students who would otherwise be difficult for him to understand. In other words, with students whose learning frameworks differ from his teaching frameworks, he is better able to assess their learning using multiple forms of assessment, including formative assessment that allows him to shift course midstream. His core belief is that students should have multiple ways to demonstrate what they have learned. Over time, this professor and others develop ways to evaluate engagement, including discussion rubrics, visual assessment of team discussions in classes, testing, papers, projects, peer feedback, observations—especially in labs and studios—and individual check-in meetings.

Group/Individual Balance in Assignments

Collaboration with and respectful critique by student peers can be very helpful to student learning and self-assessment. One professor explained that she facilitates students' responding to one another in online discussions through extra-credit points because she found that some kinds of student learning are more influenced by positive incentives such as verbal encouragement, facilitated activities, and extra-credit points than by evaluative motivators such as taking off points from a grade.

> *I went from only a few students offering respectful critique of readings or each other's comments to almost all students offering this in every discussion when I moved from points subtracted to points added on my discussion grading rubric. I also offer extra-credit points for offering professional suggestions to peers, and*

for sharing outside resources such as websites, other readings, theoretical models, and more. The funny thing is that the points are pretty negligible but they really matter to students. One student told me that by offering extra points, I clearly communicated that this type of interaction is valued and important to our learning.

—African American biology professor

Consider the Rewards

Consider the rewards of engaging in these top 10 strategies as well as additional strategies you create over time. Even if you choose only one new teaching idea, or focus on shifting toward the side opposite your strength on one cultural continuum, the results can invigorate your teaching and faculty life. Greater joy awaits us when we participate in students' growth and their excitement for learning. When students apply their natural gifts, they prosper and so do we. As we continue to reinforce existing cultural strengths and develop new teaching skills throughout the cultural frameworks continua, we are well on the way to continually enhancing learning.

7

Spreading the Cultural Word:
Faculty Development on a Larger Scale

Writing a culture and teaching autobiography was a life-changing experience for me. I think every faculty member should write one because it helped me to think deeply about who I am and how I bring that into my teaching. I've always thought of my teaching as neutral, academic. This deeply reflective activity made me understand that my teaching is very culturally based, and that I judge students based on my own cultural values. It was kind of humbling. I'm not sure how I ever believed I was neutral as a teacher and now feel really compelled not only to balance my teaching across cultural norms and values but also to spread the word and get other faculty to do this kind of reflection and hopefully develop their teaching, too. I've already presented this autobiography to other faculty at three conferences and among some of my more open-minded colleagues in my department.

—*Jewish American Earth and planetary sciences professor*

Continuous learning—especially about students, teaching, and learning—is important for educators. Every generation of students brings with it new challenges and new vistas of possibility. As college students originate in increasingly diverse cultural backgrounds it is important for us to evolve and grow as facilitators of learning across cultures. Through our own growth, we might also influence our colleagues toward developing their own understanding and abilities in culture and college teaching. We offer a few possibilities. We can encourage cultural introspection in relation to teaching, as the faculty member quoted previously does. We might also share insights we gain about students and their learning processes, informally discussing these insights from our experiences teaching across cultural frameworks. We could join or start a cohort of faculty who meet to discuss teaching across cultures, offer teaching observations to one another, and then share culturally based teaching suggestions we receive as feedback on our own teaching observations. Finally, we might share pedagogical and interactive techniques at teaching institutes on campus and present at national and international academic conferences.

In this chapter we offer suggestions for working with faculty over time in developing teaching approaches and practices that address cultural differences. In addition, we provide suggestions for how faculty can influence colleagues in their own departments and academic communities to transform teaching across cultures to improve student learning, success, and retention. Over time we worked with faculty in a variety of ways on campus, at national conferences and institutes, and through invited seminars with groups of faculty at various universities and colleges. The project we mention throughout this book (see Chapter 8 for a discussion of our development project) was a yearlong collaborative faculty development project between two universities with cohorts of faculty at both institutions. The following sections offer suggestions for a variety of ways to work with faculty on integrating cultural strengths to deepen learning among students.

On-Campus Culture and Teaching Seminars

Some campuses have faculty development programs, and many of these programs offer teaching development seminars for faculty to continuously develop their teaching practice. Seminars on integrating cultural strengths across teaching practices can be very helpful, especially to faculty who prefer to learn in groups and wish to gain discrete amounts of knowledge to apply to their teaching. On-campus seminars are especially helpful when conducted by faculty who have already applied some aspects of cultural balance to their own teaching and can share ideas and facilitate the development of pedagogical and interactive techniques appropriate for other disciplines, modes of teaching, and course levels.

Discrete teaching seminars are limited by time and opportunities for longer-term interchange among faculty. In addition, individual seminars are not as helpful for trying new strategies and then discussing them, or for forming longer-term relationships among faculty interested in exploring culture and teaching over time, something that is helpful when learning any complex practice. Seminars also do not often provide a process or time to learn, go away to reflect, and return, which is helpful to cultural introspection. Facilitators could build in shorter reflection time for this purpose in a seminar or design multiday session seminars.

Multiple-Day Culture and Teaching Institutes

Teaching institutes that take place over several days offer a chance to build relationships among faculty, hold the benefit of time away from campus and the institute in evenings for reflection and reading, and offer a chance for multiple modes of learning and practice when designed accordingly. The beginnings of culture and teaching autobiographical planning, pre-writing, and writing are possible with this longer period, though writing a full autobiography would be challenging in only a few days. Within this longer time frame, various activities become possible, including case studies, experienced faculty panels, and teaching practice (with or without observation and feedback from experienced faculty). However, even this longer format is limited by time; faculty have less opportunity to both apply what they learn to teaching practice and return to the group for reflective discussion. It is also less likely that individual consultations and observations with experienced faculty will take place because of academic schedule challenges.

Sustained Culture and Teaching Faculty Cohorts

Because of the complex nature of learning and becoming adept at cultural balance in teaching, we recommend sustained faculty cohorts for a term and preferably a full academic year. Two types of cohorts are discussed here.

Yearlong Multifaceted Culture and Teaching Faculty Cohort

We designed the full academic-year faculty development project discussed in this book (see Chapter 8 for more details) after having tried shorter and more discrete professional development seminars and institutes. We hoped to provide enough time and deeper relationships to enable learning, practicing, and developing culturally balanced teaching. We found it necessary to create a general plan and then modify it according to faculty time constraints, experience and comfort with cross-cultural interactions, and the needs of individual faculty for applying concepts to teaching practice.

A sustained cohort offers a number of benefits. An academic-year program allows time to develop trust and collegiality among faculty, which is helpful to discussion of and practice in cultural balance. Time for cultural introspection is also made more possible within a sustained project. Multiple activities were possible in our project because of the full academic-year design. Activities included monthly gatherings for learning, sharing, collective innovating, and practicing within the group; lectures by invited speakers; workshops for developing and writing a culture and teaching autobiography and sharing it with colleagues; help with sustaining cultural balancing of teaching practices in a variety of courses; individual consultations and teaching observations; and beginning and summative culture and teaching two-day institutes, during the summers on either end of the academic year. Limitations include the possible need to offer incentives for participation, to secure funding for materials and other expenses, and to appeal for longer-term commitments from faculty.

Faculty Learning Communities

A faculty learning community (FLC) focused on culture and teaching is one possibility for structuring faculty cohorts. Training sessions for facilitators and guides are available for purchase to assist with general components and processes for this kind of structure. Some campuses already have FLCs. Starting an FLC with a focus on culture and teaching might fit well into a program of topics. FLCs are limited by their common format and are not as flexible as a cohort designed specifically for the topic and the needs of faculty on a specific campus. The complexity of learning about culture, working through the challenges of discussing sensitive cultural topics, and transforming practice over time make the use of a more prescribed format less beneficial.

Websites

Online sites could serve as guides for faculty development and include a variety of learning seminars, videos, tools, reading suggestions, narratives and tips from experienced faculty, and blogs or other ways for faculty to interact and request suggestions for specific teaching challenges. They could be used within one institution or across institutions. Some faculty prefer to learn on their own or with one-on-one or more removed interactions. An online format could be available continuously, allowing faculty to use the knowledge and material when and where they have time.

Online sites would make it more challenging for teaching observations between faculty to take place, yet individuals could communicate to arrange these. In addition, we found that face-to-face interactions were very helpful in building trust, sharing innovations, and moving through sensitive materials and topics together. Our own work with teaching online suggests, however, that online written discussions have the potential to encourage significant introspection, insight, and sharing.

Individual Self-Development

Working on one's own is also a helpful mode of learning about culture and teaching. We find that many faculty fit reading, reflection, and practice into very busy schedules as they find time. Faculty we worked with found teaching observations and feedback as well as individual consultations with more experienced faculty invaluable to exploring cultural frameworks and applying new practices to their teaching. Teaching observations and consultations could become part of a modified individual self-development process.

Informal Sharing

Since working with the faculty in our project, many have reached out on their own to discuss culture and teaching with colleagues in their departments, colleges, and academic professional communities. These informal discussions often lead to them sharing materials, including consideration of cultural balance in teaching observation feedback, and offering to consult or assist other faculty in this area. We believe that this kind of ripple effect is a very powerful force among faculty and is an important form of interaction as well as an encouraging outcome of the yearlong culture and teaching project we developed and facilitated.

National and International Presentations and Institutes

Some faculty from our project have already presented formally at professional academic conferences on some aspect of what they learned about culturally balancing teaching practice. Others are finding ways to encourage specific introspection, innovation, and understanding on their own campuses, including outside their own departments and colleges. One professor spoke up at a Provost Diversity Council meeting about the need for students to engage in cultural introspection, which led to incorporation of an autobiographical assignment for students in general education courses required for all students. This same professor encouraged colleagues at a national conference to incorporate the autobiography in various projects with faculty and students and helped include a guide for writing it in a website serving the academic discipline.

Resources

Please see Appendix B for a list of resources you might find helpful in your own journey to develop a more culturally balanced teaching practice or to facilitate the development of others.

8

The Story of Our Work With Faculty

W e thought some readers would find it helpful to learn more about our work with faculty and the design of our yearlong faculty development project on culture and college teaching. This chapter includes the origins of our culture and teaching project, a summary of the work we did with faculty, and some reflections on our learning. We hope this will assist you, should you wish to develop similar initiatives on your campus.

Realizing Our Hopes

This book serves in many ways as a testament to some of the possibilities of faculty development in complex, even uncomfortable foundations of teaching. And yet it provides only a glimpse of the hopes we realized among the incredible faculty who offered of themselves to explore intersections of culture, teaching, and learning for an entire year and beyond.

Our hope for this book was to share some of what we learned through our scholarship of culture and teaching processes from students and faculty as well as from our own teaching. We hoped also to facilitate individual and shared cultural introspection among participants to facilitate understanding of their own cultural origins and the way these cultural origins influenced their teaching practices. We dreamed of creating opportunities for faculty to share and cocreate pedagogies as they strove to balance integrated and individuated cultural frameworks in their own teaching.

We are forever grateful to the brave faculty who journeyed with us during this year of cultural exploration. Their ideas and innovations, joys and frustrations permeate this book. We are forever made better by our work with this incredible group of courageous faculty.

Beginnings

A spontaneous reencounter in an elevator lobby during a 2010 conference in Chicago led to our partnership on this learning, teaching, and culture project. We renewed our connection over coffee and talked about our experiences working with students and faculty in the Southwest. Early on, we identified a shared sense of urgency about the success of college students, particularly the longtime resident Native and Hispano American student populations in Arizona and New Mexico, and our fascination with the influence of cultural identities on teaching and learning.

We decided to collaborate on work to address this urgency and discussed the need especially for work with faculty in academic arenas. We eventually focused our discussions on the scarcity of faculty development and research in the area of culture and college teaching. Alicia had conducted and published research previously about learning processes described by students of color in order to identify cultural frameworks and had also led some workshops and sessions with faculty on her campus and beyond. Susan's work previously had focused on students and their learning success, in particular with respect to campus environments, student leadership, international students, LGBT students, and students of color. Through our conversations, we realized that though significant literature exists on students in relation to their overall success as well as their success in college *outside* the classroom, less literature is available specifically on working with faculty on intersections of culture and teaching practice, and the implications for student learning and success in college courses specifically.

We focused on faculty development in our own institutions in the two adjacent southwestern states of New Mexico and Arizona to allow us to develop a longer-term project with faculty and because each of our institutions has over 30 percent enrollments of domestic and international students of color (see institutional summaries later in this chapter for more detail). We decided to fund this project almost completely from our own pockets to protect freedom and flexibility and not be restricted by the project or research design restrictions of grantors. We did secure funding from our institutions to provide faculty participants a stipend for participating in the yearlong project (neither of us took the stipend). In addition, the faculty development offices at each of our institutions provided some funding, administrative support, and expertise. We each had good relationships with our respective faculty development directors, Linda Shadiow at Northern Arizona University (NAU) and Gary Smith at University of New Mexico (UNM), and decided to invite their involvement. We each had given presentations and workshops for our faculty development programs during our time at these institutions and appreciated the expertise and interest of these directors.

The project coincided with a sabbatical year for Susan during the planning stages and for Alicia during the writing year for this book. We were each present and actively involved during the full year of faculty development. Over the five years (planning, faculty development, and writing years), we made many journeys between UNM in Albuquerque, New Mexico, and NAU in Flagstaff, Arizona, enjoying the diverse landscape by train and automobile, our conversations, and our work with faculty. We each grew immensely from our work together and from our extensive conversations about our own cultures and their manifestations in our lives and our teaching.

Coming Together and Planning

Our planning commenced with a meeting in Gallup, New Mexico, the halfway point geographically between Flagstaff and Albuquerque. Alicia, Susan, Linda Shadiow, and Gary Smith met over two days, brainstorming our vision for this project. Collaborative interactions among the four of us during this initial retreat proved very helpful to generating initial ideas and the basics of a plan for the yearlong faculty development project. We drew from our collective expertise in the study of college students, collegiate teaching, designing and facilitating faculty development, and our respective scholarship.

After this retreat, we moved ahead mostly on our own as the two faculty development directors chose to continue in mostly supportive and consultative roles for much of the project. Each of these directors provided budgetary partnerships, funding, some planning and administrative support, consultation whenever requested, and ongoing support throughout the project. Our efforts during the first academic year included more detailed planning of the faculty development activities, securing funding from our institutions, recruiting faculty, and holding a spring orientation session for faculty participants at each institution. In the second faculty development project year, Susan and Alicia focused on planning and facilitating the many faculty development activities, including beginning and summative institutes, regular faculty cohort meetings and teaching seminars, consultation with individual faculty on balancing cultural frameworks in teaching practices—including teaching observations and feedback—and assisting faculty with and reviewing the culture and teaching autobiographies required of each of the participants.

The overarching goal of the project was to improve student learning and success through faculty engagement with integrated and individuated approaches to enhance cultural inclusiveness in teaching. Because faculty are rooted in natural cultural influences that do not always align with those of students, and especially when faculty and students draw upon contrasting cultural heritages, understanding these contrasts becomes critical to student learning. One thing to keep in mind with planning, as well as how this kind of faculty development is communicated to and facilitated with participants, is to ensure a strong focus on and facilitation of developing teaching practices so that faculty move beyond the personal exploration of culture toward action— balancing pedagogies across cultural frameworks in their daily practices.

The purpose of collaboration between the two institutions was to examine the process of transforming faculty teaching practices to balance cultural frameworks of learning within the context of two different institutional types. UNM is an urban, primarily commuter, research-intensive university in a large city. Fifty-seven percent of students at UNM are minority students, many from Hispanic or Native American families who have lived continuously or almost continuously in the area since or before the mid-1500s. International students (2.9 percent) contribute to an even larger number of students of color, and large numbers of students are the first in their families to attend college. NAU is a research-intensive, primarily residential campus in a small city. Forty percent of students are first generation, and 35 percent are students of color, predominantly Latino and Native students. International students represent another 10 percent of the student population. The two public universities are similar demographically to their respective states and are representative of the southwestern United States.

A focus on these two institutions for this project allowed us to facilitate faculty development among professionals who work with large numbers of Latino, Hispano, and Native students with long histories of immersion within their own cultural communities as well as continuous conscious interactions across cultures. For these faculty, teaching across diverse cultures of students is an ongoing and conscious reality. We planned a year of activities with this in mind. We also believed and planned around the reality that there would be a diversity of levels of awareness among faculty participants about their own cultural origins. Some faculty were highly aware of their own cultural origins and regularly involved in cultural communities while others knew little about their cultural origins.

Philosophical and Organizational Underpinnings

During our meeting in Gallup, the four of us identified areas to guide the project. The core questions were:

- How does culture manifest in each person's teaching, and, most important, what does this mean for teaching practice across student cultures?

- How do differing cultural frameworks influence teaching and learning?
- What can we learn from the collective work of faculty in balancing cultural frameworks in their course designs, pedagogies, relationships with students, and self-awareness?

In addition to our core questions, we identified the following guiding principles to inform our work.

To Explore With a Positive, Inquiring, Strengths-Based Approach

One of our first tenets was to explore culture and learning with a positive, inquiring approach (which does not preclude a sometimes uncomfortable approach). We committed to a strengths-based appreciative inquiry to exploring culture, while staying true to and honoring individual experience. This commitment arose out of the realization that many conversations on our campuses and in our society about culture and race elicit denial, resistance, and blame. Instead, we wanted to build upon cultural strengths in faculty and students, drawing upon successful approaches to teaching and learning from across cultures.

One of the questions that built upon the strengths-based approach was how to balance majority or dominant cultural traits, such as individuality and linear thinking, with less common cultural traits, such as shared learning and circular thinking, as strengths in one's teaching. We wanted to identify strengths in each faculty member's unique background, core values, and stories and to acknowledge that each person's background undergirds the approach he or she takes in teaching. We believe that all cultures bring strengths to the world and are needed in the complex endeavors of teaching and learning in college.

We wanted faculty to look to the experience as a source of learning and also as a source of support and familiarity. Similar to faculty, students come into the classroom looking for ways to identify themselves. Just as we asked how students find ways to feel at home in their learning process, we asked the same of ourselves in designing this experience for faculty.

We also knew that our own growth as faculty would affect student learning, and this realization drove us forward. We were aided by the faculty development directors, with extensive experience working with faculty, and familiarity with the research that supported faculty development as a way to support students. We brought, from our own backgrounds and education about college students—their learning and success and their higher education context—insights into student and faculty cultural identity as well as Alicia's scholarship on how students with different cultural origins describe their own learning processes.

To Honor and Design for Institutional Context

Another question we had was how to honor the uniqueness of each university and engage faculty from them in ways that upheld institutional culture. For example, the groups were referred to by different names: a *faculty cohort* at UNM and a *faculty learning community* at NAU. Some state dynamics related to culture, ethnicity, and race influenced process, learning, discussions, and comfort levels differently at each institution. Also, differing funding patterns at the two institutions influenced the faculty cohort makeup for each.

To Learn Focus of Faculty Development

The learning focus was constructed around five access points:

1. Learning from students
2. Learning from colleagues
3. Learning from literature
4. Learning from self
5. Learning from existing and new teaching practices

We believed, and it became apparent during the project, that each of these access points could be entered through the vehicles or concepts of voices, stories, and practice implications. Learning from self was the most unique and least obvious access point for most faculty and was illuminated substantively through the writing of a culture and teaching autobiography.

We made some modifications as we developed our thinking about the faculty cohort year. Though we initially discussed including students in our work, we ultimately found that we did not want to include students except through literature and the sharing of faculty experiences because we were focused on supporting faculty through the challenging work of introspection. We did encourage faculty to—and most did—take time in different ways to engage, observe, converse with, culturally assess, survey, or gain insights from students to enhance their own learning and teaching processes. We also decided we did not want to facilitate the groups as formal, strictly defined faculty learning communities. The extensive literature on faculty learning communities generated expectations that we found too prescriptive for emerging, transformative work on culture and college teaching.

The Faculty Development Project

Constructing Faculty Cohorts at Two Campuses

The cohorts came together and functioned in ways we hoped and in most ways exceeded our hopes. The faculty provided support to one another and offered deep insights about their illumination of culture. Participants included 17 faculty members at UNM and 18 at NAU; the faculty rank ranged from instructor to full professor. For the most part, we sought faculty who cared about students and teaching, but we did not require any experience with culture and teaching.

Recruitment differed at the two institutions. At NAU selection was by application, and all were accepted. At UNM, recruitment varied across five participating colleges with deans who were willing to provide funding for faculty stipends. Two of the deans recommended specific faculty; one recruited faculty who were honored with UNM teaching excellence awards. One dean had an associate dean work with us to identify faculty to invite and urged us to choose those who were not as busy as the usual choices for leadership in their college. Another dean sent out an invitation to all of the faculty to invite participation and then made suggestions from this group, and one dean left it up to us to decide who to invite, urging us to work with newer faculty who, in the dean's estimation, might be more amenable to new approaches and especially cultural aspects of teaching and learning. These varied yet specific processes formed somewhat different faculty cohorts at the two institutions. UNM faculty were generally higher ranked than NAU faculty. At NAU, most participants were either instructors (five not tenure-track) or assistant professors (only five were tenured-out of 17). At UNM, all but one were tenured or tenure-track. Over half (nine) were assistant professors, six were associate professors, one was a full professor, and one was an instructor.

Materials, Supplies, Facilities, Travel, Stipends, and Website

We provided a variety of faculty development materials throughout the year and often asked faculty to read in advance of gatherings. With funding from student affairs at UNM and the faculty development offices at UNM and NAU, we purchased three books for participating faculty: *Sentipensante (Sensing/Thinking) Pedagogy: Education for Wholeness, Social Justice, and Liberation* by Laura Rendón (2009), *Look to the Mountain: An Ecology of Indigenous Education* by Gregory Cajete (1994), and *Beyond Affirmative Action: Reframing the Context of Higher Education* by Robert Ibarra (2001). These were some of the few books at the time of our project that focused directly on cultural manifestations in higher education teaching practice.

Food for the institutes and some gatherings was provided by the faculty development offices. We used a variety of gathering places, including the Native American Cultural Center for the starting institute at NAU, campus union meeting rooms and classrooms at both institutions, and the newly developed faculty development workshop rooms and learning-studio classrooms at UNM.

NAU provided technical support for the development and maintenance of a website via BlackboardLearn for the project, though this did not prove as attractive to faculty as we thought it might. With it we provided resources (articles, ideas), submitted autobiographies, and posted some of our own musings about teaching and regular announcements.

Faculty were provided an incentive of a $1,000 stipend, funded by academic deans at UNM and the provost at NAU, for a full year of participation in the project.

A culminating two-day institute was held at UNM. NAU participants traveled by train and stayed in a local hotel, and travel for this final meeting was financed by the NAU Center for International Education under the Global Learning Initiative. The Global Learning Initiative facilitates global issues in the curriculum. Global issues include tribal issues, and because this initiative exists partly to support Native students, the project was funded within the mission of global learning.

The UNM faculty development program director hosted the final institute by renting a van to transport participants between the hotel and campus as well as providing food, supplies, technological support, and facilities for the institute.

The Program

From our experiences and research about culture as well as about faculty and students, we believed that an in-depth, multifaceted program of faculty development was necessary and would be beneficial to sustaining learning. The complex nature of both teaching and culture made this a clear necessity if we were to gain insights into culture and learning as well as facilitate development and a balance of cultural frameworks in teaching among faculty participants. Our preplanning evolved to include an orientation consisting of two-day summer institutes at each institution just before the start of the academic year; monthly faculty gatherings; individual consultation meetings between one of us and each faculty participant; the writing of a culture and teaching autobiography during the first semester; observations, feedback, and suggestions on teaching for each participant; presentations by faculty at spring campus teaching institutes; and a concluding institute during the second summer to share pedagogies, process the experience, brainstorm additional teaching strategies, and celebrate the year. We hoped to get the NAU and UNM faculty groups together more, but funding was limited—though we were able to get them together for the culminating institute, which proved beneficial in numerous ways, as discussed later. The following are summaries of each project component:

Setting the Tone and Facilitating Amid the Complexity of Culture

We designed the year of faculty development to immediately facilitate respectful yet challenging discussions about culture, knowing that this would help faculty participants get through natural discomfort with the topic and get to know each other enough to share experiences, concerns, hopes, ideas, and practices. It was helpful that both of us have extensive experience facilitating complex and difficult dialogues aimed at the transformation of professional practice on college campuses. We strove to balance cultural frameworks in our own design and facilitation of institutes, seminars, meetings, and individual interactions—combining narrative sharing, scholarship, cultural introspection, pragmatic teaching strategies, and time for discussing dilemmas, as well as sharing insights developed and telling stories about positive teaching experiences.

Some dynamics served as natural catalysts for faculty motivation to develop their teaching across cultural strengths, such as an ethic of care for learning and success among a diversity of students. Some dynamics, such as the growing concerns about censorship of ethnic studies in the state of Arizona, served as catalysts for fear, hesitancy, and motivation to change and created a need to process these dynamics in relation to balancing across cultural strengths in our daily teaching.

We spoke often of the need for *academic courage*, promoting taking risks, innovating, sharing, trying new things, and getting to know students. Faculty in both cohorts humbled us with their willingness to learn and grow as well as their profound insights and innovations in teaching.

Summer Institutes

During the summer before the cohort year, we held summer institutes with the faculty at UNM and the faculty at NAU. We introduced the culture and learning project; worked through a series of exercises, reflections, and group work to begin to focus our thinking about culture and college teaching; and provided some structure to and some facilitating of the cultural autobiography assignment. Through this process, we shared from our own introspection on our cultures of origin and often used our own examples and stories as a beginning point to introduce various concepts, frameworks, and pedagogies with participants. Finally, participants developed and then shared commitments for shifting at least one foundational aspect of their pedagogical practices in the coming year. Examples of these commitments included the following:

- Explore how my background, including my culture, affects my teaching.
- Collaborate with and learn from colleagues.
- Strengthen classroom and advising work with Latina/o, Native, and African heritage students.
- Build relationships across disciplines.
- Examine what shapes curriculum decisions.
- Strengthen my role in student recruitment and persistence.
- Gain a better understanding of students' cultural experiences.
- Better understand challenges facing students.
- Participate in a yearlong interdisciplinary dialogue.
- Complicate my "knowing" of myself and my students and the curriculum.
- Expand my personal reflection on my work.
- Pursue culturally resonant teaching in my work so that I can have an impact on students and on colleagues.
- Explore the relationship between culture and motivation for learning.

Following our presentation of the Cultural Frameworks in Teaching and Learning model in Chapter 1 (Table 1.1) and facilitation of developing new teaching strategies, faculty participants generated commitments to change one aspect of their teaching in the coming year while working with the faculty cohort. The commitments to change included the following:

- Provide more time for reflection in the classroom.
- Share more personal stories with students.
- Share more cultural background with students.
- Post a picture of the instructor on the web-based course page.
- Have class outside occasionally.
- Look for critical learning moments.
- Have the courage to break the culture by allowing students to call the instructor by his first name.
- Include student participation in a large introductory freshman class.
- Share more stories in class.
- Provide questions before class to stimulate more discussion during class.

- Have students write a cultural biography.
- Invite more silence in the class.
- Facilitate discussion in which more students are invited to speak.

Throughout these conversations, and indeed throughout the year, faculty spoke about the paradox of talking about culture—always seeking nuance while generalizing—and the concerns that were generated about stereotyping or being reductionist about students and ourselves. One of our commitments was to continually and overtly acknowledge that speaking about culture, even with these risks, is preferable to keeping culture hidden and underground. We committed to start with faculty where they were and to work with them compassionately, using a consultative, spirit of inquiry, strengths-based approach throughout the year.

Monthly/Bimonthly Faculty Development Gatherings

The second year of our project represented the bulk of our work with faculty development gatherings. Each group met monthly or bimonthly to discuss culture and teaching; pedagogical strategies conceptualized or tried since the last meeting; thoughts, stories, and reflections about students; critical discussion of readings; personal and professional insights about culture; and challenges and rewards of writing cultural autobiographies. We occasionally met with guest speakers and participated in additional development activities. At NAU, we hosted Laura Rendón for a discussion of *Sentipensante (Sensing/Thinking) Pedagogy*, and at UNM, we hosted Gregory Cajete for a discussion of *Look to the Mountain* and Robert Ibarra for a discussion of *Beyond Affirmative Action*.

During these gatherings we often brainstormed to help various faculty with culture and teaching dilemmas; shared new teaching techniques developed and applied by various faculty; and offered encouragement, support, empathy, and humor to assist each other in our development.

Individual Faculty Development and Consultation

After we had met for orientation and secured commitments from faculty, we offered each of them one-on-one consultations in two forms. Our purpose was to work with faculty individually as well as collectively and give them a chance to chat with us about what they were working on and how it was going. We also wished to offer faculty assistance in working through some of the challenges and dilemmas they were facing in relation to culture and teaching. We offered suggestions, helped them process interactions and pedagogical challenges from class experiences, and sometimes offered insight about college students. We also sometimes gave general advice on promotion, relationships with colleagues, and departmental dynamics.

For those who work with faculty cohorts, we would recommend even more individual consultations and teaching observations, not only between conveners and faculty, but also among faculty, perhaps in trios, and over time. Processing of deep teaching dilemmas, opportunities, and creative ideas are enhanced significantly by one-on-one consultative and collegial dialogue.

Teaching Observations

We conducted teaching observations for almost all of the faculty during the course of the project year. After each observation, we each shared highlights from our notes with the faculty members, so they received our immediate feedback, observations, and suggestions in the suspended moments right after class. This process proved helpful because we could point out specific dimensions of the classroom, note how faculty sometimes looked to only one side, or make reference to a student who was sitting in a particular location in the classroom and her response to the teaching. We were also able to point out larger patterns in student responses to various techniques via our observations of student movement, nonverbal signs of attention, and other indicators.

We worked to provide a balance of feedback to each faculty member, usually pointing out several things in their teaching that were helpful in terms of cultural balancing for learning and one or two things they might consider modifying or adding. Throughout our teaching observations, we were acutely aware of the honor to witness master teaching across a range of disciplines, passion for students and their learning, deep cultural manifestation in individual faculty teaching practices, and a diversity of pedagogies.

We offered synopsis, interpretations, feedback, and suggestions for each segment of class by carefully recording times and teaching events in our notes. Faculty appreciated this immediate feedback; these talks proved some of our most dynamic conversations, occurring in the aftermath of energetic classroom exchanges. We offered to write letters on the observation that they could use in their promotion dossier and completed many of these throughout the following year.

Individual Consultations

We were both able to provide individual consultations with each faculty member. At UNM, Alicia provided individual consultations to most of the faculty during the fall of the project year. Consultations were used to get to know faculty better; to ask faculty what they had been reflecting on in relation to culture and teaching; to offer a chance to process culture and teaching ideas, dilemmas, and experiences; to provide additional suggestions for balancing cultural frameworks in specific courses; and to offer some assistance in working on the cultural autobiography that was due for this faculty cohort in November. Faculty in this cohort shared that these in-depth, one-on-one discussions were especially helpful in figuring out how to interpret student behavior they were seeing in their courses and to work with someone with experience reimagining pedagogies and assignments with a balance across cultural frameworks.

At NAU, Susan decided on a different approach. She scheduled individual consultations with faculty in the spring semester of the project and after teaching observations. These consultations were meant to follow up with in-depth conversations, to check in with participants about how the year was going, to assist with the cultural autobiographies, and to gather pedagogical ideas from their work during the year. Susan sometimes consulted with faculty in collaboration with Alicia and with Linda Shadiow, the faculty development director at NAU. At times she met with faculty on her own, and at other times she met with faculty participants along with Linda or Alicia.

Culture and Teaching Autobiographies

We incorporated the writing of culture and teaching autobiographies as a method of individual written introspection because of the ways writing illuminates the deep complexity of teaching and culture. We knew from our work with graduate students in the field of student affairs, as well as our work with higher education professionals in our field, that this kind of introspective writing about culture is invaluable to self-understanding and serves as a catalyst for understanding those from cultures other than our own.

We introduced the autobiography to faculty participants during the opening summer institute and facilitated several discussions, with mapping, drawing, and charting exercises to help faculty identify key values in their lives and link these visually to teaching values and practices. Throughout the project year, we offered guidance, structure, and support for the writing. Some faculty chose to gather for writing sessions while others wrote on their own. At faculty cohort meetings, we updated one another, read excerpts, and allotted time for writing. All who committed turned in an autobiography. Most have chosen to publish their work in our upcoming edited book (Longerbeam & Chávez, in press).

Perhaps not surprisingly, we noticed after reading each autobiography that faculty expressed varying conceptions of culture. In addition to ethnic cultural origins, some focused, for example, on class origins; others focused on faith; and others focused on geographic place. What was salient for each faculty member was related to their early messages about importance. The messages often came from parents, aunts, uncles, and grandparents. For some faculty, cultural influences were attributed to individual insight. Many of the faculty chose to explore their cultural roots, and these explorations led to making connections between learning and teaching processes they had not previously identified in their own experiences and their current teaching practices.

The process of writing was more difficult than most participants anticipated, sometimes joyfully so and sometimes painfully so. They identified and shared in several core themes. Among these were isolation in their families of origin and in the academy and experiences of judgment, loneliness, and humility (covered in detail in Chapter 4). Many wrote about the power of autobiographical writing about culture, particularly because they were revisiting the emotions of childhood and examining early messages about themselves and others. Faculty knew this process was unusual in academic life, and they understood and experienced its difficulty. Finally, they were continually seeking a sense of relativism and pluralism in their understanding of how culture influences their teaching. They resisted simplistic attributions to culture.

Four of the UNM faculty developed posters based on their culture and teaching autobiographies and presented them at a campus conference on college teaching in the spring of the project; afterward, the posters were hung in the faculty development center. Several more presented at national academic and teaching conferences, and some have encouraged other faculty on their campuses and nationally to engage in writing culture and teaching autobiographies. One faculty participant helped develop a website to guide other faculty in his academic field through introspection on culture and teaching (see Weissman, 2014).

E-mail and Website Reflections and Interactions

Though we primarily used e-mail rather than the website for communications, sharing of some materials, and scheduling, we did use the website in one significant faculty development way. The four facilitators offered periodic musings about our own observations of culture and teaching via the site as well as through group e-mails. Some faculty participants also chose to share insights, reflections, culture and teaching autobiographies, and experiences periodically while others queried the group for assistance, perspective, or suggestions.

Culminating Institute

The culminating institute came about through commitment and funding from both institutions (faculty development at UNM, and the Center for International Education at NAU). Most NAU faculty traveled by

Amtrak to UNM and continued our faculty conversations on the train. This second summer gathering was the first time faculty participants from both institutions met together. In Albuquerque, we enjoyed two days of focused sharing, collective brainstorming, and reflecting on the yearlong project and our learning. We continued to brainstorm teaching strategies and pedagogical insights on a variety of culture and teaching dilemmas throughout the institute, which evolved into a dynamic celebration of the year.

Some especially memorable aspects of the culminating institute included a moving cultural identity activity proposed, designed, and facilitated by NAU faculty; a PechaKucha activity to quickly and creatively share teaching strategies tried by faculty during the year, which was proposed, designed, and facilitated by three UNM faculty participants; reflections on learning from the year; application of cultural continua to specific teaching ideas; outcomes for students resulting from our work; and some discussion on where we wanted to go from there.

Cultural identity activity. A powerful activity during the culminating institute was designed and facilitated by three NAU faculty. All attendees were given markers, crayons, and newsprint and asked to create something that represented our cultural identities. We were told that we would be asked to share and explain these to the group as a whole. This storytelling activity revealed many insights, produced shared laughter and tears, and provided us with a validating way to explore and share who we are and how this matters to our teaching.

PechaKucha activity—insights, techniques, and reflections. PechaKucha is an energetic way to get started sharing ideas, and this activity was suggested and facilitated by several faculty in the UNM cohort. PechaKucha is a pedagogical tool used by architectural faculty and was originally designed by European architects working in Japan. Most of the faculty in attendance at the culminating institute used the PechaKucha format to present on some of their pedagogical innovations from the prior year by offering concrete ideas that other faculty could adopt. A wide variety of creative presentations ensued, and many innovative techniques for balancing cultural frameworks in teaching practice were shared and applauded.

For example, in the architecture field, students are usually required to give a presentation on their design, a high-stakes assignment with accordant high stress. Instead, the UNM faculty cohort member now encourages her students to share a film preview of their project with instructors several days before class; this is followed by an oral presentation in class. This modification of the high-stakes architectural presentation allows students to plan ahead for their presentations and removes much of the anxiety of presenting by first asking the instructor to preview their project. According to the faculty, students experience not only more learning but also more fun in learning by presenting their film clips before their presentation.

Reflections on learning from the year. Participants were asked during the culminating institute to reflect upon their work over the past year and to share important moments in their teaching relevant to the culture and teaching cohorts. Several faculty told us they now think of listening to students first, and not simply telling students what they know. They also reflected on how important they have discovered humility is in relationship with students, particularly by sharing in the academic experience with students as fellow learners. Part of this humility derived from writing the cultural autobiography; faculty pinpointed this as a turning point in recognizing that we cannot know students culturally until we know ourselves culturally.

Participants were asked to reflect upon how things might have changed for their students through our year of work together. Their responses were simple yet powerful. For instance, many said that students come to them more often, and they seem to be more at ease. Faculty noted a greater sense of presence from themselves and from students while sharing classroom time together. It was as though those few short hours in class together had gained more power.

Faculty were both more respectful of silence and more willing to explain their own reasoning and thinking about teaching to students. These shifts, too, came out of learning about silence in cultures and in recognizing that students who come from different cultures might be influenced by different values about what processes are most important in learning, such as the order in which to speak, listen, and reflect. Faculty realized that they needed to address these learning differences in themselves and their students and that these differences deserve explanation.

"Where do we go from here?" discussions. Some faculty were very interested in influencing others beyond our project on our campuses and in their academic disciplines. We discussed many ideas, including brainstorming campus committees in which we had members; influencing faculty in our own departments and colleges; and presenting at national, regional, and campus professional meetings. We also discussed the possibility of publishing a collection of culture and teaching autobiographies, which is now in process (Longerbeam & Chávez, in press).

Final Assessment

NAU participants completed a final assessment instrument. Faculty reflected that the culture and teaching faculty cohort influenced their work with students, especially by helping them facilitate better class discussion and create more engaged classroom environments. We asked what kinds of progress they made on their teaching goals, and they wrote that they now provide more time for reflection in the classroom, share more personal stories with students, use more stories as teaching tools, facilitate more discussion, and invite more reflective silence.

Faculty said in the orientation session that they wanted to explore how their cultural backgrounds affected their teaching, and most now believed they had achieved that goal. Faculty also noted other goals they achieved, including collaborating with and learning from colleagues, building relationships across disciplines, gaining a better understanding of students' cultural experiences, understanding challenges facing students, and participating in a yearlong interdisciplinary dialogue. Most also expanded their personal reflection on their work. Additionally, some faculty chose to observe one another's teaching and meet outside of the cohort meetings, and some continued to meet with one another beyond the cohort year.

Referencing the culture and teaching autobiography, faculty said that writing gave them insights into their cultures of origin and offered a portal to expanding the cultural continua they draw upon in teaching practice. Faculty commented on the difficulty of accessing their cultural origins and then applying those origins to teaching practice. Writing reminded them to be compassionate and understanding of the struggle students experience. One faculty member said of the writing,

> *It's been an incredibly valuable experience and stimulated thinking I've not done before about aspects of my life that I've not examined. Certainly these parts of my cultural identity have influenced my personal and professional choices, but looking for and seeing the thread of connection to my orientation to learning and teaching is new and powerful.*
>
> —Anonymous (from program assessment)

Research

Early in the project we decided to suspend most of the research aspect we originally planned so that our primary energy and focus would be on working with faculty throughout the year on their teaching development and on their culture and teaching autobiographies.

During the faculty cohort year and into the following year, we conducted faculty interviews and analyzed notes and themes from teaching
observations, cohort activities, and culture and teaching autobiographies in
preparation for this book. The research was voluntary for participants (and
not tied to the stipend for participation in the cohort) and granted institutional review board approval by each institution. We ultimately observed
and interviewed about 85 percent of participants at both campuses. Some
of the resulting themes are incorporated in this book to illustrate cultural
aspects of teaching, offer examples of techniques, and provide meaning to the
Cultural Frameworks in Teaching and Learning model applied throughout
(see Table 1.1). Future academic and practitioner journal articles are planned
with more of this research data.

Faculty Group Dynamics

We offer some thoughts about dynamics that occur in groups when culture
is overtly acknowledged and discussed. Discussions about culture require
skillful facilitation, given the emotional implications of exploring one's own
cultural identity; societal realities around ethnicity, culture, and race; and
our cultural influence and impact upon colleagues and students. Inevitably,
the larger social context becomes part of extended conversation, inclusive
of international, national, and state politics and economics. We believe it is
critical to hold and embrace these elements in conversation, while caring for
each individual and the group as a whole. Caring facilitation, through accessing our hearts, minds, and spirits, carries us through many challenging and
rewarding conversations. Our conversations were rooted in a strengths-based
approach to culture and in the knowledge that our exploration and efforts
would benefit students.

Final Reflections

Toward Learning Equity: Cultivating a
Culture of Belief in Students

No problem can be solved from the same consciousness that created it. We have to learn to see the world anew.

—Albert Einstein

Real education should consist of drawing the goodness and the best out of our own students. What better books can there be than the book of humanity?

—Cesar Chavez

In our preface for this book, we shared our belief in striving toward learning equity for students across cultures, an equity that we have yet to attain in U.S. higher education. Our faculty development project was one part of a larger cultural shift occurring at universities throughout the world. The global knowledge economy is spurring a worldwide rush among students to pursue higher education, diversifying student enrollments across cultures and other identities. Our challenge in teaching students from diverse cultures—especially those who are low-income, first-generation, and from other underserved populations—is also our opportunity. We can choose to develop our teaching practices to draw from cultural strengths that students bring with them into college. In doing so we have the opportunity to draw from the strengths of every culture in the world in service to learning.

When we hold a culture of belief in students and in the strengths they bring with them to learning, it becomes easy to see the difference we make at many community colleges, state institutions, and private colleges—all with a mission to enhance learning and increase access to and success in higher education. We have an opportunity to play an important role in facilitating whole generations through higher education. This vision and potential keep us passionate about our work, encouraging new pedagogical practices that will more effectively reach students in their own natural ways of learning and guide them toward a balance of learning across cultural frameworks. Teaching across cultural strengths enriches student learning and prepares them for wider societal and global contexts. The path ahead is full of exciting possibilities for students and for us as their teachers.

> We have a powerful potential in our youth, and we must have the courage to change old ideas and practices so that we may direct their power toward good ends.
>
> —Mary McLeod Bethune

> Our cultural strength has always been derived from our diversity of understanding and experience.
>
> —Yo-Yo Ma

> Knowledge can be learned but until it is truly experienced, it does not become wisdom.
>
> —Selo Black Crow (Lakota)

Appendix A
Guide to Writing a Culture and Teaching Autobiography

Cultural identities and epistemologies manifest in our teaching practice as well as in the ways students learn. How we interpret and evaluate students, how we design and facilitate our courses, how we interact with students, and even how we choose what to incorporate in our syllabi and other course materials are all influenced on deep levels by our own cultural upbringing.

From an anthropological perspective, our cultural identities are made up of the *values*, *assumptions*, *beliefs*, and *behaviors* that we were raised with by family, tribes, and communities, and that were further influenced by nations, cultures, spiritual traditions, religious teachings, educational environments, and even geographical locations and climates. By journeying deep within our own cultural identities, we get a better sense of how our cultures influence our teaching practice. This enhances our ability to see how the cultural norms of students we teach are likely to affect their learning. In addition, this type of self-analysis and awareness generates insight and empathy to serving students from cultures and backgrounds similar to and different from our own.

Your culture and teaching autobiography should be a narrative and interpretation about your life and *teaching practice* from within your cultural identity. Autobiographical writing is a kind of storytelling or making sense of things through narrative. This essay offers a chance for you to describe and illustrate (give examples and tell stories) this aspect of yourself and what being a part of your cultures means in your life and teaching practice.

Be sure to go deep! You are encouraged to use metaphor, artifacts such as photos, themes, or other creative means to explore this identity; yet, be sure to stay focused on deeply and specifically describing and interpreting elements of your cultural identity. Some professionals reflect informally while others find it helpful to conduct some research into their family histories, reading about specific cultures or ethnic group values and traits or having conversations with relatives.

The following are steps of analysis to assist you in your process. They provide a visual model of how specific assumptions, values, and traits manifest in your teaching practice as well as help you understand how you work with those who hold values or traits different from yours. Your own natural ways of learning will guide you as well.

Steps of Analysis

(Optional—use these if you find this kind of step-by-step process helpful.)

Getting Started

The following are some ways faculty in our culture and teaching cohort got started with their autobiographies. (Note that these were generated from questions we posted after faculty had completed their autobiogrpahies.) *What was your process of writing? How did you get to it?*

- Read my old journals
- Talked with parents, siblings, cousins, grandparents, friends, aunts, and uncles
- For very early childhood: dreaming/meditating/remembering
- Looked up personality traits of ethnicity, particularly when this exploration was new (generally Northern European Americans). For example, one participant found a description of his cultural heritage while reading as a way to prepare for his culture and teaching autobiography
- Read my own student papers and transcripts from undergraduate and graduate work
- Started by drawing a pictorial timeline of important events in my life
- Looked up mentors on the Internet
- Drew images to represent each of my main values and important traits
- Contacted and spoke with mentors

- Used Ancestry.com and other genealogy and genographic resources
- Listed my greatest values, then put them in order of priority
- Thought of a metaphor for each important value in my teaching
- Wrote out a short story of teaching events that were wonderful or upsetting
- Talked with a good friend about what they saw as my primary ways of being
- Acknowledged the centrality of our vulnerability as teachers
- Charted out key values in my teaching and in my life
- Recognized the novelty in academia of critically reflecting on and writing about our cultural backgrounds

Introduction

Describe your cultural identity in general and what you know about your cultural origins, history, family names, and generational journeys. Tell a story to capture an overall sense or spirit of the cultures in which you were raised, even if these cultures were not overtly discussed as culture within your family or community. You may find it useful to try some of the following:

- Start with key values in your teaching and think about where they originate in your life (e.g., timeliness, working through relationships, speaking up, starting with silence, hard work, empathy, responsibility, working together).
- Think back to your K–12 and collegiate educational experiences. What were some of the significant positive and negative experiences and relationships in your schooling? What values were instilled in you? How did you negotiate your educational pathway? What did you discover about your own learning?
- Draw or chart out different key traits with lines to show the relationships to or manifestations of each in your teaching.

Values Analysis

Choose three to five major values or traits that you identified during the previous exercise. (*Note*: For the following elements of this self-analysis, feel free to integrate components or steps within each value *or* use the step-by-step section approach shown here.)

- You can use the cultural assumptions, values, and behaviors in college teaching model (see Figure A.1) near the end of this appendix, if you wish, to assist you in analyzing each value or trait.

- If you are having difficulty in identifying cultural values and traits in relation to your teaching, the Cultural Frameworks in Teaching and Learning model in Chapter 1 (Table 1.1) may be helpful.

For *each* value or trait you've identified as originating in your culture(s), do the following:

- *Describe each identity value or trait*—explain and interpret each value or trait and tell stories or give examples to illustrate how this value or trait plays out in your life.
- *Discuss assumptions and beliefs underlying this value or trait* and their meaning to you. What assumptions or beliefs about others or about the world serve as a foundation for this value or theme?
  - For example, if you come from a culture that interprets most things from a shared or collective (rather than individual) perspective, then working together for the greater good is likely an underlying assumption beneath some of your values, behaviors, and beliefs. If you come from a culture or cultures that highly values individuality, then self-reliance so as not to be a burden to others is a probable underlying assumption beneath many of your values, behaviors, and beliefs.
  - If you find it helpful, you could start by discussing how this value or trait manifests itself more generally in your life and your behaviors, as well as what attitudes and motivations originate in this aspect of your upbringing. Be sure to provide examples or stories to illustrate each value or trait. These stories and examples are often helpful to deeper understanding.

Cultural Manifestations in Teaching

Describe how this value manifests in your collegiate teaching and in the way you interpret, judge, design for, and interact with students and with your subject area. Include writing about how this value or trait plays out in the following:

- Your syllabus design and content
- Your interactions with students
- The activities you facilitate during class sessions
- How much of your professional and/or personal self you share with students
- How you disseminate knowledge within a course
- What you believe is the purpose of education/learning
- What your role is in relation to student learning

- How you evaluate and judge student behavior (what encourages your approval or disapproval)
- What kinds of skills you expect students to already have and what you expect to teach them
- How you design evaluations within a course

Describe how this value or trait is *helpful* to your effectiveness as a teacher of a diversity of learners (perhaps focus on learners most comfortable in individuated *and* in integrated cultural frameworks).

Describe how this value or trait is *limiting* to your effectiveness as a teacher of a diversity of learners.

Be sure to provide stories or examples to illustrate what you mean. If you are more of an emerging teacher, discuss how you believe your values will be both helpful and limiting.

Balancing Across Cultural Frameworks

Analyze each of your identified cultural traits or values within a balance of cultural frameworks.

Analyze each value or trait you identified previously in relation to *how you currently facilitate or could facilitate student learning with students who have different cultural values or traits*. For example, how could you design teaching for a student who learns collectively or in shared ways if you usually prioritize individuality and learning individually?

Analyze the effect of your cultural identity on your *view of and work with students*—interpretations, assumptions, generalizations, judgments made about students you teach and advise. Focus especially on how you work with students who have *different* values from those that originate in your own culture(s).

- For example, what is your value in relation to students' speaking up in class? Do you often interpret silence as a sign of thoughtfulness, apathy, deep listening, disengagement, respectfully waiting to be called on, or something else?

Analyze the effect of these values/themes on your *behavior toward students and toward yourself* in your work as a teacher.

- How do you or could you teach in ways that are supportive of students with different cultural frameworks while still honoring those valued in your culture(s)?

- How might you harness students' cultural strengths and abilities toward their own and others' learning? For example, how might you facilitate student learning through both silence and discussion?
- How might you learn in relation to your teaching both from students who are culturally similar to you *and* from students who are culturally different from you?

Discuss some of the ways you might facilitate learning effectively with a diversity of students in a specific class.

- How might you maximize your own cultural strengths as well as minimize cultural limitations in your teaching?
- How might you design a course using a balance of cultural frameworks?
- How might you incorporate a variety of pedagogies, kinds of assignments and evaluations, and interactions to balance across cultural frameworks?

Summarize What You Learned

Synthesize some of the key things you learned through this culture and teaching self-reflection and some ways you wish to continue growing as a faculty member who teaches across cultures.

Figure A.1 Cultural Assumptions, Values, and Behaviors in College Teaching

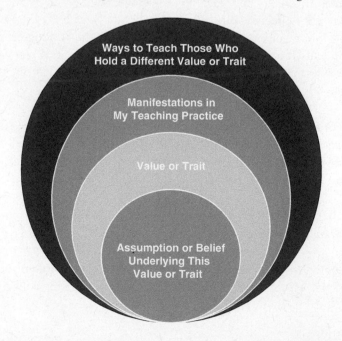

Appendix B
Resources

We need many more books that make us appreciate the mental stimulation of teaching and learning.

—Maryellen Weimer

We offer a few resources that we find helpful in our own work. Though we found little on the influence of faculty cultures on their teaching or on student learning in higher education, components of each of these topics are available in other books (culture and teaching in higher education, culture and teaching in K–12 education, faculty teaching introspection, and learning theory and research). We look forward to research and writing on understanding the confluences of culture, teaching, and learning in college.

Theory and Research on Culture and Teaching in Higher Education

Cajete, G. (1994). *Look to the mountain: An ecology of Indigenous education*. Rio Rancho, NM: Kivaki Press.

Ginsberg, M. B., & Wlodkowski, R. J. (2009). *Diversity and motivation: Culturally responsive teaching in college* (2nd ed.). San Francisco, CA: Jossey-Bass.

Ibarra, R. A. (2001). *Beyond affirmative action: Reframing the context of higher education*. Madison, WI: University of Wisconsin Press.

Rendón, L. I. (2009). *Sentipensante (sensing/thinking) pedagogy: Education for wholeness, social justice, and liberation.* Sterling, VA: Stylus.

Tisdell, E. J. (2003). *Exploring spirituality and culture in adult and higher education.* San Francisco, CA: Jossey-Bass.

Teaching Guides Related to Culture and Teaching: Collegiate, K–12, and Adult Learning Sources

Banks, J. A., & Banks, C. A. M. (1997). *Multicultural education: Issues and perspectives* (3rd ed.). Boston, MA: Allyn & Bacon.

Delpit, L. D. (2006). *Other people's children: Cultural conflict in the classroom.* New York, NY: New Press.

Gay, G. (2000). *Culturally responsive teaching: Theory, research, & practice.* New York, NY: Teachers College Press, Columbia University.

Ladson-Billings, G. (2001). *Crossing over to Canaan: The journey of new teachers in diverse classrooms.* San Francisco, CA: Jossey-Bass.

Nieto, S. (1999). *The light in their eyes: Creating multicultural learning communities.* New York, NY: Teachers College Press, Columbia University.

Faculty Teaching Introspection

Flores Carmona, J., & Luschen, K. V. (2014). *Crafting critical stories: Toward pedagogies and methodologies of collaboration, inclusion, and voice.* New York, NY: Peter Lang Publishing.

Ghaye, T. (2010). *Teaching and learning through reflective practice: A practical guide for positive action.* New York, NY: Routledge Press.

Longerbeam, S. D., & Chávez, A. F. (in press). *Going inward: The role of cultural introspection in college teaching.* New York, NY: Peter Lang Publishing.

Shadiow, L. K. (2013). *What our stories teach us: A guide to critical reflection for college faculty.* San Francisco, CA: Jossey-Bass.

Learning Theory and Research

Ambrose, S. A., Bridges, M. W., DiPietro, M., Lovett, M. C., & Norman, M. K. (2010). *How learning works: Seven research-based principles for smart teaching.* San Francisco, CA: Jossey-Bass.

Brown, P. C., Roediger, H. L., III, & McDaniel, M. A. (2014). *Make it stick.* Cambridge, MA: Harvard University Press.

Mayer, R. E. (2001). *Multimedia learning.* Cambridge: Cambridge University Press.

Medina, J. (2011). *Brain rules: Twelve principles for surviving and thriving at work, home, and school.* Victoria, Australia: Scribe Publications.

Zull, J. (2002). *The art of changing the brain.* Sterling, VA: Stylus Publishing.

References

Ambrose, S. A., Bridges, M. W., DiPietro, M., Lovett, M. C., & Norman, M. K. (2010). *How learning works: Seven research-based principles for smart teaching.* San Francisco, CA: Jossey-Bass.

American College Personnel Association. (1975). *A student development model for student affairs in tomorrow's education.* Tomorrow's Higher Education Project, Phase II. Washington, DC: American College Personnel Association.

American Council on Education. (1937). *The student personnel point of view.* Washington, DC: American Council on Education. Retrieved from http://www.myacpa.org/pub/documents/1937.pdf

American Council on Education. (1949). *The student personnel point of view.* Washington, DC: American Council on Education. Retrieved from http://www.myacpa.org/pub/documents/1949.pdf

Banks, J. A., & Banks, C. A. M. (1997). *Multicultural education: Issues and perspectives* (3rd ed.). Boston, MA: Allyn & Bacon.

Baxter Magolda, M. B. (1999). *Creating contexts for learning and self-authorship: Constructive-developmental pedagogy.* Nashville, TN: Vanderbilt University Press.

Baxter Magolda, M. B. (2001). *Making their own way: Narratives for transforming higher education to promote self-development.* Sterling, VA: Stylus.

Becker, J. R. (1995). Women's ways of knowing in mathematics. In P. Rogers & G. Kaiser (eds.), *Equity in mathematics education: Influences of feminism and culture* (pp. 163–174). Bristol, PA: Falmer Press.

Belenky, M. F., Clinchy, B. M., Goldberger, N. R., & Tarule, J. M. (1986). *Women's ways of knowing: The development of self, voice, and mind.* New York, NY: Basic Books.

Bennett, J. M., & Bennett, M. J. (1994). Multiculturalism and international education: Domestic and international differences. In G. Althen (ed.), *Learning across cultures* (pp. 145–165). Washington, DC: Association of International Educators.

Biggs, J. (1999). What the student does: Teaching for enhanced learning. *Higher Education Research and Development, 18*(1): 57–75.

Bloom, B. S. (1956). *Taxonomy of educational objectives, Handbook I: The cognitive domain.* New York, NY: David McKay Co.

Boas, F. (1911). *The mind of primitive man.* New York, NY: Collier Books.

Bonwell, C., & Eison, J. (1991). *Active learning: Creating excitement in the classroom.* ASHE-ERIC Higher Education Report No. 1. Washington, DC: George Washington University.

Bourdieu, P. (1977). Cultural reproduction and social reproduction. In J. Karabel & A. H. Halsey (eds.), *Power and ideology in education* (pp. 90–130). New York, NY: Academic Press.

Brendtro, L. K., & Brokenleg, M. (1996). Beyond the curriculum of control. *Journal of Correctional Education, 47*(4): 160–166.

Brown, P. C., Roediger, H. L., III, & McDaniel, M. A. (2014). *Make it stick.* Cambridge, MA: Harvard University Press.

Cajete, G. (1994). *Look to the mountain: An ecology of Indigenous education.* Rio Rancho, NM: Kivaki Press.

Chang, M., Denson, N., Sáenz, V., & Misa, K. (2006). The educational benefits of sustaining cross-racial interaction among undergraduates. *Journal of Higher Education, 77*(3): 430–455.

Chantal. (1999). Gotta keep climbin' all de time. In R. Kilkenny, T. L. Robinson, & J. V. Ward (eds.), *Souls looking back* (pp. 186–202). New York, NY: Routledge.

Chávez, A. F. (2007). Islands of empowerment: Facilitating multicultural learning communities in college. *International Journal of Teaching and Learning in Higher Education, 19*(3): 274–288.

Chávez, A. F., Guido-DiBrito, F., & Mallory, S. (2003). Learning to value the "other": A model of diversity development. *Journal of College Student Development, 44*(4): 1–17.

Chávez, A. F., & Ke, F. (2013). *Web-based teaching and learning across culture and age.* New York, NY: Springer Science + Business Media.

Chávez, A. F., Ke, F., & Herrera, F. (2012). Clan, sage, and sky: Indigenous, Hispano, and Mestizo narratives of learning in New Mexico context. *American Educational Research Journal, 49*(4): 775–806.

Chickering, A. W., & Gamson, Z. F. (1987). Seven principles for good practice in undergraduate education. *AAHE bulletin*, 3–7.

Choudhury, I. M. (n.d.). *Culture.* Retrieved from http://www.tamu.edu/faculty/choudhury/culture.html

Corey, G. (1996). *Theory and practice of counseling and psychotherapy.* Pacific Grove, CA: Brooks/Cole.

Deal, T. E., & Peterson, K. D. (2009). *Shaping school culture: Pitfalls, paradoxes, and promises* (2nd ed.). San Francisco, CA: Jossey-Bass.

Delpit, L. D. (2006). *Other people's children: Cultural conflict in the classroom.* New York, NY: New Press.

Flores Carmona, J., & Luschen, K. V. (2014). *Crafting critical stories: Toward pedagogies and methodologies of collaboration, inclusion, and voice.* New York, NY: Peter Lang Publishing.

Freire, P. (1993). *Pedagogy of the oppressed.* New York, NY: Continuum Books.

Fried, J. (1995). *Shifting paradigms in student affairs: Culture, context, teaching, and learning.* Washington, DC: American College Personnel Association.

Fried, J. (2012). *Transformative learning through engagement: Student affairs practice as experiential pedagogy.* Sterling, VA: Stylus.

Gardner, H. (2006). *Multiple intelligences: New horizons.* New York, NY: Basic Books.

Gay, G. (2000). *Culturally responsive teaching: Theory, research, and practice.* New York, NY: Teachers College Press, Columbia University.

Ghaye, T. (2010). *Teaching and learning through reflective practice: A practical guide for positive action.* New York, NY: Routledge Press.

Gilgun, J. F. (2002). Completing the circle: American Indian medicine wheels and the promotion of resilience of children and youth in care. *Journal of Human Behavior in the Social Environment, 6*(2): 65–84.

Gilliland, H. (1999). *Teaching the Native American* (4th ed.). Dubuque, IA: Kendall/ Hunt Publishing.

Ginsberg, M. B., & Wlodkowski, R. J. (2009). *Diversity and motivation: Culturally responsive teaching in college* (2nd ed.). San Francisco, CA: Jossey-Bass.

Gomez-Chavez, J. (2014). *How do peer mentors impact college students in undergraduate gateway courses at a large public university?* Unpublished dissertation. Department of Teacher Education, Educational Leadership and Policy, University of New Mexico.

Gurin, P., Dey, E. L., Hurtado, S., & Gurin, G. (2002). Diversity and higher education: Theory and impact on educational outcomes. *Harvard Educational Review, 72*(3): 330–367.

Hall, E. T. (1959). *The silent language.* Greenwich, CT: Fawcett.

Hall, E. T. (1966). *The hidden dimension* (2nd ed.). New York, NY: Anchor.

Hall, E. T. (1981). *Beyond culture* (2nd ed.). New York, NY: Anchor.

Hall, E. T. (1984). *The dance of life: The other dimension of time* (2nd ed.). New York, NY: Anchor.

Hall, E. T. (1993). *An anthropology of everyday life.* New York, NY: Anchor.

Hassanali, S. (2007). My permanent home. In A. Garrod & R. Kilkenny (eds.), *Balancing two worlds* (pp. 169–184). Ithaca, NY: Cornell University Press.

Hender-Giller, R. (2011). *The neuroscience of learning: A new paradigm for corporate education.* The Maritz Institute. Retrieved from http://www.maritz.com/~/media/ Files/MaritzDotCom/White%20Papers/Institute/Neuroscience-of-Learning.pdf

hooks, b. (1994). *Teaching to transgress: Education as the practice of freedom.* New York, NY: Routledge Press.

Howard, K., & Stevens, A. (Eds.). (2000). *Out and about campus: Personal accounts by lesbian, gay, bisexual, and transgendered college students.* Los Angeles, CA: Alyson Books.

Hu, S., & Kuh, G. D. (2003). Diversity experiences and college student learning and personal development. *Journal of College Student Development, 44*: 320–334.

Hurtado, S. (1992). The campus racial climate: Contexts of conflict. *Journal of Higher Education, 63*: 539–568.

Hurtado, S. (2007). Linking diversity with the educational and civic missions of higher education. *Review of Higher Education, 30*(2): 185–196.

Ibarra, R. A. (2001). *Beyond affirmative action: Reframing the context of higher education.* Madison, WI: University of Wisconsin Press.

Jackson, A. P., Smith, S. A., & Hill, C. L. (2003). Academic persistence among Native American college students. *Journal of College Student Development, 44*(4): 548–565.

Jaschik, S. (2013). They aren't retiring. *Inside Higher Education.* Retrieved from http://www.insidehighered.com/news/2013/08/02/new-study-shows-difficulty-encouraging-professors-retire

Joint Task Force on Student Learning. (1998). *Powerful partnerships: A shared responsibility for learning.* Washington, DC: American Association for Higher Education, American College Personnel Association, and National Association of Student Personnel Administrators.

Katz, J. H. (1985). The sociopolitical nature of counseling. *Counseling Psychologist, 13*(4): 615–624.

Ke, F., & Chávez, A. F. (2013). *Web-based teaching and learning across culture and age.* New York, NY: Springer Science + Business Media.

Kim, B. S. K., Atkinson, D. R., & Yang, P. H. (1999). The Asian values scale: Development, factor analysis, validation, and reliability. *Journal of Counseling Psychology, 46*(3): 342–352.

Kolb, D. (1984). *Experiential learning: Experience as the source of learning and development.* Englewood Cliffs, NJ: Prentice Hall.

Kuh, G. D. (1993). *Cultural perspectives in student affairs work.* Lanham, MD: American College Personnel Association.

Kuh, G. D., & Hall, J. E. (1993). Using cultural perspectives in student affairs. In G. D. Kuh (ed.), *Cultural perspectives in student affairs work* (pp. 1–20). Lanham, MD: American College Personnel Association.

Kuh, G. D., Kinzie, J., Schuh, J. H., & Whitt, E. J. (2010). *Student success in college: Creating conditions that matter.* San Francisco, CA: Jossey-Bass.

Ladson-Billings, G. (2001). *Crossing over to Canaan: The journey of new teachers in diverse classrooms.* San Francisco, CA: Jossey-Bass.

Ladson-Billings, G. (2014). Culturally revelvant pedagogy 2.0: aka the remix. *Harvard Educational Review, 84*(1): 74–84.

Lamont, M., & Lareau, A. (1988). Cultural capital: Allusions, gaps, and glissandos in recent theoretical developments. *Sociological Theory, 6*(2), 153–168.

Leaver, B. L. (1997). *Teaching the whole class.* Thousand Oaks, CA: Corwin Press.

Lee, M. W. (Producer and Director). (1994). *The color of fear* [Motion picture]. Oakland, CA: Stir Seminars and Consulting.

Longerbeam, S. D. (2010). Developing openness to diversity in living-learning program participants. *Journal of Diversity in Higher Education, 3*: 201–217.

Longerbeam, S. D. (in press). Challenge and support for the 21st century: A mixed methods study of college student success. *Journal of the First-Year Experience & Students in Transition.*

Longerbeam, S. D., & Chávez, A. F. (in press). *Going inward: The role of cultural introspection in college teaching.* New York, NY: Peter Lang Publishing.

Lukes, S. (1974). *Power: A radical view.* London, England: MacMillen.

Maslow, A. (1968). *Toward a psychology of being.* New York, NY: Van Nostrand Reinhold Company.

Mayer, R. E. (2001). *Multimedia learning.* Cambridge, MA: Cambridge University Press.

McCarthy, J., & Benally, J. (2003). Classroom management in a Navajo middle school. *Theory Into Practice, 42*: 296–304.

McDermott, L. C., Rosenquist, M. L., & van Zee, E. H. (1983). Strategies to improve the performance of minority students in the sciences. *New Directions for Teaching and Learning, 16*: 59–72.

Mead, M. (1971). *Coming of age in Samoa.* New York, NY: Harper Perennial.

Medina, J. (2011). *Brain rules: Twelve principles for surviving and thriving at work, home, and school.* Victoria, Australia: Scribe Publications.

Merriam, S. B., Caffarella, R. S., & Baumgartner, L. M. (2007). *Learning in adulthood: A comprehensive guide* (3rd ed.). San Francisco, CA: Jossey-Bass.

Milem, J. F. (2003). The educational benefits of diversity: Evidence from multiple sectors. In M. J. Chang, D. Witt, J. Jones, & K. Hakuta (eds.), *Compelling interest: Examining the evidence on racial dynamics in colleges and universities* (pp. 126–169). Stanford, CA: Stanford University Press.

Mortiboys, A. (2012). *Teaching with emotional intelligence* (2nd ed.). New York, NY: Routledge.

Myers-Briggs, I. (1995). *Gifts differing* (2nd ed.). Boston, MA: Nicholas Brealey Publishing.

Nieto, S. (1999). *The light in their eyes: Creating multicultural learning communities.* New York, NY: Teachers College Press, Columbia University.

Pai, Y. (1990). Cultural pluralism, democracy and multicultural education. In B. Cassara (ed.), *Adult education in a multicultural society* (pp. 24–56). London, England: Routledge.

Parham, T. A., White, J., & Ajamu, A. (1999). *The psychology of Blacks: An African-centered perspective.* Upper Saddle River, NJ: Prentice Hall.

Perry, W. G. (1978). Sharing in the costs of growth. In C. A. Parker (ed.), *Encouraging development in college students* (pp. 267–273). Minneapolis, MN: University of Minnesota Press.

Plank, G. A. (1994). What silence means for educators of American Indian children. *Journal of American Indian Education.* Retrieved from http://jaie.asu.edu/v34/V34S1sil.htm

Pope, R., Reynolds, A., & Mueller, J. (2004). *Multicultural competence in student affairs*. San Francisco, CA: Jossey-Bass.

Prince-Hughes, D. (Ed.). (2002). *Aquamarine blue 5: Personal stories of college students with autism*. Athens, OH: Ohio University Press.

Rendón, L. I. (2009). *Sentipensante (sensing/thinking) pedagogy: Education for wholeness, social justice and liberation*. Sterling, VA: Stylus.

Rendón, L. I., Nora, A., & Kanagala, V. (2014). *Ventajas/Assets y Conocimientos/Knowledge: Leveraging Latin@ strengths to foster student success*. San Antonio: Center for Research and Policy in Education, the University of Texas at San Antonio. Retrieved from http://education.utsa.edu/center_research_policy_education/

Sanford, N. (1966). *Self and society*. New York, NY: Atherton Press.

Sanford, N. (1967). *Where colleges fail: A study of the student as a person*. San Francisco, CA: Jossey-Bass.

Schoem, D. (Ed.). (1991). *Inside separate worlds: Life stories of young Blacks, Jews, and Latinos*. Ann Arbor, MI: University of Michigan Press.

Schreiner, L. A., & Anderson, E. "Chip." (2005). Strengths-based advising: A new lens for higher education. *NACADA Journal, 25*(2): 20–29.

Seligman, M. E. P. (2002). *Authentic happiness: Using the new positive psychology to realize your potential for lasting fulfillment*. New York, NY: Simon & Schuster.

Shade, B. J., Kelly, C., & Oberg, M. (1997). *Creating culturally responsive classrooms*. Washington, DC: American Psychological Association.

Shadiow, L. K. (2013). *What our stories teach us: A guide to critical reflection for college faculty*. San Francisco, CA: Jossey-Bass.

Shakespeare, W. (1999/1611). *The tempest*. Mineola, NY: Dover Publications.

Smith, G. A. (2008, September). First-day questions for the learner-centered classroom. *National Teaching and Learning Forum, 17*(5): 1–4.

Snyder, C. R. (2010). *Positive psychology: The scientific and practical explorations of human strengths*. Thousand Oaks, CA: Sage Publications.

Stanley, C. A. (2006). *Faculty of color: Teaching in predominantly White universities*. San Francisco, CA: Jossey-Bass.

Stone, L. (2008). *Continuous partial attention*. Retrieved from LindaStone.net

Sue, D. W. (2004). Whiteness and ethnocentric monoculturalism: Making the "invisible" visible. *American Psychologist, 59*(8): 761–769.

Sue, D. W. (2010). *Microaggressions in everyday life: Race, gender, and sexual orientation*. Hoboken, NJ: John Wiley & Sons.

Sue, D. W., & Sue, D. (2007). *Counseling the culturally diverse: Theory and practice* (5th ed.). Hoboken, NJ: John Wiley & Sons.

Sue, D. W., & Sue, D. (2013). *Counseling the culturally diverse: Theory and practice* (6th ed.). Hoboken, NJ: John Wiley & Sons.

Symonette, H. (2006). Making evaluation work for the greater good: Supporting provocative possibility and responsive praxis in leadership development. In K. Hannum, J. W. Martineau, C. Reinelt, & L. C. Leviton (eds.), *The leadership handbook of evaluation* (pp. 111–136). San Francisco, CA: Jossey-Bass.

Symonette, H. (2008). Cultivating self as responsive instrument: Working the boundaries and borderlands for ethical border crossings. In D. Mertens &

P. Ginsberg (eds.), *The handbook of social research ethics* (pp. 279–294). Thousand Oaks, CA: Sage Publications.

Takaki, R. (1993). *A different mirror: A history of multicultural America*. Boston, MA: Little, Brown, and Company.

Thomas, R. (1991). *Beyond race and gender: Unleashing the power of your total workforce by managing diversity*. New York, NY: AMACOM.

Tisdell, E. J. (2003). *Exploring spirituality and culture in adult and higher education*. San Francisco, CA: Jossey-Bass.

Tisdell, E. J. (2004, October). The connection of spirituality to culturally responsive teaching in higher education. *Spirituality in Higher Education Newsletter, 1*(4): 1–11.

Tsuchiya, L. (2014). *A case study in mathematics education: Initiating diverse learning opportunities by engaging Indigenous ways of knowing and learning*. Unpublished manuscript. Department of Educational Leadership and Organizational Learning, University of New Mexico.

Tuohy, D. (1999). *The inner world of teaching: Assumptions which promote change and development*. Philadelphia, PA: Falmer Press.

United States Department of Education, National Center for Education Statistics, Integrated Postsecondary Education Data System, Faculty Data, Digest of Education Statistics. (2012a). *Full-time instructional faculty in degree-granting institutions, by race/ethnicity, sex, and academic rank*. Retrieved from http://nces.ed.gov/programs/digest/d12/tables/dt12_291.asp

United States Department of Education, National Center for Education Statistics, Integrated Postsecondary Education Data System, Student Data, Digest of Education Statistics. (2012b). *Percentage of first-time full-time bachelor's degree-seeking students at 4-year institutions who completed a bachelor's degree, by race/ethnicity, time to completion, sex, and control of institution: Selected cohort entry years, 1996 through 2005*. Retrieved from http://nces.ed.gov/programs/digest/d12/tables/dt12_376.asp

Viernes Turner, C. S. (1994). Guests in someone else's house: Students of color. *Review of Higher Education, 17*(4): 355–370.

Viernes Turner, C. S., & Myers, S. L. (1994). *Faculty of color in academe*. New York, NY: Pearson Education.

Vygotsky, L. S. (1978). *Mind in society*. Cambridge, MA: Harvard University Press.

Weimer, M. (2002). *Learner-centered teaching: Five key changes to practice*. San Francisco, CA: Jossey-Bass.

Weissman, G. (2014). Develop cultural competency. *InTeGrate: Interdisciplinary Teaching About Earth for a Sustainable Future*. Northfield, MN: Carleton College. Retrieved from http://serc.carleton.edu/dev/integrate/programs/diversity/dev_cultural_comp.html

Whitt, E. J. (1993). Making the familiar strange: Discovering culture. In G. D. Kuh (ed.), *Cultural perspectives in student affairs work* (pp. 81–94). Lanham, MD: American College Personnel Association.

Wilson, E. O. (2010). *The diversity of life*. Cambridge, MA: Belknap Press.

Woodard, D. B., Mallory, S., & DeLuca, A. (2001). Student assessment retention model. *NASPA Journal, 39*(1): 53–83.

Yosso, T. J. (2005). Whose culture has capital? A critical race theory discussion of community cultural wealth. *Race, Ethnicity, and Education, 8*(1): 69–91.

Zull, J. (2002). *The art of changing the brain*. Sterling, VA: Stylus Publishing.

About the Authors

Alicia Fedelina Chávez is an associate professor of educational leadership and policy at the University of New Mexico. She has served as a collegiate leader, student affairs professional, and faculty member in universities around the country. Her scholarship is centered in facilitating understanding and balance between cultural epistemologies and ways of being in professional practice. She works from a belief that higher education institutions and societies benefit from garnering the strengths of many peoples, cultures, and nations.

Chávez has published in areas of culture and college teaching as well as identity and collegiate leadership. Her publications include a coauthored book on culture and college teaching, *Web-Based Teaching and Learning across Culture and Age* (Springer, 2013), as well as two coedited books on identity and leadership in higher education, *Identity and Leadership: Informing Our Lives, Informing Our Practice* (NASPA, 2013) and *Indigenous Leadership in Higher Education* (Routledge, 2015). Her academic journal articles include "Clan, Sage, and Sky: Indigenous, Hispano, and Mestizo Narratives of Learning in New Mexico Context;" "Toward a Multicultural Ecology of Teaching and Learning;"and "Learning to Value the 'Other': A Model of Diversity Development."

Susan Diana Longerbeam is an associate professor of educational psychology at Northern Arizona University, where she leads a graduate student affairs program. She served as a university health services director and interim dean of students at Oregon State University and holds a PhD in college student personnel from the University of Maryland, an MA in health services administration from Antioch University, and a BA in community studies from the University of California, Santa Cruz. She served on the ACPA Commission on Professional Preparation and the NASPA Faculty Fellows and Council.

Longerbeam's scholarship focuses on culture, campus climate, and student success in higher education. Recent publications include "'We Cannot Reach Them': Chinese Undergraduate Student Perceptions of the U.S. Campus Climate" (*Journal of Student Affairs Research and Practice*, 2013); "Putting Old Tensions to Rest: Integrating Multicultural Education and Global Learning to Advance Student Development" (*Journal of College and Character*, 2013); "Developing Openness to Diversity in Living-Learning Program Participants" (*Journal of Diversity in Higher Education*, 2010); and "Challenge and Support for the 21st Century" (forthcoming); and reflective work: "Encounters with Angels: A Struggle to Return Home From Study Abroad" (*About Campus*, 2015); "One Journey of Compassion: My Search for Inspiriting Leadership" (NASPA, 2013); "You Home? Meet Me on the Stairway: Lessons of Living Together" (NASPA, 2009).

Index

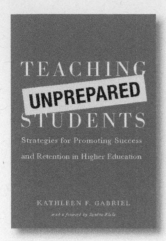

Teaching Unprepared Students
Strategies for Promoting Success and Retention in Higher Education
Kathleen F. Gabriel
Foreword by Sandra M. Flake

"Teaching is a tough job, especially when your pupil is underprepared. *Teaching Unprepared Students* is a guide for this all-too-common situation where students are dangerously in over their heads in the class they are in. Aiming for students to get the resources they need to turn a subpar student into a superb one, *Teaching Unprepared Students* is an invaluable manual for when traditional methods just aren't good enough."—***Midwest Book Review***

"Gabriel has put together an inspiring tableau of what constitutes good teaching and learning for the majority of faculty in their interactions with current students. I believe that most of our students are at risk; those that would get through without much help from us are cheated out of an excellent education.

"I especially enjoyed the interweaving she consistently does between issues of teaching effectiveness and assessment of student learning. Gabriel has created a professor-friendly discussion for all those concerned with classroom success."—***Judy Diane Grace***, *Center for Learning and Teaching Excellence*

Sty/us

22883 Quicksilver Drive
Sterling, VA 20166-2102

Subscribe to our e-mail alerts: www.Styluspub.com

Sentipensante (Sensing/Thinking) Pedagogy
Educating for Wholeness, Social Justice, and Liberation
Laura I. Rendón
Foreword by Mark Nepo

"What would happen if educators eschewed the silent agreements that govern institutions and established a new set of working assumptions that honor the fullness of humanity? In this visionary study, Laura Rendón lays the groundwork for a pedagogy that bridges the gap between mind and heart to lead students and educators toward a new conception of teaching and learning. Grounding her work in interviews of scholars who are already transforming the educational landscape, Rendón invites the reader to join a burgeoning movement toward more inclusive classrooms that honor each learner's identity and support education for social justice. Her book is vital reading for anyone seeking to create more inclusive institutions for students and teachers alike."

—*Diversity & Democracy (AAC&U)*

"Challenging, inspiring, beautifully written, and unusual, this book calls readers to find ways to link mind and heart—thinking and feeling—to transform teaching and learning in higher education.

"I commend this book to readers. Laura Rendón has illustrated how one can unite one's deep beliefs, values, and feelings, with one's keen analytical and intellectual abilities.

"Many faculty members, and certainly many graduate students considering work in academe, are interested in how to shape careers where their passions and values are central, and how to find satisfactory and meaningful balance in their commitment to both the professional and personal dimensions of their lives.

"Laura Rendón's volume offers insights, examples, questions, and inspiration that will help those grappling with such issues.

"The book or any of its individual chapters can be used by individuals thinking through their own values and practice, in classes designed to prepare future faculty members, or in faculty development programs organizing dialogues about teaching and academic life. . . . An important, thought-provoking, and unique addition to the literature on teaching, learning, and the academic life."—*The Review of Higher Education*

(*Continues on preceding page*)

MEMBERSHIP HAS ITS PRIVILEGES!

NISOD is a membership organization committed to promoting and celebrating excellence in teaching, learning, and leadership at community and technical colleges.

INNOVATION ABSTRACTS

This weekly publication features best ideas from community and technical college practitioners about programs, projects, and strategies that improve students' higher education experiences.

EXCELLENCE AWARDS

The NISOD Excellence Awards, the most coveted award among community and technical college educators, have honored more than 25,000 recipients since their inception.

MONTHLY WEBINARS

Monthly webinars are led by community and technical college leaders and other experts in the field. This benefit provides action-oriented, measurable, and learning-focused objectives to help faculty members improve their teaching techniques.

ANNUAL CONFERENCE

NISOD's International Conference on Teaching and Leadership Excellence is the definitive gathering of faculty, administrators, and staff exploring best and promising practices designed to improve student achievement.

SCOTT WRIGHT STUDENT ESSAY CONTEST

Three winning students and three faculty members, staff members, or administrators receive a $1,000 check. In addition, the winning colleges receive a complimentary NISOD membership.

DIVERSITY AWARDS

The Promising Places to Work in Community Colleges Award identifies and recognizes exceptional commitment to diversity at NISOD member colleges. This benefit can be used by recipient colleges to promote their commitment to providing campuses where all individuals and groups feel welcomed, respected, and valued.

STUDENT ART CONTEST

Students at NISOD member colleges are invited to design the official Conference Program cover for NISOD's International Conference on Teaching and Leadership Excellence. The artist of the winning design receives $1,000 as well as other benefits. The student's college receives a complimentary NISOD membership.

For a complete list of benefits, go to www.nisod.org.

NISOD provides budget-friendly, high-quality, and faculty-focused programs and resources for community and technical colleges that want to make the most of their professional development dollars. For nearly 40 years, NISOD's customer-focused approach has helped align our wide array of benefits with the needs of our members, which explains why the American Association of Community Colleges named NISOD, "The country's leading provider of professional development for community college faculty, staff, and administrators."

College of Education • The University of Texas at Austin